POWER

for
Pro Tools 10

POWER TOOLS

for
Pro Tools 10

Master Avid's Pro Audio and Music Production Application

INCLUDES DVD-ROM!

Glenn Lorbecki

HAL LEONARD BOOKS
An Imprint of Hal Leonard Corporation

Published in 2012 by Hal Leonard Books
An Imprint of Hal Leonard Corporation
7777 West Bluemound Road
Milwaukee, WI 53213

Trade Book Division Editorial Offices
33 Plymouth St., Montclair, NJ 07042

Printed in the United States of America

Book design by Kristina Rolander

Library of Congress Cataloging-in-Publication Data is available upon request.

ISBN 978-1-4584-0035-2

www.halleonardbooks.com

Contents

CHAPTER 4
BUILDING AND MANAGING
YOUR VIRTUAL STUDIO   75

CHAPTER 5
PLAYBACK AND RECORDING   107

MASTERING OVERVIEW

Preface

If time is a river, as the saying goes, then technology is surely the whitewater rapids. As time goes by, we see a doubling of technological capability every 18 months (Google "Moore's Law"). Example: in just 12 months, AVID has introduced Pro Tools 9 and another whole-number release, Pro Tools 10, in a lightning-fast move toward employing the latest technologies and processing capabilities in their flagship Digital Audio Workstation platform. While it may be hard to keep up with the changes, those who work in digital audio and need to take advantage of these improvements to increase their output and streamline their workflow find it necessary to accept the investment of time and money in keeping pace with the most recent software and hardware versions.

This iteration of the software includes many upgrades in performance and feature sets for all users, but particularly the post-production user. In the "What's New" section, we will explore the new features and functions and show you how to get the most from this latest exciting release of Pro Tools.

THE CRYSTAL BALL

There is no way to predict what the future holds for the professional user base, yet the release of Pro Tools 10 in the fall of 2011 seems to confirm AVID's commitment to a major software upgrade once a year. "32-bit floating point" was the buzz term on the AES show floor; will next year find the industry buzzing about a fully functional 64-bit Pro Tools 11 application? That certainly seems like the next major upgrade on the list. HDX processing cards were announced in 2011 as well, which puts HD and HD Accel users on notice that they have limited hardware support beyond Pro Tools 11.

If I could put one thing on my wish list for future development (after a 64-bit app), it would be support for seamless recording and playback of high track counts using 24-bit/96 kHz audio. The professional recording industry wants to move toward higher-definition audio production; the consumer is being primed for broad acceptance of higher-quality playback; the technology certainly exists to deliver 24/96 audio files to end-users. If AVID can deliver reliable performance at high bit/sample rates, one hopes that we can finally achieve a new high-water mark in the quality of the listening experience and fulfill the promise of digital audio as it was introduced to us some 30 years ago.

Finally, drop me a line; let me know if this is helpful information, or suggest other information that you would find useful. Ping me: PT@GlennSound.com

Updates

Occasionally, information will be updated to reflect new software releases or revisions. Check my website from time to time to see what's new in the world of Pro Tools as it relates to this book. You will also find a list of selected links to support websites, manufacturers, and other resources that will help you in your pursuit of audio excellence.

Acknowledgments

It takes a good deal of time to write a book—more than one might think, certainly more than I ever thought! There are people in my world who have accommodated my wacky schedule, and I would like to thank Evan and Erika and their mom for understanding, and Kisha Kalahiki for taking up the slack and helping me decide what stays and what goes. Thanks to my friends Eric Schilling, Bob Ludwig, David Miles Huber, Eric Kuehnl, Andy Cook, and Dave Gross for the never-ending technical advice. Andy Hagerman and Jenny Amaya did some painstaking (and painful) research and allowed me to share it with you. Dusty from Mojave Microphones let me use their terrific mics. Bruce from iZotope helped us understand their amazing processing line of products. Coady from ShortCutStickers. com breathed new life into my Pro Tools keyboard. ELS made my year with the Layla 5.1 mixes. My gratitude goes to Jeff Beck for being amazing. As always, special thanks to my mom for making all things possible.

Introduction

Welcome to the Power Tools guide to Pro Tools 10! Whether you're a student or a professional engineer, this book is a tool to help guide you through the process of understanding how to record, edit, mix, and master digital audio in Pro Tools 10, one of the most powerful DAW platforms in the world. The latest version of Pro Tools builds on the solid platform established and refined by Digidesign/AVID since 1991, and is used by top recording engineers and producers to create music and soundtracks in nearly every imaginable genre. Pro Tools has become the de facto standard for music production, audio post-production for visual media, and game audio production, and you will find it in virtually every major recording facility and project studio worldwide. Because of this ubiquity, it is to the advantage of every serious engineer to learn the platform thoroughly, in order to work efficiently and get the most from every session. Whether you're working at home or trading files with someone across the globe, Pro Tools is a complete environment for producing audio at the highest professional level of quality.

Let's take a moment to outline our goals: In order to get the most out of this book, you should be serious about improving your engineering skills and learning new production techniques. My goal is to help you become familiar with all basic functions of the Pro Tools environment and to demonstrate how to use these functions. Pro Tools is a complex application, and you will need to commit a good deal of time to learn all the techniques required to become proficient. If you put in the effort—and use this book as a guide—you will be producing audio tracks that sound better than ever before.

Thank you for letting me be a part of your creative journey. I hope you enjoy the ride!

WHAT SHOULD YOU BRING TO THE PARTY?

In addition to having access to your own working Pro Tools rig, you'll need to have a few skills to take full advantage of the information presented to you in this book.

Computers: You must possess an above-average understanding of computers to make the most of your Pro Tools software and, indeed, of any professional DAW software system.

Engineering: You should have a working knowledge of audio engineering concepts, signal flow, and gain structure, and have an understanding of the language of audio production.

Music: It helps to have a background in music. It may seem obvious, but there are terms and concepts in music production that we use constantly, and these terms are not always self-evident—such as verse, chorus, and bridge; or tempo, crescendo, and intonation. This is the language of music, and it's very handy for understanding and communicating ideas.

Music Theory: It also helps to have had some music theory education, even if self-taught. A good producer can tell if a particular note or chord is working within a song, and can make suggestions and fixes when it's not working. (This, of course, is subjective—never assume that a half-step harmony interval is a mistake.)

Patience: Pro Tools is a very deep and complex program, and it can take years to fully understand all the features. I've been using Pro Tools for over a decade, yet have learned many new things in the course of researching the Pro Tools book series. I will give you basic information on each subject initially, then delve into deeper levels of understanding and complexity. Get familiar with the basics and practice your skills, so you can move on to the more challenging material with confidence.

Learn More Than One Way to Do Things: This will come in handy in many situations, such as when you are editing audio and need to cut out a clip and drag it to another track. I can think of at least four different ways to do it, each with its own set of advantages, each depending on the situation and the editing tool I have currently selected. Learn to be versatile and practice with the tools often; through repetition you will become an expert.

HOW TO USE THIS BOOK AND RELATED DVD MATERIALS

This book is designed to quickly bring you up to speed on the power and capabilities of Pro Tools 10, and to make you a more competent and confident Pro Tools user overall. A good deal of this confidence will come from knowing that your system is properly installed and configured.

Some people are visual learners—that is, they need to see an image in order to get a solid understanding of abstract subjects. Throughout the book, you will see pictures or screen captures that illustrate the function or process as described in the text. Use these to be sure you comprehend the information or screen being discussed on that page.

Not all information is applicable to both host-based and TDM systems. Where there is a difference, I will point out the distinction.

Since we'll be learning a lot of new key command shortcuts in each chapter, you will find a table of the pertinent keystrokes at the end of each chapter. All keystroke examples will be given in Mac user format. Since PC users will be using this text as well, here is a comparison table for basic Mac versus Windows key equivalents to get started:

MAC OS X	WINDOWS 7
Control key (Ctrl)	Control key (Ctrl)
Option key (Opt)	Start key (Win) also called Windows key
Command Key (⌘, Apple)	Alt
Return key	Enter key, main keyboard only
Delete key	Backspace key

There will also be a brief self-exam at the conclusion of each chapter, so you can brush up on important chapter material before moving on. Experienced Pro Tools users will find this to be a particularly useful exercise, as some of the operations in Pro Tools 10 may have been changed or modified from previous versions of the software.

I will give you as many practical uses and examples as possible so that you can benefit from some shortcuts and a more streamlined workflow. Work with these exercises as much as you can; it will make the techniques seem like second nature.

Since most of the work you'll be doing is in stereo, we will assume that stereo is the main default output or destination format for examples given in the book.

Feel free to do what I do when reading a book like this: dog-ear the pages, take notes in the margins, use a highlighter, paste sticky notes on important pages, keep it next to your DAW—whatever it takes to make this info easily accessible so that you'll be more inclined to use it.

Terminology

There are some terms with which you may be unfamiliar or which may be used in different ways in this book. Take a moment to review definitions of these common terms in the glossary section at the back of the book.

Video Content

We have prepared a number of videos showing in detail some of the operations discussed in this book. You can watch the videos anytime just by selecting a video file from the DVD-R directory and double-clicking it. This requires QuickTime or other video playback software for your Mac or PC.

Session Data and Audio Files

You will also find on the enclosed DVD-R a number of Pro Tools sessions, so that you'll have access to the audio and session setups for many of the exercises or operations described in the book. Just copy the session files and folders to the local hard drive you have already set up for Pro Tools sessions.

You may want to create a new folder or directory named "Demo Exercises"; just be sure this data is kept separate from your other sessions. As you create or open these sessions, select "Save As…" in the Pro Tools File menu, and name the session using your initials as the first characters of the filename. This way you can easily locate your version of the exercises and still be able to open the original files if you should lose some data or need to start over.

In the event that you are unable to read or import session data, you can import audio files into a new session by pressing Shift + Command + I and selecting the audio files to be imported. When prompted, create a new track for each file and align them all to the sequence start time. Using this method, you will have to import or re-create other session settings, but the audio files should all be in sync.

Additional Materials

We have dedicated a section of our website to provide you with easy access to download handy and important files to aid you in your productions. These include pre-production planning worksheets, input lists, tracking sheets, a list of common Pro Tools error codes, and even a key command roadmap to help you work faster and more efficiently. Here's the link: www.GlennSound.com/PT.

Pro Tools 10 Primer

First order of business: your Pro Tools system needs to be running properly before working on any of the techniques in this book. If you already have Pro Tools 10 installed and your hardware is operating properly, then you're ready for the "What's New" section of the book.

It is very important that you follow all of the instructions in the Pro Tools software and hardware installation guides that come with your Pro Tools system purchase. This book can help guide you through system settings and configuration, but the installation of your particular software modules and hardware I/O is unique to you, so you should always refer to the "Getting Started" guides and "Read Me" files included on your original Pro Tools 10 software installation disks in order to get your Digital Audio Workstation (DAW) up and running. Once you have the basic system operating properly, use this book as a guide to fine-tune system performance and get the most out of your Pro Tools configuration.

If you encounter problems with the initial installation of your software or hardware, you should visit (and bookmark) the section of the AVID audio forums website dedicated to addressing up-to-the-minute changes and "known issues." This is referred to as the Digi User Conference, or DUC; the website URL is http://duc.avid.com/.

It can be frustrating to encounter computer problems while trying to get up to speed on new software. While Pro Tools is equally stable on both OS X and Windows 7 platforms, you still need to have a machine with sufficient RAM, disk space, and data I/O ports. It's important to check your computer's specifications to be sure they are compatible with the current release of Pro Tools software. See the "Studio Basics" chapter of this book to determine if your computer is compatible and capable of running the software according to AVID specs. There is also a list of supported OS versions maintained on the AVID website: http://avid.custkb.com/avid/app/selfservice/search.jsp?DocId=353265.

WHAT'S NEW IN PRO TOOLS 10

The last major Pro Tools software update was in 2010 with version 9.0; since then, the folks at AVID have been working on an upgrade schedule that appears to include a whole-number upgrade every year, and we can probably expect that schedule to continue. They have incorporated many of the features users have been clamoring for, and have paved the way for a new approach to hardware as well. With the release of version 10, Pro Tools users will see more than 50 new or improved features. Here's a look at what's new…

Digidesign Is Now AVID

AVID has owned Digi since 1995, and 2010 marked the emergence of AVID as the main brand identity for all their audio/video software and hardware lines. As a result, the Digidesign brand name is being phased out. However, the Pro Tools name lives on, as does its reputation for being the industry standard platform for professional audio production.

Now let's take a brief look at some of the new features of AVID's Pro Tools 10 that will have an impact on the way we work.

Support for More Audio Formats

Pro Tools 10 sessions can use multiple file formats in the same project—including stereo interleaved.

You can record and mix using 32-bit floating-point files.

Many of the Most-Requested Features

- Improved disk scheduling, disk cache, and real-time fades.
- Clip gain adjustment to speed up editing and mixing.
- Host-based systems can now access a 16k ADC setting for bigger mixes with more plug-ins. (This feature is not available on TDM systems.)
- AudioSuite processing improvements, including handles and preservation of metadata.
- New global solo and mute status indicators on the main counter display.

Pro Tools HDX

With the release of Pro Tools 10, AVID unveils a new PCIe processing card, featuring better performance and specifications per card as compared with HD TDM.

MORE POWER:
- Up to 5 x more DSP power per PCIe card.
- 4 x the voices (256 per card up to 768 with three cards).

- 4 x the delay compensation (16K sample mode).
- Twice the I/O per card (64 channels).
- Scalable up to three cards per system.

HIGHER RESOLUTION, MORE HEADROOM
- Higher plug-in resolution with 32-bit floating point math.
- Increased mixer headroom with 64-bit floating point math.

New Pro Tools Audio Engine

With Pro Tools 10, AVID has added support for third-party I/O. Now you can use any audio interface with supported Core Audio or ASIO drivers installed. This is an enormous step in the right direction for those who have not previously opted to purchase Digi or M-Audio hardware.

Not only can you use third-party I/O, but you can use the internal audio on a Mac as well. Imagine booting up your Pro Tools sessions without external I/O—on a laptop in your car or on a plane!

Increased Track Counts

With the exception of HD TDM systems, track counts are up for most other systems. See the table below for the new specs.

FEATURE	PT10	CPTK	HD NATIVE	HDX	HD TDM
Voiced Tracks	96 mono/ stereo tracks	256	256	256 per card up to 768 with three cards	192 (hard-ware limit)
Total Audio Tracks	128	768	768	768	768
Aux Input Tracks	128	512	512	512	512
VCA Master Tracks	n/a	128	128	128	128
Instrument Tracks	64	128	128	128	128
Master Fader Tracks	64	64	64	64	64
MIDI Tracks	512	512	512	512	512
Total I/O	32	32	64	192 (64 per card)	160 (32 per card)
Sample Rates	192	192	192	192	192
Maximum ADC	16,383 samples	16,383 samples	16,383 samples	16,383 samples	4095 (hard-ware limit)

Near-Zero Latency—Regardless of Buffer Setting

From a low of .7 ms with HDX hardware, to a max of 10 ms using an Mbox Mini!

Clip Gain

You can now adjust playback volume of individual clips in the edit timeline, independent of volume automation.

Disk Cache

Improved Disk Scheduler drivers dramatically improve performance for all user levels.

Extended Disk Cache for Pro Tools HD/CPTK users allows you to leverage 64-bit OS X ability to access large amounts of RAM for instantaneous cached audio/video playback.

Plug-in Improvements

- All versions of Pro Tools 10 now include a Channel Strip plug-in based on the Euphonix System 5 console.
- New Down Mixer.
- New Mod Delay III.
- Improved UI for many Avid Rack Plug-Ins.
- Pro Tools 10.0.1 will include new native versions of (previously) TDM-only plug-ins: ReVibe, Impact, Reverb One.

AAX Plug-ins

AVID has introduced an improved floating-point plug-in platform designed to:

- Run native on all systems (including legacy HD).
- Run as DSP-accelerated on HDX.
- Be ready for 64-bit operating systems.
- Employ broad third-party support from existing plug-in partners, with many more coming.

Audio Suite Enhancements

- Now you can open multiple AudioSuite plug-ins windows.
- Store and recall plug-ins and settings using Window Configurations.
- Select user-definable handles, including "whole file" option.
- New creative "Reverse" option for reverb- and delay-based AudioSuite plug-ins.

Improved Collaborative Workflows

Pro Tools 10 has been called the upgrade "for audio post-production users." Workflow enhancements for collaborative projects include:

- Export selected tracks as new session.
- Import session data enhancements.
- Set Session Start Time based on incoming session or AAF.
- Import Clip gain from Media Composer to Pro Tools.
- Import AAF Volume Automation to Pro Tools Volume Automation.
- Mixed bit depths and file formats in the same session.
- 16-bit, 24-bit, and 32-bit floating point files.
- AIFF and WAV.
- Interleaved audio.
- Change mid-session using Session Setup window.
- Export directly to SoundCloud and iTunes.
- 24-hour timeline.

Interoperability Improvements

Now you can load, run, and store Pro Tools sessions on nearly any type of storage, with these features:

- NAS (Network Attached Storage) storage support.
- Improved performance with NAS storage.
- Full track counts and faster responsiveness.
- Faster load time.
- Field recorder support.
- Media Composer interoperability.
- Round-trip workflows with 5.1/7.1 files and Clip gain.
- OMF/AAF support for real-time fades.

New EUCON Controller Enhancements

Access nearly 500 new Pro Tools functions in the AppSet.

- New integrated control support for:
- VCA slaves
- HEAT
- Satellite Link
- XMON

Complete Production Toolkit Upgrades

CPTK users can access the complete HD toolset, including:

- Track Input monitoring
- Destructive Punch record

Aggregate I/O

This is where all of your I/O hardware comes together to create the ultimate in system flexibility. You will be able to hook up your MBox Pro, your Eleven Rack, and your Apogee Duet—all at once. The new Pro Tools audio engine allows you to connect and select from your list of I/O options, in many cases without having to restart Pro Tools.

Automatic Delay Compensation (ADC)

This is a huge benefit for LE users. Beginning with version 9, Pro Tools incorporated optional ADC into every session, with a full range of features previously available only to HD TDM users.

Delay Compensation view is now available in the Mix window on all systems. ADC is automatically suspended during recording for low-latency monitoring.

Unified Installer

One software installer package now loads all system options, the features of which are accessed depending on the level of your iLok authorization (or "auth" for short).

No more M-Powered, Essential, SE, LE, or HD versions, each with its own installer and authorization options.

Pro Tools offers three levels of performance:

1. Pro Tools, the standard Pro Tools host-based software mode.
2. Pro Tools with Complete Production Toolkit (CPTK) offers extended performance and capability.
3. Pro Tools HD unlocks the full power of your Pro Tools software and hardware from your desktop computer, using HDX, PCIe, PCIe Accel, or HD Native cards.

Session Import/Export

Now all Pro Tools users will be able to import and export OMF and AAF formatted files without having to purchase or install additional software. This is great news for Pro Tools operators who regularly exchange files with users of other DAW systems.

There are advanced Import Session Data options, which were formerly available only with Pro Tools HD systems. For example, you now have the ability to bounce MP3 files to disk, which formerly required purchase of the MP3 Export option.

New Terminology

As Pro Tools moves closer to the operational functions of other AVID products such as Media Composer 6, some of the nomenclature has changed as well. This table gives you a comparison of the terminology used in Pro Tools 9 with that used in Pro Tools 10:

PRO TOOLS 9	PRO TOOLS 10
Region	Clip
Region List	Clip List
Region Group	Clip Group
Trimmer tools	Trim Tools
Timeline selection start marker	Timeline selection In point
Timeline selection end marker	Timeline selection Out point
Edit selection start marker	In point
Edit selection end marker	Out point
Time Code	Timecode
Locators to import (Import Session Data)	Markers to import (Import Session Data)
Process (AudioSuite)	Render (AudioSuite)

We will examine some of these new features in detail as we get into the various chapters of this book. There will be examples of how to maximize your system performance, activate and access your I/O, and make the most of the production techniques available with these new and expanded tools.

It's good to know that all of your Pro Tools skills will now translate equally between the different levels of software. This is an amazingly versatile DAW platform; learning how to navigate through the program and use all of its secrets will make you a better engineer, and as a result, your music and soundtracks will sound better too.

Configuring Your Pro Tools System

With the release of Pro Tools 10, AVID supports three levels of performance, and these modes are now integrated into one installation package.

SOFTWARE OVERVIEW

Even the basic version of Pro Tools incorporates some of the features and functionality of Pro Tools HD:

Automatic Delay Compensation is perhaps the greatest benefit of moving up to Pro Tools. Every version of Pro Tools now offers ADC, which allows you much more flexibility in selecting and applying plug-ins, and saves tons of time having to manually calculate latency.

You can use any ASIO or Core Audio–compliant audio interface.

I/O settings have changed; busses now include output busses as well as internal-mix busses. Output busses can overlap, facilitating sharing of physical outputs. I/O settings can be imported or ignored on opening a session.

DigiBase search and catalog functions have been enhanced.

The AVID PRE mic pre-amp is supported.

You can import and export OMF/AAF sequences. Various timecode and synchronization features have been added.

HARDWARE OVERVIEW: THREE LEVELS OF PERFORMANCE

Pro Tools provides a single software solution for all supported AVID hardware, and now, for the first time, Pro Tools offers support for third-party audio interfaces that utilize compatible Core Audio and/or ASIO drivers. If you're a longtime user of Pro Tools, this will be a revolutionary change in the right direction. With your iLok attached, Pro Tools will even run your session without any hardware interface attached. This is another major change in Pro Tools 10.

The level of Pro Tools performance will be determined by the mode you have installed on your iLok device.

Level 1: Pro Tools 10.x

- This is the standard software mode for Pro Tools when a non-HD audio engine is selected.
- Requires a Pro Tools 10 iLok authorization.

FEATURES
- Up to 32 channels of I/O.
- Up to 96 tracks (depending on sample rate).
- Up to 64 Instrument tracks.
- 512 MIDI tracks.
- 160 Aux tracks.
- 256 busses.

HARDWARE REQUIREMENTS
- Can be used with any supported AVID or M-Audio interface on Mac or PC. (Pro Tools 10 does not support the 001 family or the first, first-generation Mbox.)
- See the website for revised listings: http://avid.custkb.com/avid/app/selfservice/search. jsp?DocId=380563.
- Any ASIO or Core Audio–supported I/O should be recognized by the system.
- A number of audio interface manufacturers are now touting their Pro Tools 10 compatibility, including Apogee, MOTU, Presonus, and others. Check your local pro audio dealer, or consult the Interwebs for more info.See the section on Aggregate I/O for more info on how to access your interface(s) within Pro Tools.

CONNECTION
Depending on your audio interface, any USB or FireWire port on the computer itself should work like a charm. Ports attached to USB keyboards typically do not have enough current to power hard drives or interfaces. Check the AVID website to find out if your legacy Digidesign I/O device is supported.

CALIBRATION
Each manufacturer has its own calibration or setup protocol, depending on which I/O you choose. See the later section on system calibration for more details on DIY calibration methods.

PLUG-INS

Pro Tools comes with an extensive bundle of plug-ins and virtual instruments designed to get you up and running right away.

See the website for details: http://www.avid.com/US/products/Pro-Tools- Software/.

Level 2: Pro Tools 10.x with Complete Production Tool Kit (CPTK)

- This is the intermediate software mode for Pro Tools when a non-HD audio engine is selected.
- Requires a valid Pro Tools 10 iLok authorization, plus a CPTK auth.
- This is the operating mode for your system when you have a valid Pro Tools HD authorization on your iLok but no HD hardware is present.
- This means you can open and play back HD sessions on your laptop (minus the TDM plug-ins, of course).

FEATURES

Start with Pro Tools 9, then add CPTK and get:

- Track counts up to 512.
- 48 to 192 voices (depending on sample rate).
- Surround mixing capability.
- Multi-channel tracks (for surround recording and mixing).
- QuickPunch support for up to 64 tracks.
- Up to 128 Instrument tracks.
- Up to 64 video tracks.

Level 3: Pro Tools HD 10.x

- Pro Tools runs in this mode when you connect supported HDX, HD TDM, or HD Native hardware, and have selected the appropriate interface in your audio engine settings.
- Requires a valid Pro Tools HD10.x iLok authorization.
- Will function as Pro Tools 10 CPTK without HD hardware connected.

FEATURES

Includes everything in Pro Tools 10 CPTK, plus:

- Near-zero latency record monitoring.
- 64-bit floating point mixer (HD Native).
- TDM systems take on the heavy-lifting part of DSP using 48-bit fixed point processing (HD Core and Accel Core).

- The 48-bit mix bus gives you dynamic range of nearly 288 dB with +54 dB of headroom.

HARDWARE

- Use either Pro Tools HD Native, HD, or AVID compatible interfaces. All require HDX or HD Accel PCIe Core cards.
- An HD Native Core card gives you up to 64 I/O channels and 192 tracks using host processing (no TDM).
- HD Native can be used with the HD OMNI, HD I/O, and HD MADI interfaces, in addition to the prior generation 192 I/O and 96 I/O interfaces.
- The HD Core or Accel Core cards offer up to 160 channels of I/O.

CONNECTION

- A multi-pair cable connects the PCIe card to the outboard audio interface(s).
- If you use more than three cards (HD4 or higher), you will need an expansion chassis, a PCIe controller card, and a cable to connect to the PCIe controller card in your computer. (The expansion chassis includes card and cable.)
- A maximum of three HDX cards can be used with this system.

CALIBRATION

- The HD I/O, 192, and 96 audio interfaces offer access to rear panel calibration pots. See the later section on calibration for details.

PLUG-INS

Pro Tools HDX can run AAX, TDM, and RTAS plug-ins. Pro Tools HD can run TDM and RTAS plug-ins. See the AVID website for more info and up-to-date availability.

Outboard Gear

The really cool part about working with outboard gear in Pro Tools is the ability of the system to calculate and compensate for delays introduced by using outboard signal processing devices in a send/return configuration. In other words, you can take analog audio from any interface, send it to an outboard compressor (for example), return the compressed audio to the interface, and let Pro Tools calculate the round-trip delay. You can then set the system to compensate for that delay. This is a great solution for digital/analog hybrid-system users.

Refer to the section on hardware inserts for instructions on how to connect your outboard gear.

iLok

Pro Tools copy-protection authorizations currently reside on an iLok USB dongle, which comes with your Pro Tools software. Most plug-in manufacturers now authorize their software via iLok as well.

- **The Pluses:** Portable, safe, convenient, reliable. A great way to store all of your authorizations in one place and easily transport them from studio to studio or machine to machine.

- **The Minuses:** An iLok is small and can be lost or broken if you're not careful. Replacing authorizations can be very costly, unless you buy "Zero down-time" license protection.

There is a recent trend moving away from iLok authorizations for some plug-in developers. Check the developer websites for up-to-the-moment information on installing and authorizing your plug-ins.

Fig. 2-1

System Calibration

To be certain your hardware and software are passing audio properly, you should devise a regular regimen for calibrating your system. Since audio equipment operates best within its own range of input/output voltages, it's a good idea to set up each piece of gear so that it can connect to the next piece of gear in line and still be within its comfortable operating voltage range.

The basic principle is to apply a fixed-level input signal to a hardware input, then adjust each gain stage in the system to maintain optimal operating level. This level is typically 0 dBVU (-14 dBFS).

Some audio I/O hardware may have physical input and output calibration accessible via trim pots. See the owner's manual for exact calibration instructions for your interface.

PRO TOOLS CALIBRATION MODE
(USERS WITH HD I/O, 192 I/O, OR 888|24 I/O ONLY)
Pro Tools HD users with the above I/O attached can use Calibration mode to help adjust input and output levels. There are detailed instructions here included in the 192 I/O manual, but the shorthand version looks like this:

1. Connect a Pro Tools output to a VU meter on a console or other recording device.
2. Use a Signal Generator plug-in on a channel to send a 1 kHz tone through an output channel to the meter.
3. Adjust level via the Output Trim pot on the back of the I/O unit until the VU meter reads 0 dB. Repeat these steps for each physical output channel.
4. Connect all of the I/O device outputs directly to the I/O inputs.
5. Route the Signal Generator track output to all outputs.

6. Select Calibration mode from the Options menu. All Track Names will flash, and small arrows at the bottom of each track will point up or down to indicate whether you need to adjust the Input Trim pot up or down to achieve the level you've selected in the calibration level Preferences menu.

7. Adjust the I/O Input Trim pot accordingly. When you've trimmed to the exact level on a track, that Track Name will stop flashing. Modify the levels in this procedure to match your configuration.

UPGRADING FROM PRO TOOLS 9 TO PRO TOOLS 10

If you're making the jump from Pro Tools 9 to Pro Tools 10, here are a few hints on making the transition as smooth and trouble free as possible.

Let's assume that your Pro Tools 9 rig is up and running properly with all plug-ins registered and functioning, and that you have paid for and registered your upgrade with AVID. Follow these initial steps to upgrade your system, regardless of platform:

1. Download all of the latest assets to your iLok.
2. Download all of the latest Pro Tools 10 installers from AVID.
3. Disconnect your audio I/O device(s).
4. Download and install the latest driver for your I/O device before installing Pro Tools 10.

This is where the process diverges for the two OS's.

Upgrading on Mac OS Systems

1. Run the Pro Tools 10 installer from the downloaded DMG file.
2. Follow all system prompts along the way.
3. When finished, connect your I/O device and restart your Mac.
4. Launch Pro Tools 10, and check all components and plug-ins.
5. Get to work!

Upgrading on Windows OS Systems

1. From Control Panel > Programs, choose Uninstall Avid Pro Tools 9.x. (If you try to install Pro Tools 10 without uninstalling Pro Tools 9, the installer will stop you.)

Note: When running the uninstaller from the Control Panel, you must choose the option to uninstall Pro Tools 9.x and the HD Driver. No more, no less. Do not uninstall any other components.

2. After completing the uninstall process, restart your computer when prompted.

3. If you haven't already done so, install the latest driver for your I/O device.
4. Restart when prompted.
5. Install Pro Tools 10 from the downloaded installer.
6. Click Finish when prompted.
7. When installation is complete, wait patiently to exit installation.
8. Install Avid Virtual instruments from the VI installer (if applicable).
9. Click Finish when prompted.
10. Connect your I/O device; be sure your iLok is attached.
11. Launch Pro Tools 10.
12. When the registration window opens, choose "I have upgraded my Pro Tools software," then "Exit Registration."
13. Create a new session, and check all components and plug-ins.

If you get an error message when trying to use Xpand2!, take the following steps:

1. Create a new Instrument track in the session, insert the Xpand!2 plug-in on the track, and wait for Xpand!2 to load.
2. When Xpand!2 loads, you should see a translucent gray window appear over the plug-in window that says, "The Factory Content Was Not Found..."
3. Click Browse and navigate to this file path, then select the last folder in the path (the Xpand2 folder): C:\Program Files (x86)\Avid\Avid Virtual instruments\Xpand2.
4. With the Xpand2 folder selected, choose OK.
5. You should now have access to all of your Xpand!2 content.

Now get to work!

(The Windows upgrade sequence comes to you courtesy of Jenny Amaya from www. commercialmusiclab.com.)

OPTIMIZING THE PRO TOOLS ENVIRONMENT

Tweaking Pro Tools for each application is a little different; recording and overdubbing benefit from preferences and system configurations that differ from the settings you might use when mixing. It's a fairly simple operation, and you can use this section as a guide to walk you through the steps in getting the most out of your Pro Tools rig for each application.

System Usage Window

Having this window open on your desktop will keep you informed on the performance of your Pro Tools session by displaying system status in real-time. On non-HD systems, you will see three meters in the Activity window:

- **CPU (RTAS):** Shows current RTAS usage as a percentage of the allocated processing capacity.
- **CPU (Elastic):** Shows current Elastic Audio usage as a percentage of allocated processing capacity.
- **Disk:** Displays the amount of activity on the disk bus or busses as a percentage of total capacity.

FOR HD|TDM SYSTEMS

The Activity window displays the CPU and disk use as above, but you will also see a meter for PCI bus usage.

- **TDM:** Displays number of Voices Allocated compared to total available, and the number of Time Slots used compared to total available.
- **HD Core PCIe #1:** Displays DSP usage as a percentage of available processing for the Pro Tools HD Core Card. This section also tells you which plug-ins and/or mixer functions are associated with this particular DSP card.
- **HD PCIe (or Accel PCIe):** If you have additional process cards installed, this section displays DSP usage as a percentage of available processing for the Pro Tools Process Card. This section also tells you which plug-ins and/or mixer functions are associated with this particular DSP card.

Playback Engine

Whether you are using Pro Tools or Pro Tools|HD software, you will need to adjust the parameters for host-based operation. This is referred to as Optimizing Host-Based Pro Tools Performance. HD Native and standard Pro Tools users rely on host-based processing for recording, playback, mixing, and real-time effects processing. Even if you are using TDM DSP cards, the computer host still handles the chore of real-time effects processing.

- First, access the Playback Engine menu by choosing

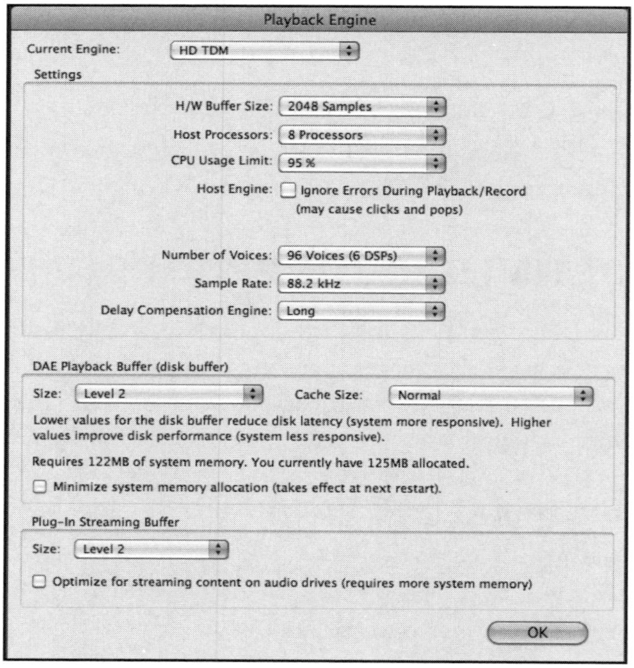

Fig. 2-2

Setup > Playback Engine ... Your current engine will be displayed in the drop-down menu at the top of the Playback Engine window.

- This menu will display a list of available connected I/O devices. Select your preferred device from the list. If you are selecting Pro Tools Aggregate I/O or any hardware other than the current device, Pro Tools will ask you to quit and restart in order to make that device active.

Buffer Settings

When recording, you should use the minimum buffer settings. This will allow you to do faster audio processing, and it keeps audio latency (delay) to a minimum. Locate the H/W Buffer Size menu, then select the lowest setting available for your system.

When mixing, you should use the maximum buffer settings. Since latency is not an issue during mixing, you can opt for maximum buffering to accommodate high track counts and intense plug-in processing without audible glitches. Locate the H/W Buffer Size menu, then select a higher setting for your system.

Host Processors

Modern computers employ multi-core or multiple processors, which allow you to designate how much processor power to dedicate to specific computing demands. The Host Processors menu lets you know how many processors you have available and allows you to enable multi-processor support for RTAS processing. This setting is used in combination with the CPU Usage Limit setting to determine how your computer system carries out Pro Tools tasks.

Note: If you are looking to upgrade or buy a new computer in order to run Pro Tools, remember that faster processors are generally better than more processors. CPU processing is performed in series by these chips, so more does not automatically mean faster.

In the Playback Engine window, choose the Host Processors drop-down menu. From this menu, select the number of processors you would like to allocate.

- Selecting a greater number of processors will allocate more CPU capacity for RTAS processing.
- Selecting a lower number of processors will reserve more CPU capacity for other Pro Tools functions such as automation, screen redraw, and video playback. It will also reserve performance for stand-alone apps running alongside Pro Tools, such as Reason, Melodyne, Live, and so forth.Suggestion: Determine how many processors you have available, then divide that by two. Your Host Processors setting should be 50 percent of available processing.

CPU Usage Limit

This setting allows you to set the maximum percentage of CPU resources allocated to performing Pro Tools host processing.

- Higher CPU usage settings allocate more power for Pro Tools processing and will be better for working on mix sessions with high track counts and lots of RTAS processing.
- Lower CPU usage settings allow you to reserve CPU resources for operating system function, running other apps, and screen redraw. If your system is getting sluggish or running slower than usual, try lowering your CPU usage settings.Suggestion: Set the CPU Usage Limit for 70 to 80 percent on most multi- processor systems to start. You should be able to run your CPU usage limit all the way up to 99 percent without affecting system performance.

Host Engine

This check-box option asks if you would like to ignore errors during playback or record. The next statement says it all: "May cause clicks and pops." Ignore this command entirely, and leave the box unchecked.

Delay Compensation Engine

ADC (Automatic Delay Compensation): This setting lets you determine the maximum delay limit for ADC. The setting options are None, Short, and Long. The delay will be displayed in samples, which will vary depending on the sample rate of your session. TDM systems can compensate for up to 4,095 samples of delay; host-based systems can now compensate for up to 16,383 samples of delay. This is an important performance increase for Pro Tools 10 users.

Suggestion: Use minimal plug-ins, and leave ADC off for the recording and overdub process. ADC works by calculating the longest plug-in delay propagated in any channel, then delaying all track outputs to match that delay. This makes it increasingly difficult for musicians to play with accurate timing when listening to delayed individual tracks or delayed general output. Turn ADC back on for editing and mixing.

Remember: You can easily turn ADC on or off: select Options > Delay Compensation to toggle the on/off state.

DAE Playback Buffer

The DAE (Digidesign Audio Engine) Buffer setting reserves a particular amount of RAM as a disk buffer for audio operations such as recording and playback.

- Higher buffer settings will improve playback performance on large sessions with high track counts, lots of edits, or slow disks. Do you ever see error code -9073 ("Disk too slow or fragmented")? Increasing your buffer settings traditionally helps alleviate this problem. With the new Pro Tools 10 disk caching capabilities, larger amounts of system RAM will now compensate for slow disks and facilitate the launching of sessions from virtually any mountable disk volume.

- Conversely, lower buffer settings tend to improve the speed at which your system responds to commands, so recording and playback will commence more quickly.

Suggestion: The optimum buffer size for most operations is 1500 ms, Level 2. This is also the default setting, so you may not need to change it.

Cache Size

This relates to Elastic Audio processing and the RAM that DAE allocates for pre- buffering audio. The standard setting is Normal, though you may need to raise the cache size if you encounter Elastic Audio errors, or lower it to free up memory for other system performance requirements.

Plug-in Streaming Buffer

This is applicable only if you're using the Structure Professional Sampling Workstation plug-in, and relates to the amount of memory DAE reserves for streaming from disk. The standard setting is 250 ms, Level 2.

Apply Changes

When you have made all applicable changes to your Playback Engine, click OK to exit. Again, if you have made changes to your Hardware I/O Engine, you will have to quit and restart Pro Tools.

Very Important Note!

If you start Pro Tools without the previously selected Hardware I/O connected and powered up, Pro Tools will not launch! Instead, it will go part way through the boot process, then pause to display an error message that reads, "Pro Tools could not initiate the current playback device. Please make sure that the device has been configured correctly."

Don't worry; just click OK, then relaunch Pro Tools while holding down the "N" key. This will bring up the Playback Engine dialog, which will allow you to select another interface or use the computer's built-in I/O. Click OK, and you're off and running. In fact, if you like, you can use the hardware I/O modifier key command to call up the Playback Engine dialog every time you launch Pro Tools.

Hardware Settings

- The Pro Tools Hardware Setup menu gives you the option to set word clock source, sample rate, and digital I/O for your hardware, depending on the type of audio interface you have connected to your computer.
- Any device that is supported by Core Audio drivers (Mac) or ASIO drivers (PC) can be configured in this menu, including your computer's built-in sound options via Pro Tools Aggregate I/O.
- Choose Setup > Hardware to access the Hardware Setup window.

Peripherals

This window identifies the connected I/O device, or allows you to select the device to be configured if you have multiple I/O devices connected.

Sample Rate

- If no session is open, you can use this window to select the default sample rate for Pro Tools operation. This would apply to new sessions as you create them. Note: you can also specify a sample rate in the dialog window when creating a new session.
- In opening an existing session, Pro Tools would assume the sample rate at which that session was created. In which case, the Sample Rate option would not be available for modification.

Clock Source

This drop-down menu lets you select the digital clock source Pro Tools will use as a reference.

- **Internal:** Select this if recording analog audio, unless you have an external clock source connected.
- **S/PDIF (RCA):** This setting is for use when recording from the S/PDIF RCA digital input, and will synchronize Pro Tools to the output of the external digital device.
- **Optical:** Use this setting when recording from an optical digital source. You will have to select Format from the following menu in order to match the source signal.

Optical Format

- **ADAT:** Choose this setting from the drop-down menu if your source is emitting ADAT Optical digital multi-channel output (Lightpipe) connected via fiber-optic cable. Supports session sample rates up to 48 kHz only.

- **S/PDIF:** This refers to optical 2t-channel S/PDIF digital signal input via optical TOSLINK cable only.

Launch Setup App

Use this command when setting up your third-party I/O device. This will launch the control panel specifically designed for your audio interface.

Disk Allocation

This menu refers to the location of the folder from which your audio will be played back—per track.

Suggestion: If your session is displaying audio waveforms and playing back audio correctly, do not change these settings.

I/O Settings

Choose Setup > I/O to access the I/O settings for your specific audio interface. From this window, you can select the following:

- **Input:** Here you can name any input channel, per input, per device. You may also turn any input on/off, change routing, or add new input paths to your configuration.
- **Output:** This menu is where you name output channels, activate or deactivate output paths, change routing, or add new output paths. You may assign an Audition Path for Audio Suite previews, Clip List auditions, and so forth. You may also assign a destination for the solo bus, if you choose to send it somewhere other than the main outputs.
- **Bus:** There are major changes in bus assignments beginning with Pro Tools 9. Whereas you used to see all available busses in this tab, now you only need to see the ones you create for your session.

In fact, that's a good place to start. Let's set up a sample bus page for monitor outputs:

- **Step 1:** Open the I/O > Bus tab and delete all bus paths. Yes, you read correctly, delete all bus paths. Now you can create a new, clean routing page with only the info you need for your session.
- **Step 2:** Click on the New Path button. In the pop-up dialog, create one new Stereo path, name it "Monitor Out," then click OK. The new path will appear in the Bus window.
- **Step 3:** Tick the box next to the Mapping to Output window; this will create a link between the Monitor Output path you created and the I/O hardware output pair A 1–2. The Monitor Out bus will now become the main output assignment for all of the tracks in your session.

- **Step 4:** You can create new busses in this window, or you can use the "new track…" command from the Send pane of the Edit or Mix windows to create a new Aux Input path as required for your session. Find that menu by clicking on the Send button, then click "new track…"
- **Step 5:** To make a reverb send, create a Stereo Aux Input, sample based, and name it "Reverb," tick the box marked "Create next to current track," then click Create. In one simple operation, you have created a reverb send/return path with all assignments readymade.

Repeat these steps as necessary to create new destinations for your session.

Note: This send/return operation is described in greater detail in chapter 4: "Building and Managing Your Virtual Studio."

PREFERENCES

The look, feel, and function of Pro Tools have a lot to do with how the preferences are set up. To access the Preferences options, choose Pro Tools menu > Preferences, or Setup > Preferences. This will display the Pro Tools Preferences dialog window, in which you can set your preference for various behaviors in Pro Tools operation. These prefs may change from project to project, so it's a good idea to know where to find them and how to change them.

The Pro Tools Preferences window has a series of tabs across the top, each of which contains a page of preferences for that subject, and options or adjustments for each. To change the preferences, click the subject tab you wish to change. Make your changes on the page, and click OK when you're finished. This will save your preferences and close the Preferences window.

Most of the preference settings are systemwide, or Global Preferences. This means that any new sessions will adhere to the settings you have defined as default settings. There are several preferences that relate only to the session currently open, and these are called Local Preferences. Quite often, the defaults in place when creating a new session will serve most users well. I will offer some general comments in this section, but more specific pref settings suggestions will appear in notes throughout the book.

Let's take a look at the Pro Tools Preferences window and some of its components.

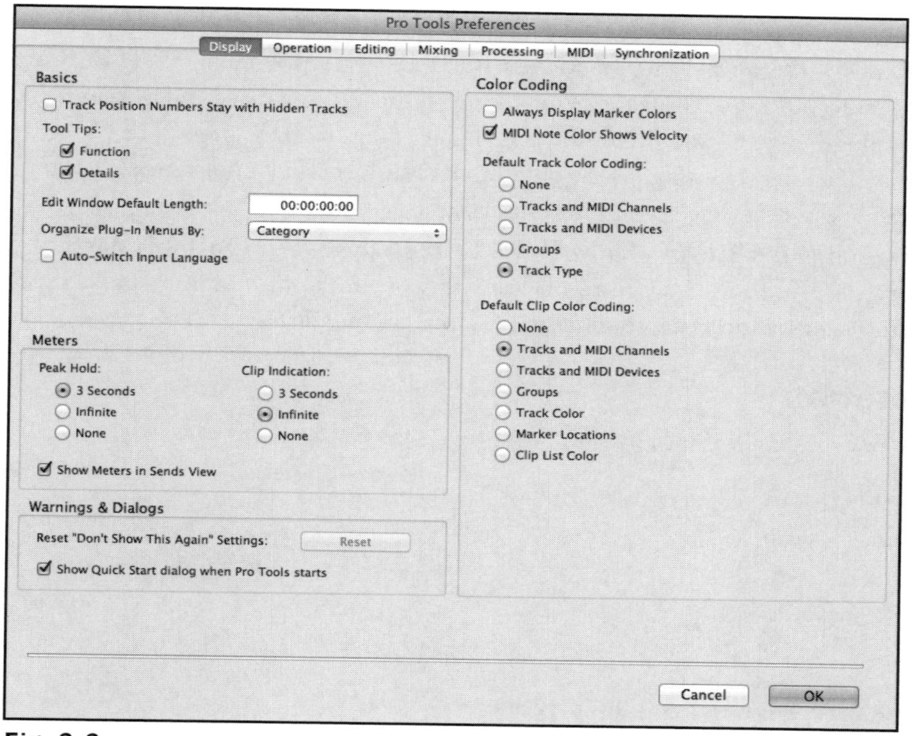

Fig. 2-3

Display

These prefs are divided into four groups:

- Basics
- Meters
- Warnings & Dialogs
- Color Coding

  The Local, or current session preferences on this page are:

- Edit Window Default Length
- Always Display Marker Colors
- Default Track Color Coding options
- Default Clip Color Coding options

COMMENTS
- **Basics > Organize Plug-In Menus By:** Your options here are Flat List, Category, Manufacturer, and Category and Manufacturer. If you have more than a handful of plug-ins, you should consider organizing plug-ins by Category or Category and Manufacturer. Hunting for the plug-in in a Flat List (a list alphabetically organized by name) can be a time consuming and frustrating task.
- **Warnings & Dialogs > Show Quick Start Dialog when Pro Tools starts:** If you're new to Pro Tools, I suggest you leave this on until you become familiar with the process of creating new sessions and finding existing ones.

Operation

These prefs are divided into five groups:

- Transport
- Auto Backup
- Video
- Record
- Misc.

The Local Preferences on this page are:

- Custom Shuttle Lock Speed
- Back/Forward Amount
- PEC/Direct Style Input Monitoring
- DestructivePunch File Length

COMMENTS
- **Transport > Numeric Keypad:** If for some reason your numeric keypad refuses to operate the Transport, look here first. The default setting should always be "Transport," but sometimes this gets changed without explanation.
- **Auto Backup:** While this should always be enabled, you should tweak it to your working style. If you tend to save your sessions manually on a regular basis, set the backup for 15-minute increments. If you don't save often, leave it set to backup every 5 minutes and increase the number of backups to 20.
- **Misc > Clip Auto Fade In/Out Length:** Leave this set at 0 ms unless you are doing a lot of voice editing or are editing a clip with lots of background noise. It can save a ton of manual fade-creation work if you set the auto fade time to 10 ms (10 milliseconds).

Editing

These prefs are divided into five groups:

- Clips
- Tracks
- Memory Locations
- Fades
- Zoom Toggle

   There are no Local Preferences on this page.

COMMENTS

Levels of Undo: The maximum number of Undo levels in Pro Tools is 32; you should leave it set at 32. If you get in too deep on an edit, or if track sync has slipped, this can be a huge lifesaver, along with the Revert To Saved command.

Mixing

These prefs are divided into three groups:

- Setup
- Controllers
- Automation

   The Local Preferences on this page are:

- Coalesce Trim Automation Options

COMMENTS

- **Setup > Default EQ and Default Dynamics:** Take a moment to select your favorite EQ and dynamics plug-ins here, or just use the awesome new Channel Strip plug-in. Your selections will now show up at the top of the list when you click on an insert button. This is a huge time-saver.

Processing

These prefs are divided into four groups:

- AudioSuite
- Import
- TC/E
- Elastic Audio

The Local Preferences on this page are:

- Imported WAV Files To AES31/BroadcastWave

COMMENTS

Import > Sample Rate Conversion Quality: Leave this set on "TweakHead (Slowest)." It's not exactly clear how you can have a setting that's better than "Best" (see their list of options), but there is no reason to ever use anything other than the highest-resolution option for conversion quality when importing audio files.

MIDI

These prefs are divided into four groups:

- Basics
- Note Display
- Delay Compensation for External Devices
- MIDI/Score Editor Display

  The Local Preferences on this page are:

- Play MIDI Notes When Editing
- Display Events as Modified by Real-Time Properties
- Automatically Create Click Track in New Sessions
- Default Thru Instrument
- Pencil Tool Resolution When Drawing Controller Data
- Delay for External Devices Options

Synchronization

These prefs are divided into two groups:

- Machine Control
- Synchronization

  There are no Local Preferences on this page.

HARD DRIVES

Pro Tools allows you to record and play back from a variety of hard drives, including the internal computer drive, or system volume. While this is possible, it is not recommended, as performance will not be as good as recording and playback from external or non-system drives.

Mac and PC Compatibility

You should dedicate an external FireWire (Mac) or USB (PC) drive with sufficiently high performance for all of your recording and playback needs. If you try to run a USB drive on a Mac or a FireWire drive on a PC, you may encounter playback or system errors.

Sharing sessions between Mac and PC is fairly simple; just be sure that Mac drives are formatted as HFS or HFS+, and PC drives are formatted as NTFS drives. Some PCs running Windows OS can record and play back audio using Mac HFS+ formatted drives; check your system settings to see if your computer is compatible.

Workspace Volume Settings

The Workspace menu gives you the ability to designate particular drives or partitions as Performance Volumes or Transfer Volumes.

- **Performance Volumes:** These are drives that are suitable for audio and video media recording or playback, and are designated as Record and Playback (R), or Playback Only (P), in the Workspace window.
- **Transfer Volumes:** These are volumes that either do not support recording or playback, such as CDs or DVDs, or have been designated as Transfer (T) drives by the system or the user. Use the Workspace menu to manage and modify hard drive permissions.

When recording audio multiple tracks simultaneously, it may be helpful to designate the system volume as Playback (P) or Transfer (T) only, to avoid having random audio tracks written to this drive and fragmenting your session files.

Monitoring Hard Drive Space

Concerned about running out of disk space? Pro Tools has a Disk Usage window to show you the remaining space available for each partition of your hard drive(s).

Choose Window > Disk Space

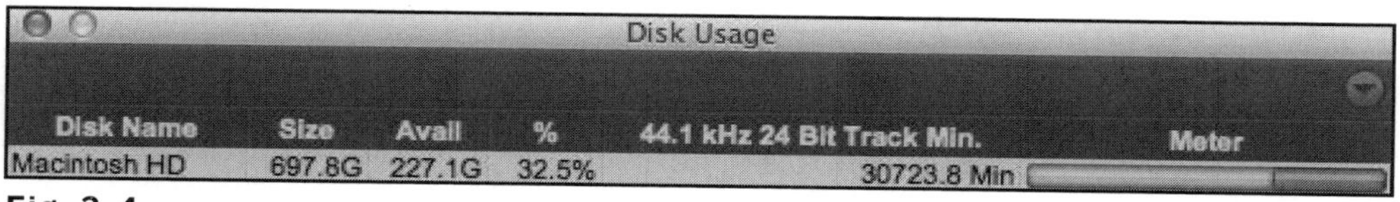

Disk Name	Size	Avail	%	44.1 kHz 24 Bit Track Min.	Meter
Macintosh HD	697.8G	227.1G	32.5%	30723.8 Min	

Fig. 2-4

You can view capacity in graphic "gauge" or text format, selectable from the Disk Usage menu in the upper-right corner of the window display.

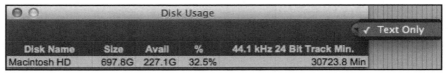

Fig. 2-5

MIDI SETUP

Pro Tools is designed to work with an external MIDI interface, allowing you to integrate MIDI-based controllers, keyboards, and other devices smoothly into your workflow. Each OS and every device has its own MIDI setup procedure; you should consult the manual when configuring each new device.

Mac OS MIDI Studio Setup

OS X users will be able to configure their individual MIDI studio and audio preferences on their computer systems by using the Audio MIDI Setup (AMS) utility included in the Mac OS Applications > Utility folder. This utility is also accessible in Pro Tools by choosing Setup > MIDI > MIDI Studio. From here you will be able to add new MIDI devices and configure your MIDI studio preferences. See your Mac OS manual for more information.

Windows OS MIDI Studio Setup

Users of Windows 7 and above will be able to configure their individual MIDI studio preferences by using the MIDI Studio Setup utility. This utility is accessible in Pro Tools by choosing Setup > MIDI > MIDI Studio. From here you will be able to add new MIDI devices and configure your MIDI studio preferences. See your Windows OS manual for more information.

CHAPTER 2 REVIEW

1. With the introduction of _____, AVID no longer supports Pro Tools M-Powered or LE.
2. Automatic _____ compensation and third-party _____ support are now part of Pro Tools 10 software.
3. Pro Tools requires the installation of a USB _____ in order to authorize the system for operation of Pro Tools 10.
4. Pro Tools _____ is the basic software level for Pro Tools systems.
5. Pro Tools 10 with _____ iLok authorization has many extended operational features, which allow you to run HD sessions on a laptop.

6. Pro Tools|HD 9 features near-zero latency record _____ with AVID _____ audio interfaces.

7. In order to run both RTAS and _____ plug-ins, you will need to have an iLok authorized for Pro Tools|HD 9, a set of HD _____ cards installed in your computer, and an AVID interface designed for _____ operation.

8. AVID HD|TDM systems have dedicated cards for TDM processing, which are called the _____ Card and the _____ Card.

9. The System _____ window tells you at a glance what percentage of _____ power you are using.

10. The Playback Engine dialog is used to fine-tune _____ performance.

11. _____ Hardware Buffer settings will result in greater latency, but are preferable during mixing to allocate more power to effects processing and _____ plug-ins.

12. Setting a _____ limit on _____ usage is better for sessions with high track-counts and RTAS demands.

13. The delay compensation engine has three settings: _____, _____, and _____.

14. When experiencing slow disk playback or disk errors, increasing the DAE _____ can make the system run more smoothly.

15. Starting Pro Tools software holding the ____ key will bring up the Playback Engine dialog, enabling you to designate a specific _____ device.

16. In Pro Tools 10 HD or CPTK, the Setup > Hardware Settings > Clock Source menu lets you select the session clock reference, whether _____ or _____.

17. Pro Tools has two optical input settings, _____ and _____ Lightpipe.

18. You configure all input and output assignments using the _____ menu.

19. The four main Edit modes in Pro Tools are _____, _____, _____, and _____ mode.

20. Name the six main Edit tools:

   a)_____ tool

   b)_____ tool

   c)_____ tool

   d)_____ tool

   e)_____ tool

   f)_____ tool

21. The tool that performs multiple functions depending on the position within the track is called the _____ tool.

22. Pro Tools usually has several ways to complete an editing function. In addition to mouse-clicking commands, you can use numerous _____ shortcuts to complete tasks.

Pro Tools Basics

TERMINOLOGY

In order to navigate properly and identify the tools we will be using, you should understand a few of the terms we will be using to describe the screen layout in Pro Tools.

- **Window:** This refers to a main display component, such as the Edit window or a plug-in window.
- **Pane:** This refers to a subsection of an open window. An example would be the Track Name pane in the Edit and Mix windows.
- **Button:** This would be any clickable graphic that enables/disables functions and choices, or gives you access to a sub-menu. For example, the OK button at the bottom of a pop-up window.
- **Drop-Down Menu:** Any menu that opens to display more options when clicked is referred to as a drop-down menu. The Window menu at the top of the Pro Tools menu bar is a drop-down menu.
- **Pop-Up Window/Menu:** This could be a menu of functions or a new window that opens to display controls. Clicking on an assigned insert button displays a plug-in pop-up window.
- **Dialog Box:** This refers to any window or pop-up that requires text input: naming a track, a send, a session, or a file to be bounced.

CREATING, SAVING, AND OPENING SESSIONS

Every Pro Tools project begins with creating a new session. When you launch Pro Tools, you will see a Quick Start session dialog giving you the opportunity to create a new session or open an existing session.

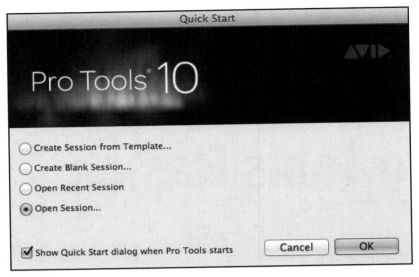

Fig. 3-1

The choices on this screen are:

- Create Session from Template
- Create Blank Session
- Open Recent Session (displays a list of the 10 most recently opened sessions)
- Open another session on your system

Create Session from Template

Session templates are a good place to start exploring Pro Tools capabilities and flexibility. Templates can help you understand how to create sessions and handle routing within Pro Tools. In the Quick Start dialog, select and open one of the session templates in the list to see examples of track layout, plug-in configuration, use of Aux busses, creation of a headphone mix, and more. You can modify session parameters

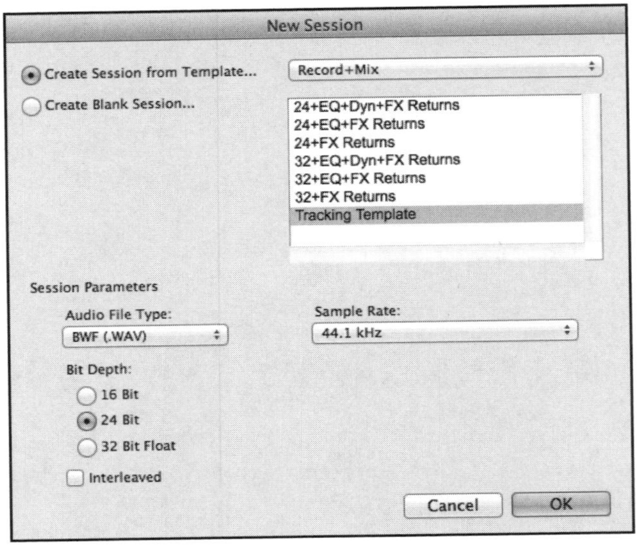

Fig. 3-2

such as file type, bit depth, and sample rate, then click OK to bring up the Save dialog, which allows you to name the session, choose a destination for the session to be saved, and then click Save to write the session to the drive of your choosing.

See "Using Session Templates" later in this chapter.

Create Blank Session

If you select the Create Blank Session option from the Quick Start dialog, you will choose file type, bit depth and sample rate, and I/O settings, similar to using templates. The difference is that this session will open with no tracks or routing assignments, as you will be creating these from scratch per your needs. Clicking the OK button will bring up the Save dialog, as above.

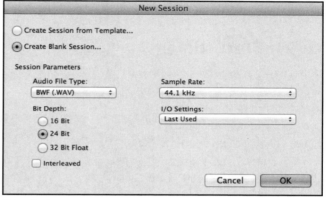

Fig. 3-3

Open Recent Session

If this is the first time you've launched Pro Tools, the Quick Start dialog will not include the option to Open a Recent Session. If you have previously opened Pro Tools sessions, the 10 most recent sessions will appear on the list to the right. You may select one of the sessions on the list and click OK to open.

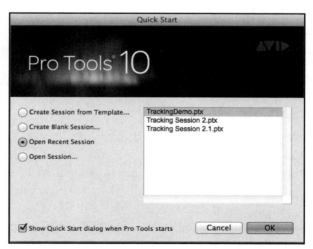

Fig. 3-4

Open Session

This option allows you to open any session on a currently mounted disk and brings up the Choose a Session dialog, allowing you to navigate to and select the desired session. Click Open to complete the task.

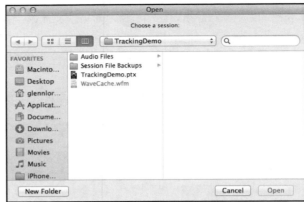

Fig. 3-5

Quick Start Dialog

You may choose to disable the Quick Start dialog on launching Pro Tools: just deselect the box next to Show Quick Start Dialog when Pro Tools Starts. To restore this display option, choose Setup > Preferences, then click on the Display tab. Locate the Warnings and Dialogs section of the Display Preferences page, and choose Show Quick Start Dialog when Pro Tools Starts. Click OK to change the preference.

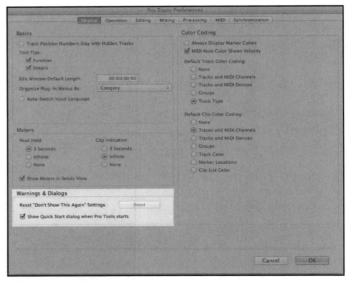

Fig. 3-6

Choosing Bit Depth and Sample Rate

How do you know which bit depth to use? What's the best sample rate setting? The answers to these questions will depend on the type of project you're working on, the number of tracks, the performance of your system, and your budget for hard drives. You also have to think about compatibility with other systems if you're sharing session data, and the overall sound quality of the recording. No small feat. Consider this: the higher your bit depth and sample rate, the better your project will sound. (Usually, that is; some hip hop producers would argue that 16 bit/44.1 kHz is the best way to get "that sound.") Also consider that the higher bit and sample rates will use more disk space, reduce track counts, and generally use more system resources. Think about these factors, think about the final release format for the project (CD, MP3, video game, and so on), then use the highest bit depth and sample rates your project will permit.

Bit Depth

- **16-Bit:** This is the standard for audio CDs and video soundtracks.
- File size is minimal, but you may sacrifice audio quality, headroom, and plug-in processing accuracy.
- **24-Bit:** This is the standard for most professional productions, as you get improved headroom and noise floor specs, as well as improved plug-in processing and overall sound quality.
- A 24-bit file is one-third larger than a 16-bit file.
- **32-bit Floating Point:** This high-quality option is new in Pro Tools 10, and it improves rendering performance in Audio Suite processing, as well as helping to avoid rounding errors when converting bit-depth. This occurs typically during playback or real-time plug-in processing.
- 32-bit FP files are one-third larger than 24-bit files, and twice as large as 16-bit files, which will use more disk space and cut down on the number of tracks your system can play back simultaneously. This is due to the limitations of audio streaming bandwidth and hard disk access speed.
- Be aware that not all DAW systems can read/write 32-bit FP files. Keep this in mind if you are collaborating with a non–Pro Tools 10 partner. Session bit depth can be changed in the Session Setup window: choose Setup > Session, then choose your bit depth from the drop-down menu.

Sample Rates

- **44.1 kHz:** This is the most common sample rate used in music production. It is also the specified sample rate for red book (audio) CDs.
- **48 kHz:** This sample rate is commonly used in video production and audio post-production. It is the standard sample rate for DVD-video. 48 kHz is the maximum sample rate for multi-channel audio transmission using Lightpipe (fiber optic cable).
- **Higher Sample Rates:** The higher the sample rate, the more resolution and higher-frequency response you will capture in your recordings. Your plug-in processing will sound better, as that higher resolution will tend to aid time-based plug-in processing and help avoid noise from aliasing.
- Pro Tools recording and playback at these higher sample rates requires hardware capable of supporting higher resolution.

- **88.2 kHz and 96 kHz:** In addition to being double the sample rate for CD and audio-for-video content, files recorded at these sample rates use double the disk space.
- **172.4 kHz and 192 kHz:** These files are four times the sample rate and size of standard 44.1 kHz and 48 kHz files, respectively. These are the highest sample rates currently available for Pro Tools production, and require hardware capable of supporting these resolutions. Production with high sample rates will usually reduce the number of tracks available for simultaneous playback. As with higher bit depth, this is due to the limitations of audio streaming bandwidth and hard disk access speed when playing high-bandwidth files.
- Note: There is some debate in the audio community as to whether or not the quality of audio encoded at sample rates higher than 96 kHz does indeed sound better than audio encoded at 96 kHz or below. The current state of A/D-D/A hardware technology leaves some room for doubt. As in all things audio, you should rely on your own ears and experience to show you the best way to proceed.

File Formats

Pro Tools 10 can import audio from a variety of formats, but will use only WAV and AIF files in the session.

A WAV file, when written in in Pro Tools, is actually a version of a BWF, or Broadcast Wave File. Technically, this is an AES31 Broadcast Wave file and contains additional information in the file, such as timecode stamp and other information about the file.

Pro Tools sessions prior to version 8.0.3 had the option to use SDII (Sound Designer II) files; if you open or import a session in an older format, you will be prompted to save audio files in either WAV or AIF formats.

Mixed File Formats

Pro Tools will now allow you to use WAV and AIF audio file formats within the same session without having to convert them on import. You can also change the file format for all audio files in your session by choosing Setup > Session; then, in the Audio Format selector, choose WAV or AIF.

Interleaved Audio Files

In versions prior to Pro Tools 10, the program would convert any multi-channel or interleaved files to multiple-mono files on import. With this release, you can import interleaved stereo or multi-channel audio files without having to convert them to multi-mono files. You can still split stereo or multi-channel tracks into multiple-mono files in order to process or edit them separately.

When a session is open, you can change its interleaved setting in the Session Setup window. All files recorded or imported from that point forward will conform to the new setting.

SESSION FILES AND FOLDERS

Pro Tools uses a simple method to keep track of all of the files and other elements of each session. Whenever you create a new session, a folder is created with the same name as your Pro Tools session. Inside this folder is the Pro Tools session file or files—up to six sub-folders containing files and settings, and a WaveCache file.

Pro Tools Session Files

When you create a new project, these are the actual files that store the information about your session and all of its components. You can have multiple session files within the session folder, but you may only have one session open at a time. Pro Tools 10 session files use the .ptx suffix. Session files belonging to Pro Tools versions 9 and earlier use the .ptf suffix.

WaveCache File

The WaveCache file stores all of the waveform display data for the session. This allows sessions to be opened more quickly. If a WaveCache file is deleted, Pro Tools will automatically generate a new one the next time that session is opened. This may cause your session to take longer to open. WaveCache files use the .wfm suffix.

Audio Files Folder

This folder contains all of the audio files you have recorded, created, or imported into your session. You can select an alternate hard disk path for audio files in the Disk Allocation window (Setup > Disk Allocation…), but it is strongly suggested that you keep all audio files within the main Audio Files folder.

Renamed Audio Files Folder

When you import audio files with incompatible characters in the name, or if you open a Pro Tools session that does not support long filenames, the original files will be stored here, and a new file created that ensures system compatibility.

Fade Files Folder

Pro Tools 10 uses real-time fades, so newer sessions will not use the Fade Files folder. Older versions of Pro Tools would write a physical fade file for every fade you created in your session. These files live in the Fade Files folder.

Rendered Files Folder

Any temporary files created in the process of using Elastic Audio will live in this folder.

Clip Groups Folder

Clip Groups exported from your session are stored in this folder. (Clip Groups were formerly referred to as Region Groups.)

Session File Backups Folder

If you have Session File Auto Backup enabled in the Preferences window, those backups will be stored in the Session File Backups folder. It is strongly advised that you enable this feature.

OPENING SESSIONS

You can open an existing session in Pro Tools using one of the following methods:

- Select File > Open Session from the main menu bar.
- Select File > Open Recent Session from the main menu bar.
- Type Command + O when Pro Tools is launched.
- Double-click on a Pro Tools session file from the DigiBase browser.
- Double-click on a Pro Tools session file from the Finder or top level of your computer.

The Pro Tools session will begin to open, and you will see tracks, windows, or other displays that were open when the session was last saved.

In some cases, you will be presented with a dialog box or other window reporting on the status of the session you are about to open, and prompting as to whether or not any action will need to be taken to complete the task.

Opening Sessions with Unavailable Files

If you open a session that is missing some files, or if the system cannot readily find all of the files, the DigiBase window will display a list of offline files and give you options for finding or ignoring those files.

Opening Sessions from a Transfer Volume

If some files exist on volumes designated for Transfer only (including CD or DVD), Digibase will prompt you to save the session on a Performance Volume. All media files will be copied to the specified drive and converted as required.

Opening Sessions with Unavailable Resources

When opening a session created on a Pro Tools system that was configured differently or used different system resources from your own, the Unavailable Resources dialog box will appear, reporting a list of the session components that are missing or otherwise unavailable. This can include differing DSP resources, I/O paths, voices, or plug-ins.

You will have an opportunity to save a detailed version of this report as a text file (.txt) by clicking the Yes button at the bottom of the dialog box. This file can be saved in a location of your choosing for future reference.

Here's what happens when you open a session with unavailable resources:

- Unavailable I/O paths and sends will be made inactive.
- Inserts with unavailable plug-ins will be made inactive.
- On sessions with high track counts, tracks exceeding the maximum number of available voices will be set to "voice off" (host-based systems) or "made inactive" (TDM systems).

Opening Sessions with Fade Files

Since Pro Tools 10 uses real-times fades, it will neither use nor create fade files. Any fades in the Fade Files folder will remain unused; no new files will be created.

Opening Legacy Sessions Saved with +6 dB Fader Gain

Since Pro Tools version 7, all sessions have had the capacity for up to +12 dB of fader gain. Sessions saved with older versions offered a maximum of +6 dB. When you open one of these legacy sessions, the fader settings will remain as saved, but the capacity for change will increase by +6 dB to a maximum of +12 dB.

Note: When saving a session in an earlier format—e.g., saving for Pro Tools 6.x—any fader gain or automation in excess of +6 dB will be truncated.

Opening Sessions Saved with Illegal Characters

By saying "illegal characters," we're not referring to criminal activity. Rather, there are some ASCII keystrokes/characters that are not recognized in Pro Tools naming conventions. You should avoid naming audio tracks or audio files using these characters.

If you open a session containing audio files that contain these characters in the name, you will be prompted to save a report of these filenames to the Session folder. Next, Pro Tools automatically makes copies of the files in question and saves them to the Audio Files folder with new names. The underscore character ("_") will be inserted in place of the illegal character in the filename, and the original, unaltered file will be placed in the Renamed Audio Files folder.

Here is a table of those illegal characters for your reference:

ASCII	DESCRIPTION
/	Forward Slash
\	Backslash
:	Colon
*	Asterisk
?	Question Mark
" or "	Quotation Marks
< or >	Less-Than or Greater-Than symbol
|	Vertical Line / pipe
Also not supported	Any character created using a combination of keys

Opening Recent Sessions

We have already learned how to open recent sessions using the Quick Start window. Now we'll look at other methods.

- Choose File > Open Recent to choose from the list of sessions, and click on the one you want to open. Pro Tools remembers the last 10 sessions opened.
- Type Command + Shift + O to open the most recent session.

To clear the Recent Sessions sub-menu, choose File > Open Recent; choose Clear from the list.

Opening Sessions with Plug-ins Deactivated

At some point, you may wish to open a Pro Tools session without activating all of the plug-ins. If you want to quickly audition the session without taking time to load the plug-ins, or maybe you are working on a system that doesn't support all of the plug-ins in that session, you can easily open a session with the plug-ins deactivated. Choose File > Open Session; locate and select the session you wish to open; then Shift + Click on the Open button. Your session will load with all of the inserts made inactive.

To re-activate the inserts, you can either activate them individually or choose File > Revert to Saved to re-open the session with all inserts (and available plug-ins) activated.

SAVING SESSIONS

As I am prone to tell my students, "Only save when you like the work you've done and want to keep it." In other words, save early and often, every few minutes at a minimum. Even though you can set up your software to save a backup of the session file every 15 minutes, it's safer to know that the last 12 minutes of intense editing won't have to be reconstructed from scratch if you should lose power. It happens.

To save your session file, choose File > Save. Alternately, you can press the Command + S keys.

The Save As Command

When working on a session that calls for iterations or versions, you can use the Save As command to create a new version of the session with a modified name. This file can be saved to the same directory or to another hard drive. This command saves a version of the session file that contains the edits, but does not move or duplicate any of the other files or folders in the session folder.

Saving versions should be a part of your workflow. As you add parts to a project or experiment with new edits, saving iterations along the way will allow you to go back to the exact version of the session before major changes were made. In music sessions, I will typically have a version of each session saved as "Song X_Tracking," a version saved as "Song X_Overdubs," a version saved as "Song X_Edits," and umpteen versions saved as "Song X_Mix01," "Song X_Mix02," and so forth.

Choose File > Save As, name the file, then click Save.

The Save Copy In Command

There are a variety of reasons to copy a session:

- Creating backups.
- Versioning.
- Sharing a session with other users.
- Consolidating large sessions into a smaller and more manageable session.
- Changing audio file type, bit depth, or sample rate.
- Prepping a session for use with another program or an earlier version of Pro Tools.

To save a copy of the session:

- Choose File > Save Copy In.
- In the Save Session Copy dialog box, type a name for the new session, then select a destination for the session to be saved.
- From the Session Format menu, select the desired Pro Tools version, from Pro Tools 3.2 through the latest version. (Pro Tools version 5.x is the earliest version for Windows PC users.)

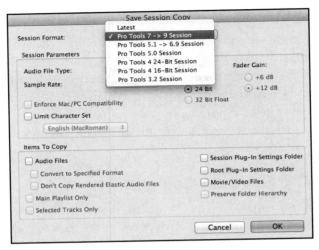

Fig. 3-7

- From the menu, choose the Audio File Type for the new session. Select BWF (WAV) or AIFF.
- Choose the sample rate and bit depth for the new session.
- Set the Fader Gain level for +6 dB or +12 dB as applicable.
- If you are saving a Pro Tools 7 or higher session to a lower version that may need to be compatible with both Mac and PC systems, click on the Enforce Mac/PC Compatibility button. This will create new files compatible with both systems.
- Select Limit Character Set when saving from a newer version to an older version of Pro Tools. The drop-down menu allows you to select a single language for the new session file.
- Select the applicable Items to Copy for the new session.
- Click Save to create the new session.

Note: Using the Save Copy In command does not close the session currently open in Pro Tools nor does it open the copy just created; it merely creates a new session with the parameters you have selected.

USING SESSION TEMPLATES

In an earlier section of the book, we discussed using the Quick Start Dialog to create a new session. Now we'll take a more detailed look at using existing templates, and creating and saving your own custom session templates.

Creating a New Session from a Template

Let's review the process for opening a Pro Tools Session Template and saving it as a new session.

1. Choose File > New, or press the Command + N key command.
2. From the New Session dialog box, select Create Session from Template. You can also open a template from the Finder level (Mac) simply by double-clicking a template file. Pro Tools templates use the .ptt file suffix.
3. Choose from the list of session templates on the right side of the dialog box. You will see that the templates are grouped by category.
4. Choose a category that describes the project in general terms, then select a template from the list that most closely matches your session.

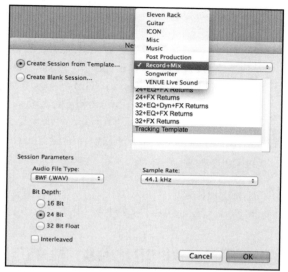

Fig. 3-8

5. Choose the Audio File Type, Sample Rate, and Bit Depth; then check the Interleaved box if you wish to record or import stereo audio files in the interleaved format rather than multiple mono files.
6. Click OK.
7. The Save New Session As dialog box will pop up and prompt you to choose the hard drive destination where the new session will be saved. Type a name for your session, then click Save to complete the operation.

Creating Your Own Session Templates

If you are a songwriter, guitar player, or engineer who tends to use the same or similar session configurations on a regular basis, you can save much time and many steps just by saving your own Pro Tools session templates for use in creating new projects. Once you have built a session containing the number of tracks, inserts, sends, and other elements that you require, you can save this session as a template by following these steps:

1. Choose File > Save As Template.

2. In the Save Session Template dialog box, you can choose to "Install template in system" or "Select location for *template...*" By installing the template in the system, you are actually saving the file to the same System folder used by the Quick Start dialog to show you template options. From here, you can select a category from the drop-down menu. Conversely, if you choose a different location for the template to be saved, it will not show up in the Quick Start dialog menu.

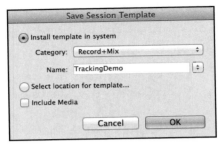

Fig. 3-9

3. If you wish to include any media files with your template, select the Include Media button. Note that this will include all media files (audio, video, MIDI) associated with your session. Make sure your session only contains the necessary media elements before saving.

4. Name the template and click OK.

CLOSING SESSIONS, QUITTING PRO TOOLS

You will only be able to have one session open at a time in Pro Tools. If you have a session open, you'll need to close it in order to open a new session.

Before you close a session or quit Pro Tools, you should perform a manual Save or Save As command. Even though you are prompted to save when closing or quitting, you should get in the habit of saving first. No sense in tempting fate.

To close a session, choose File > Close Session, or type Shift + Command + W.

To quit Pro Tools, choose Pro Tools > Quit Pro Tools, or type Command + Q.

You will be prompted to Save, Don't Save, or Cancel the operation.

ACCESSING PRO TOOLS MENUS

There are 13 main menus in the menu bar at the top of the screen that give you access to configure the vast majority of available Pro Tools functions. These menus are available to you regardless of whether you're working in the Edit or Mix windows. Refer to this list when following menu selection instructions.

🍎   Pro Tools   File   Edit   View   Track   Clip   Event   AudioSuite   Options   Setup   Window   Marketplace   Help

Fig. 3-10

- **Pro Tools**: This menu lets you access version info, and preferences; and hide or quit the program.
- **File**: Open sessions, create new sessions, save versions, bounce audio and video, import/export options, general info.
- **Edit**: Undo, cut/copy/paste options, clip editing commands.
- **View**: Select display options.
- **Track**: Create and manage audio and MIDI tracks, manage track automation data.
- **Clip**: Manage audio and MIDI clip, including clip groups, looping, sync points, quantizing, and Elastic Audio properties.
- **Event**: Manage Time, Tempo, and Key operations for audio and MIDI tracks; activate Beat Detective.
- **Audio Suite**: Access to all Audio Suite functions for processing audio clips. (See the Audio Suite section of this book for new rendering options in Pro Tools 10.)
- **Options**: Manage record modes, transport control, and many other functional options for Pro Tools operation.
- **Setup**: Optimize system configurations, hardware routing, and access preferences.
- **Window**: Show, hide, and memorize screen display and window configurations.
- **Marketplace:** Access online information about your AVID account, available plug-ins, Support and Training, and Upgrades, using an in-app AVID browser.
- **Help**: Online and offline help is available on a variety of topics.

MAIN PRO TOOLS WINDOWS

Pro Tools gives you two main operating environments, the Edit window and the Mix window, both with complementary functions. You may prefer working mainly in one or the other, but you can move effortlessly between the two for maximum flexibility in manipulating tracks during recording, editing, and mixing. Select Window > Edit to show the Edit window, and Window > Mix to show the Mix window. Command + "=" toggles between these windows.

OTHER WINDOWS

In addition to the two main environments, there are several other types of windows you will learn to use:

- **The Transport Window** gives you access to navigation controls and all transport-related functions.

Fig. 3-11

- **Plug-in Windows** give you access to plug-in parameter adjustments.

Fig. 3-12

- **MIDI Edit Windows** allow you to edit MIDI information.

Fig. 3-13

- The **Score Edit Window** allows you to edit MIDI information as musical notation.

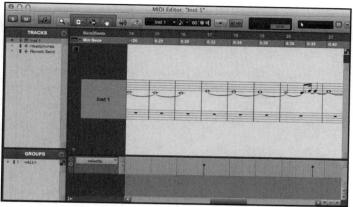

Fig. 3-14

- **DigiBase Browsers** give you access to session media and allow you to manage media, as well as to audition and import files.

Fig. 3-15

- There are also **In-App Web Browsers** to give you access to Pro Tools Online and the AVID Marketplace.

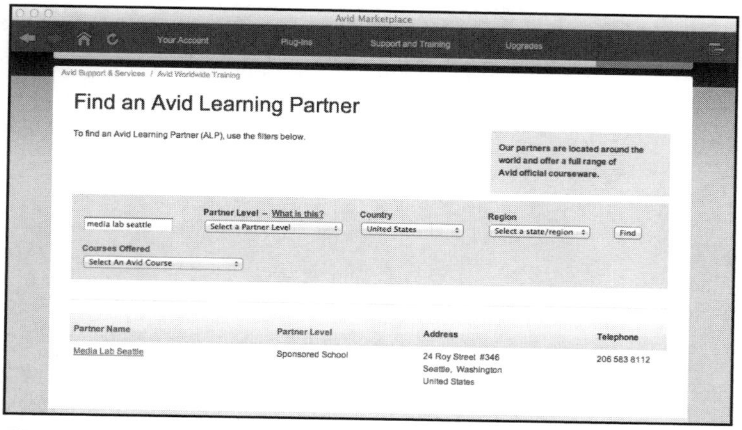

Fig. 3-16

THE MIX WINDOW

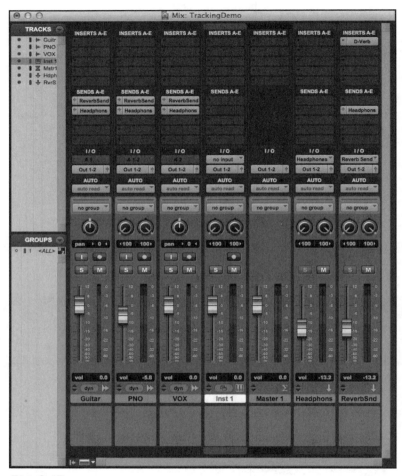

Fig. 3-17

The Mix window shows tracks as vertical channel strips with meters, much like a recording console. This window also shows controls for:

- Inserts
- Sends
- Input and output assignments
- Volume
- Pan
- Record Enable

- Track Input monitoring
- Automation mode
- Solo
- Mute
- Instrument controls
- Mic preamps
- HEAT controls (Pro Tools HD only)

To view the Mix window, select Window > Mix.

To view all display options, select View > Mix Window > All.

THE EDIT WINDOW

Fig. 3-18

The Edit window gives you a timeline-based display of all tracks, audio and video clips, and MIDI events active in your session. This is also the main window for recording and editing audio, MIDI, and automation data. The tracks show controls for record enable, Solo, Mute, and Automation modes, and additional information display can be easily modified to show as much or as little as desired.

To view the Edit window, select Window > Edit.

To view all display options, select View > Edit Window > All.

Fig. 3-19

There are several display modules that are always available to you in the Edit window, and their views may be modified to provide options for accessing a variety of functions. These are:

- Edit Mode buttons
- Edit tools
- Counters
- Edit Selection indicators
- Grid and Nudge selectors

The order in which these modules appear in the window can be changed simply by holding the Command key and dragging the module to the desired location at the top of the Edit window.

There are also optional displays you can choose to add to the Edit window view. These are selectable via the Edit Window toolbar in the upper-right corner of the Edit window.

Let's take a tour of the options and functions available to you in the Edit Window displays.

EDIT MODES

There are four basic editing modes in Pro Tools: Shuffle, Slip, Spot, and Grid modes. There are two Grid modes, which we will explore in a moment. The Edit modes are selectable via the Edit mode buttons in the upper left-hand corner of the Edit window display. You can click the appropriate Shuffle, Slip, and Spot mode button to select the mode; with Grid mode you can click and hold the button to display the option for choosing Absolute or Relative Grid modes. Once you have selected, you may simply click the Grid

Fig. 3-20

mode button. Alternately, you can cycle through the main Edit modes by using the Accent key (`), right next to the number "1" on your alpha keyboard. Each press of the Accent key advances to the next mode.

Following are the detailed descriptions of each mode and its functions.

Shuffle (Key Command: FI)

Shuffle mode allows you to add clips to the timeline without gaps in between, move clips in the timeline without leaving gaps, or insert new regions between adjacent clips while forcing subsequent clips downstream. Trimming a clip in Shuffle mode will affect the timing of all clips downstream. If you change the order of clips in a sequence, you will notice that the clips will always snap to each other's boundaries. The exception here is this: if a gap already exists between clips, moving a clip into that position using Shuffle mode will maintain the gap.

An edit made in Shuffle mode is also known as a ripple edit.

Shuffle mode does not apply to MIDI notes.

SHUFFLE LOCK

When editing a project in which clip timing must be maintained, you can invoke Shuffle Lock, which effectively locks out the Shuffle mode function. This prevents accidental timing changes using the Shuffle editing mode. To lock the Shuffle mode and make it inactive, Command-click the Shuffle button. You will now see a Lock icon on that button display. When locked, Shuffle mode can no longer be selected by mouse-click or key command. Command-click the Shuffle button again to unlock Shuffle mode.

Fig. 3-21

Note: You must be in an edit mode other than Shuffle in order to enable Shuffle lock.

Slip (Key Command: F2)

As the name suggests, this mode allows you to move or *slip* clips in time or between tracks without time constraint. Using slip allows you to position clips with gaps between clips, or overlap them, without regard to the position of any clips that may already be placed in the timeline.

Slip is the default mode for most editing operations.

Spot (Key Command: F3)

Clicking on a clip in Spot mode brings up a dialog box that enables you to type in a precise timecode or bar/beat start, end, or sync point for that clip. Dragging a clip from the Clip list, Finder, or DigBase browser into the timeline also brings up the Spot dialog.

This is particularly handy if you've accidentally moved a clip from its original recording time and need to get it back to where it once belonged.

Grid (Key Command: F4)

When inserting, moving, or trimming media clips or MIDI notes, Grid mode allows you to snap clips and MIDI notes to precise time increments, whether minutes/seconds, feet/frames, or bars/beats. You can specify the Grid increment in the Grid selector window.

Moving a note, clip, or marker using the Absolute Grid setting snaps the event start exactly to the nearest time increment on the grid, even if the event was initially between beats or other grid markings.

Fig. 3-22

Relative Grid aligns the note or clip to the grid relative to its initial starting position. For example, if clip A is between beats 1 and 2 of the bar and your grid is set for quarter notes, the clip will be moved left or right in quarter-note increments but will retain its original timing between beats. This feature is demonstrated in a video on the DVD included with this book.

You can Shift-click on the Grid mode button to toggle Absolute and Relative Grid mode states.

To temporarily defeat snapping to Grid, press the Command key while moving or trimming a clip or note with the mouse. Releasing the key returns you to normal snap to Grid operation.

Note: When moving or editing video in Grid mode, the time reference of a video clip is automatically and irrevocably set to frames. Even if moved to an exact bar/beat Grid line, a video clip will default to placement on the nearest frame if the bar/beat should fall between frames.

DISPLAYING GRID LINES

In the Edit window, you can show or hide the Grid lines by clicking the Grid button in the Grid selector window, or by clicking the name of the Timebase Ruler that is currently selected.

Fig. 3-23

USING SNAP TO GRID WITH OTHER EDIT MODES

You can use a combination of modes to give you more flexibility when editing clips in the timeline. In Shuffle, Slip, or Spot mode, Shift-click the Grid mode button to enable a combination mode that can be very useful for editing to a grid.

GRID VALUES

Grid values are governed by two factors: timebase (minutes/seconds, bars/beats, and so on) and increments (seconds/milliseconds, whole/quarter/eighth/sixteenth notes, and so on). When clicked, the small Triangle icon next to the Grid selector window reveals a pop-up window of optional values for the Grid display.

In addition to the regular timebase options for Grid value, you can select Follow Main Time Scale to have the Grid value follow the Time Scale as selected in the ruler.

Choosing the Clips/Markers option from the Grid Values menu "magnetizes" the clips and markers so that they can snap to the nearest edit or marker when dragged, if so desired. Clips and markers still behave as they would in Slip mode, but they tend to snap to other clips or markers when in close proximity. This makes it much easier to line up takes sequentially without gaps or overlaps.

Note: MIDI notes do not conform to the Clips/Markers grid settings; they will behave as they would in Slip mode.

Fig. 3-24

EDIT TOOLS

The Edit Tools module gives you access to the tools you'll be using to manipulate audio and video clips, MIDI data, automation—just about everything you can touch in Pro Tools.

Fig. 3-25

Zoom Buttons

The Zoom buttons magnify the audio and MIDI track displays both vertically and horizontally. Not the track *height*, just the height of the waveform or MIDI notes visible within the track. Click and hold one of the buttons, and drag left/right or up/down to scroll continuously.

- **Vertical Audio Zoom:** Use the audio vertical zoom buttons to increase or decrease the height of the waveform visible in the display. You can also use Command + Option + "[" to zoom out, and Command + Option + "]" to zoom

  Fig. 3-26

  in. If you hold the Command key down for a few moments, the display will zoom continuously.

- **Vertical MIDI Zoom:** Use the MIDI vertical zoom buttons to increase or decrease the height of the note data visible in the display. You can also use Command + Shift + "[" to zoom out, and Command + Shift + "]" to zoom in. If you hold the Command key down for a few moments, the display will zoom continuously. Note: MIDI vertical zoom is not active when the Track view is set to Clips or Blocks view.

- **Horizontal Zoom, All Tracks:** Use the horizontal zoom buttons at the left and right sides of the Zoom options box to increase or decrease the length of the time period visible in the display. You can also use Command + "[" to zoom out, and Command + "]" to zoom in; or simply use the "R" key to zoom out and the "T" key to zoom in. If you hold the Command key down for a few moments, the display will zoom continuously.

- **Previous Zoom Level:** To return to the previous zoom level, either Option- click one of the Zoom buttons, or type Command + Option + E.
- **Zoom Preset Buttons:** Below the Zoom controls are five memory Preset Store/Recall buttons used for quickly recalling horizontal magnification. By default, these buttons are set for increasing degrees of magnification, and can easily store user preset Zoom levels.

To store a Zoom preset:

1. Adjust your desired horizontal track zoom using the Zoomer tool or other key command.
2. Click and hold one of the five preset buttons.
3. From the pop-up menu, select Save Zoom Preset.
4. The Zoom preset button will flash briefly, signaling that your preset information has been stored to that button location. Any previous preset information will be overwritten.

Zoom presets are stored with the session and can be different for each project.

Zoomer Tool

The Zoomer tool zooms in and out on the timeline horizontally. Choose the Zoomer tool, then click once in the timeline to magnify by one level. Use Option-click to decrease magnification level.

Fig. 3-27

In **Normal Zoom** mode, the Zoomer tool remains selected even after the zoom is complete.

Single Zoom mode allows you to use Zoom once; the cursor then reverts to the previously selected non-zooming tool.

Use the F5 key to select the Zoomer tool, and to toggle between Normal and Single Zoom modes.

Continuous Zoom is activated by holding down the Control key while dragging the Zoomer tool up or down to increase or decrease vertical magnification. Use Control + drag left or right to increase or decrease horizontal magnification.

You can also drag up or down on the Audio Zoom button, MIDI Zoom button, or the left or right Zoom buttons to zoom continuously.

View Entire session. To view the entire length of the horizontal session timeline, double-click the Zoomer Tool icon or type Option + A. Using this command also resets the vertical waveform zoom to the default setting, and shows all MIDI notes on the vertical plane.

Trim Tool

There are four options for the Trimmer tool:

- **Standard:** Shortens or extends the duration of an audio clip or MIDI note by clicking and dragging the start or end of the clip or note.
- **TCE:** The Time Compression/Expansion tool uses an AudioSuite plug-in to process the contents of a clip. You can speed up or slow down playback of a clip without changing the pitch. The resulting clip is rendered at that speed, and a new file is created and saved to disk. This file is placed into the timeline and the Clip list.

  The TCE plug-in can be specified in the Preferences window. Choose Setup > Preferences, then click on the Processing tab. In the TC/E pane, select the plug-in of choice from the TC/E Plug-in menu. In the Default Settings menu, choose the setting that most nearly matches the type of track you'll be editing.

- **Scrub:** The Scrub Trim tool allows you to scrub the ends of a clip to hear the audio as you adjust the clip length. Drag the end of a clip to hear the audio; let go of the mouse button when you have found the appropriate spot in the track. This is handy for finding the edge of a beat or the beginning of a breath. For finer resolution, hold down the Command key while scrubbing.

  This tool is available to Pro Tools HD and CPTK users only.

- **Loop:** Use the Loop Trim tool to duplicate clips back to back in a sequence or to adjust the length of a looped clip. Whether the subject is a drum loop or room ambience, this is the quickest way to create a continuous audio loop.

  To edit the length of a loop series, position the Loop Trim cursor near the middle of the right edge of the last clip, then click and drag to adjust. To edit the original clip on which the loop is based, position the cursor along the bottom edge of a looped clip, then click and drag to adjust the length.

Selector Tool

Selects an area within a clip or track for editing or playback. You can define a region in a track or in the Timeline ruler above the tracks. To select an entire clip with the Selector tool, double-click anywhere in the clip.

Grabber Tool

The Grabber tool enables you to select an entire clip and move it within the track or to other tracks within the timeline. There are three options for the Grabber tool:

- **Time:** With this tool, you can select an entire clip within the timeline by clicking once on the clip. You can then move the clip to another position on any track.
- **Separation:** This option allows you to grab and move a clip or a defined edit region within a clip. It is best when used with the Smart tool; you'll see why a few paragraphs from now.
- **Object Grabber:** The Object Grabber tool allows you to select non-contiguous clips, or clips that are not next to each another. This is handy for moving a group of time-related clips without selecting the other audio material between those clips. The Object Grabber is also good for defining clips to be included in Clip Groups. Note: This tool cannot be used with the Smart tool.

Smart Tool

Click on this gem to have immediate access to a combination of the Selector, Grabber, and Trim tools, depending on where the cursor hovers over a track, clip, or automation lane. The Smart tool also performs single-click fades and cross-fades. Since these functions are all dependent upon where the cursor is positioned, you should take some time to get familiar with the feel of using this tool. For repetitive operations, such as breath editing, it may be more efficient to use a dedicated tool; but the Smart tool can be a real time-saver if you're performing multiple duties, such as defining edits, cutting or truncating clips, moving clip segments, and adjusting automation parameters.

EDITING AUDIO:

- To activate the **Trim** tool, move the cursor to the start or end of a clip until the left or right Bracket icon appears.
- To activate the **Selector** tool, hover over the upper half of a clip in the middle of a track until the I-Beam icon appears.
- To activate the **Grabber** tool, hover over the lower half of a clip in the middle of a track until the Hand icon appears.

EDITING AUTOMATION

First, change the track view to display automation data, or open the automation lane display beneath an audio track.

To activate the Trim tool, move the cursor near the top of a clip until the horizontal Bracket icon appears. Dragging the automation bar up or down will create new automation breakpoints for the clip being adjusted. Use the Command key modifier with the Trim tool for higher-resolution moves.

To activate the Selector tool, hover over the lower portion of a clip until the I-Beam icon appears. Use this to select a region within a clip or track, then use the Trim tool to adjust or delete automation. Double-clicking a clip in Selector mode will select the whole clip.

Use a modifier key in conjunction with the Grabber to change the state of the Grabber tool when editing automation data.

- **Command:** Hold the Command key to add a single automation breakpoint or node.
- **No Modifier Key:** Release the Command key to move the breakpoint with the Grabber tool.
- **Shift:** Constrain Grabber tool node adjustment to the vertical plane by holding the Shift key.
- **Option:** Hold down the Option key to use the Grabber to delete individual automation breakpoints.
- **Control:** Hold the Control key to turn the Grabber into a Pencil tool. You can use this tool to draw automation data according to the pattern selected in the Pencil tool menu.

EDITING MIDI NOTES

- To activate the **Trim** tool, move the cursor to the start or end of a MIDI note until the left or right Bracket icon appears.
- To activate the **Selector** tool, move outside of a MIDI note in the middle of a track until the Crosshair icon appears.
- To activate the **Grabber** tool, hover over the middle of a MIDI note until the Hand icon appears.

THESE ARE A FEW OF MY FAVORITE TOOLS

I leave the cursor tools set on Smart tools all the time, except when I need a job-specific tool, such as TC/E or the Pencil tool. Of the three choices for tools, I use the Standard Trim tool, the Selector tool, and the Separation Grabber. These allow me to trim the beginning and end of a clip, highlight a region within a clip, and easily move regions or notes. The addition of the Separation Grabber allows me to highlight areas for deletion, copying, or moving without disturbing the original region or having to change to another tool.

Fig. 3-28

You can easily change edit tools by using the Right-click button to select from the pop-up menu, or by toggling through options by using function keys F5 to F10.

Scrubber Tool

Drag the Scrubber tool across audio tracks in the Edit window to locate an edit point or to hear a particular section within an audio region. We used to "scrub" tape back and forth over the playback head on a reel-to-reel tape recorder to find a musical downbeat for editing or cuing; this is the digital equivalent.

When scrubbing a stereo track, holding the Scrubber tool in the top half of the track will scrub the left side of the stereo audio track; holding the Scrubber tool in the bottom half of the track will scrub the right side of the stereo audio track; holding the Scrubber tool in the middle of the track allows you to scrub (and hear) both sides of the stereo track.

Pro Tools will scrub up to two stereo audio tracks at a time. To scrub two tracks, position the Scrubber icon on the line between two adjacent tracks. Drag in the track to scrub audio.

Hold the Command key for higher resolution while scrubbing.

- **Scrub Shuttle Mode:** Whereas normal Scrubber mode will scrub audio as long as you move the mouse forward or back, Scrub Shuttle mode allows you to shuttle-play audio continuously, forward or backward, as long as you hold the mouse button down. To activate Scrub Shuttle, simply press the Option key when you begin scrubbing. There is no need to hold the Option key down continuously. Releasing the mouse button exits Scrub Shuttle mode.

- **Numeric Keypad Shuttle Mode:** If you set the numeric keypad to Shuttle mode in the preferences, you will be able to play back a selected region just by pressing and holding various keys on the numeric keypad. Release the key to stop playback.

To activate Numeric Keypad shuttle mode:

1. Open the Preferences window by choosing Setup > Preferences.
2. Click the Operation tab and locate the Transport pane.
3. Click the button to activate Numeric Keypad: Shuttle.
4. Select a starting point in a track or tracks.
5. Press and hold the following keys to initiate playback from that point, in forward or reverse:

SHUTTLE SPEED	REWIND KEY	FORWARD KEY
1 X speed	4	6
4 X speed	7	9
1/4 X speed	1	3
1/2 X speed	4 + 5	5 + 6
2 X speed	7 + 8	8 + 9

You may press successive keys to change direction or speed; release the key to stop playback.

Remember to change the Numeric Keypad mode preferences back to Transport when finished with this operation.

Pencil Tool

You can use the Pencil tool to draw Pro Tools data in the following ways:

- Use to redraw waveforms so as to eliminate a click or pop in an audio file. (Must be zoomed in to the sample view level in order to activate.)
- May be used for drawing MIDI notes in MIDI or Instrument tracks.
- May be used for drawing automation breakpoints. Can draw various shapes for automating pan, volume, and other parameters. Shapes include line, triangle, square, random, and freehand.
- Note: Draw Tempo information in the Tempo ruler. The Pencil tool is made active by clicking the icon in the Edit toolbar. It can be activated temporarily by holding the Control key when the Smart tool is in use.

Edit Tool Modifier Keys

The modifier keys are the Shift, Control, Option, and Command keys. (On a PC, those keys are Shift, Control, Windows, and Alt.) Pro Tools allows you to modify keystrokes and mouse-clicks depending on the modifier key. In some cases, various combinations of modifier keys will be used to achieve different results. For example, while Command + Click (Alt + Click on PC) brings up a tool menu for the cursor, Control + Command + Click (Control + Alt + Click on PC) performs a variety of functions, depending on the menu clicked.

The mouse Right-click will bring up a contextual menu of options as well.

See a list of topic-specific key commands at the end of each chapter.

Selection Modifiers

The row of buttons beneath the Edit tools give you ready access to Pro Tools views and functions without having to hunt deep in menus.

Fig. 3-29

ZOOM TOGGLE

This is a handy feature when you need to edit something at a very high level of magnification—for example, when editing a click or pop in a recorded track. Using the Selector tool, define the region you want to edit. Click the Zoom Toggle button, then adjust the vertical and horizontal magnification to blow up the region display on the screen. When you click the Zoom Toggle button again, you will return to the previous track view with all magnification settings returned to normal. Now you can use the Zoom Toggle button to closely examine any region or clip you have highlighted in the timeline.

The key command for Zoom Toggle is "E."

TAB TO TRANSIENT

When the Tab key is highlighted, each key-press enables the cursor to advance from one transient peak to the next transient peak within a selected track. Option + Tab reverses direction so that each key-press rewinds to the previous transient peak.

If you turn off Tab to Transient, the Tab key advances from edit to edit with each key-press. Option + Tab reverses direction so that each key-press rewinds to the previous edit.

MIRRORED MIDI EDITING

When editing MIDI clips, enable this command to have any edits of that clip apply to all copies of the clip. This is useful when editing MIDI loops.

The Mirrored MIDI Editing button flashes red once when you have made an edit that applies to more than one MIDI clip.

AUTOMATION FOLLOWS EDIT

When this button is highlighted, any automation data associated with audio or MIDI clips will travel with the clips when they are moved from their original location in the timeline. Turning off this function allows you to move a clip without moving the automation on that track. I am still trying to find a use for this function.

You can also turn the Automation Follows Edit function on or off by selecting Options > Automation Follows Edit.

LINK TIMELINE AND EDIT SELECTION

The default setting for this selection modifier links the timeline and Edit selection, and defines the range for playback and recording.

Turning this function off allows you to select a region for editing, or a playback start point in the timeline; and audition or play another part of the timeline without disturbing the initial edit selection. This can be helpful when you want to retain a playback position, yet need to audition material from another point on the timeline.

To play another selection in the timeline, highlight a region, then press Control + "[" to play that selection. If Loop Play is selected, the selection will continue to play repeatedly until stopped.

Click the Link Timeline and Edit Selection button to activate or deactivate the link. You can also select or deselect Options > Link Timeline and Edit Selection.

LINK TRACK AND EDIT SELECTION

In normal operations, Pro Tools does not automatically link an edit selection in the timeline with associated tracks. In other words, if you select clips on two tracks, both Track Names will not be highlighted. Clicking the Link Track and Edit Selection button highlights all Track Names when an edit selection is made across multiple tracks. This is particularly helpful when you wish to make a track view change, activate Zoom Toggle, or view automation data across selected tracks.

In addition to clicking the button, you can activate or deactivate this mode by choosing Options > Link Track and Edit Selection.

INSERTION FOLLOWS PLAYBACK

With this button activated, the point at which you stop playback will be the point at which the next playback begins. In other words, the cursor stays where it was when you stopped playback. If you deactivate this function, playback will begin from the same starting point no matter where you stop playing. You will probably find both states useful when editing.

In addition to clicking the button, you can activate or deactivate this mode by pressing the "N" key.

Counters

The Counter display shows the current cursor position in the timeline as measured in the currently selected timebase. You can choose from:

Fig. 3-30

- Bars/Beats
- Minutes/Seconds
- Timecode
- Feet + Frames
- Samples

You can also activate a secondary or sub-counter, displaying a second timebase for reference.

The counter display uses the Start/End/Length pane to show you the position of the play start point, the end point of an edit selection, and the length of an edit selection (if any).

There is a button for toggling playback of MIDI notes when editing.

Beneath the basic Counter display is another row of status indicators:

- Current Cursor Location
- Current Cursor Value
- Timeline Data Online Status
- Session Data Online Status
- Delay Compensation Status
- Solo Status
- Mute Status
- Default Note Duration selector

Grid and Nudge Settings

This module displays current Grid and Nudge increment settings and gives you access to customizing those settings.   **Fig. 3-31**

Basic Transport Controls

This smaller version of the Transport window shows just the basic Transport controls, including:

Fig. 3-32

- Sync Online
- Stop
- Play
- Record Enable
- Return to Zero
- Rewind
- Fast Forward
- Go to End

This truncated Transport also has status indicators for Record Enable Status and Input Status.

MIDI Controls

The MIDI Controls window gives you Edit window access to the following controls:

Fig. 3-33

- Count Off enable/disable button
- Count Off bar number indicator (double-click to access click and count off options)
- Meter indicator (double-click to insert meter change)
- Tempo resolution and BPM display

   Beneath this display pane are four MIDI control buttons:

- Wait for Note (when recording MIDI) on/off
- Metronome on/off
- MIDI Merge control on/off
- Conductor Track on/off

Synchronization Controls

When operating Pro Tools in a timecode or MIDI Timecode environment, the Synchronization controls allow you to put Pro Tools into Online mode (waiting to respond to external timecode for playback or record) and generate MTC on/off. Clicking the button activates that function.

Fig. 3-34

Edit Window Toolbar

In the upper-right corner of the Edit window is a small Triangle icon, which hides the Edit Window Toolbar menu. In this menu, you can choose which components of the toolbar you wish to have visible in the Edit window by clicking on the name of the option. The options are:

Fig. 3-35

- Zoom Controls
- Transport
- MIDI Controls
- Synchronization
- Minimal (shows only the four basic Edit window displays)
- All (shows all Edit window display options)
- Expanded Transport (shows all Transport window display options)
- Track List

- Clip list
- Universe
- MIDI Editor

Key Commands

Most of the common operations in Pro Tools can be activated by a mouse-click or a keystroke. If you have a two-button mouse, there is a whole list of shortcuts available to you by performing a Right-click on a menu or pane. There are nearly 30 pages of key command shortcuts in Pro Tools. Far too many to list here, but I will include the most-used commands as they pertain to each topic of the book. Memorizing these commands will save you lots of time and many miles of mousing.

There are custom keyboards, keyboard overlays, and stickers available from AVID and other third-party suppliers. If you work in Pro Tools a lot, it may be worth your while to look into those options to improve your workflow and speed up your process. Since I totally wore out the original stickers that came with Pro Tools 6, my favorite new Pro Tools keyboard stickers come from a company called "The Best Pro Tools Stickers Ever." I am inclined to agree. Check them out, see if you concur: www.ShortcutStickers.com.

Keyboard Focus

The Pro Tools Keyboard Focus determines how the alpha keys function on your keyboard. There are three modes of operation, which will allow you to directly select clip in the clip list, enable or disable groups in the group list, or perform an edit or playback command. Only one Keyboard Focus mode can be active at a time, which disables the other two temporarily. Here are the different modes:

COMMANDS KEYBOARD FOCUS

Selected in the Tracks pane of the Edit window. This enables a wide variety of single-key editing and playback commands accessible from the Edit window.

Note: Even if Commands Keyboard Focus mode is disabled, you can still access the command by using Control + the usual key.

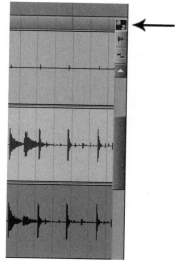

Fig. 3-36

CLIP LIST KEYBOARD FOCUS
Selected in the upper-right corner of the Clip pane.

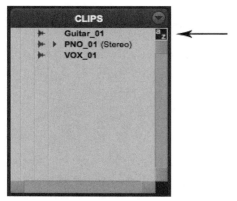

Fig. 3-37

When enabled, you will be able to select audio and MIDI clip by typing the first few letters of the name.

GROUP LIST KEYBOARD FOCUS
Selected in the upper-right corner of the Groups pane.

When enabled, you will be able to enable or disable groups by typing the Group ID letter that corresponds with the desired group.

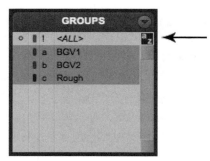

Fig. 3-38

KEYBOARD FOCUS ACCESS
Either click the a–z button in the panes as described or type one of the following key commands:

KEYBOARD FOCUS SETTING	COMMAND + OPTION +...
Commands Keyboard Focus	1
Clip or Region List Keyboard Focus	2
Group List Keyboard Focus	3
Tracks Pane Keyboard Focus	4
MIDI Editor Pane Keyboard Focus	5

TRANSPORT WINDOW

Pro Tools uses a Transport window to access all transport functions; in addition, there are dedicated key commands for transport control. To bring up the Transport window, choose Window > Transport, or simply type Command + 1 on the numeric keypad.

Fig. 3-39

The basic transport controls are, from left to right:

- **Online:** Puts Pro Tools into Sync mode, allowing recording or playback when synchronized to an external timecode source.
- **Return to Zero:** Moves the cursor to the beginning of the session. Key command: Return on the main keyboard.
- **Rewind:** Moves the cursor earlier in the timeline when pressed or held. Key command: "1" on the numeric keypad. Holding the Rewind button moves the cursor continuously. Clicking the Rewind button once moves the cursor earlier by time increments depending on the scale you have selected in the Main Time Scale window. Clicking the Rewind button repeatedly moves the cursor earlier by increments.

REWIND/FAST FORWARD INCREMENTS

TIME SCALE	INCREMENT
Bar|Beats	1 bar earlier/later
Min:Secs	1 second earlier/later
Time Code	1 frame earlier/later
Feet+Frames	1 foot earlier/later
Samples	1 second earlier/later

- **Fast Forward:** Moves the cursor later in the timeline when pressed or held. Key command: "2" on the numeric keypad. Holding the Fast Forward button moves the cursor continuously. Clicking the Fast Forward button once (or more) moves the cursor later by time increments dependent on the scale you have selected in the Main Time Scale window. Clicking the Fast Forward button repeatedly moves the cursor later by increments.

TRANSPORT COMMANDS

FUNCTION	KEY
Play/Stop	0
Rewind	1
Fast Forward	2
Record	3
Toggle Loop Playback mode	4
Toggle Loop Record mode	5
Toggle QuickPunch mode	6
Click On/Off	7
Countoff On/Off	8
Toggle MIDI Merge/Replace mode	9

- **Go to End:** Locates the cursor at the end of the last clip in your session. Key command: Option + Return.
- **Stop:** Click the Stop button to stop the transport. Key command: spacebar or "0" on the numeric keypad.
- **Play:** Begins playback from the current cursor location. Click the Play button. Key command: spacebar or "0" on the numeric keypad. Right-clicking the Play button allows you to choose playback modes from a pop-up menu:

  Half-Speed

  Prime for Playback

  Loop Playback

  Dynamic Transport

You can cycle through the playback modes by Control-clicking the Play button when stopped. See the following section on Playback mode for more detail.

- **Record:** Clicking the Record button arms Pro Tools to record on all record-enabled tracks; clicking Play begins the recording. Key commands: pressing Command + spacebar, F12, or "3" on the numeric keypad will each begin recording immediately. Right-clicking the Record button allows you to choose recording modes from a pop-up menu:

  Normal

  Loop Record

  Destructive Record

  Quick Punch

Track Punch (HD systems only)

Destructive Punch (HD systems only)

You can also cycle through the recording modes by Control-clicking the Record button when stopped. See the following Recording mode section for more detail.

There are two additional indicators in the transport window, a Track Record Enable Indicator, and a Track Input Monitor Indicator. The upper box turns red to indicate if you have at least one record-enabled track, gray if there are none.

Fig. 3-40

The lower box turns green to indicate that at least one track is set to monitor Input Only (regardless of record-enable status), gray if all tracks are set to monitor Auto Input.

Fig. 3-41

Transport Window Menu

The Transport window can show as much or as little information as you desire. Choose from display options by clicking the Triangle icon on the right side of the Transport window. You will see a menu listing your display options, including:

COUNTERS

This shows or hides the main and secondary counter displays.

Fig. 3-42

MIDI CONTROLS

This shows or hides the MIDI control section of the transport, which displays click/tempo/meter information and count-off status, and allows you one-click access to toggle four MIDI-related states:

• **Wait for Note:** When this is selected, recording will not begin until Pro Tools senses that a MIDI event has been received. Use this when you want recording to begin at the exact time you begin playing a MIDI instrument or send some other MIDI data.

Fig. 3-43

- **Metronome:** When this mode is selected, Pro Tools will generate a regular rhythmic beat that can trigger internal or external MIDI sounds, providing a click track for use in recording or playback. You must create a click track or Instrument track in order to assign a sound source input/output for the metronome click to be heard. The click will correspond to the tempo you have set in the Tempo window or Conductor track. Double-click the Metronome button to open the Click/Countoff Options dialog window used to configure the metronome.

- **MIDI Merge Mode:** When this is highlighted, any newly recorded MIDI information will be merged and added to any existing MIDI information on that track. When deselected (also called "Replace mode"), any newly recorded MIDI information will replace whatever was previously recorded on that track.

- **Conductor Track:** Also called the Tempo Ruler Enable button, this activates the Tempo map as defined in the Tempo ruler of the Edit window. When it is deselected, Pro Tools reverts to Manual Tempo mode and will ignore the Tempo ruler information. Manual Tempo mode allows you to enter a numeric BPM value in the Tempo field, or tap the desired tempo by tapping the "T" key on your main keyboard.

Display the MIDI Controls window by selecting View > Transport > MIDI Controls, or Command-clicking the Expand/Collapse "+" button in the Transport window.

SYNCHRONIZATION
This window displays three buttons:

- **Online:** Puts Pro Tools into Sync mode, allowing recording or playback when synchronized to an external timecode source.

- **Gen MTC:** When Gen MTC is active, Pro Tools will generate MIDI timecode and send the signal out to all connected devices capable of receiving MIDI TC.

- **Gen LTC:** When Gen LTC is active, Pro Tools will generate Linear timecode in the format specified in your session setup.

MINIMAL
This command minimizes the size and content of the Transport window. Unless you have selected the Expanded Transport option, the Transport window will only show the main Transport control buttons.

ALL

This selection expands the transport to show all available Transport Module windows.

EXPANDED TRANSPORT

This option expands the Transport window display to add more information to the display, including secondary counter, pre-roll and post-roll settings, and the Metronome setting details.

MIDI IMPLEMENTATION IN PRO TOOLS
MIDI Is Not Audio

Contrary to popular belief, MIDI is not audio. MIDI, which is an acronym for Musical Instrument Digital Interface, is an instruction set containing control information common to all MIDI-capable devices and programs. In 1982, US music technology pioneer Dave Smith developed a standard specification for communication of control data between synthesizers and other music devices. Ikutaro Kakehashi, founder of the Roland Corporation, helped institutionalize the standard by incorporating MIDI I/O in all Roland synthesizers. Since then, MIDI has become the DAW standard for storing, synchronizing, and transmitting information about musical performances, including notation, patch change information, continuous controllers, SYSEX data, and many other control protocols. The MIDI 1.0 spec is also the standard music communication protocol for computers, cell phones, game consoles, and other devices.

In recent releases, Pro Tools has emerged as a powerful tool for recording, editing, and manipulating MIDI data. The importance of MIDI integration into any modern DAW is beyond debate, and MIDI implementation Pro Tools 10 has by far surpassed previous efforts. In addition to recording, manual data entry, editing, and playing back MIDI data on MIDI or virtual Instrument tracks, Pro Tools gives you four different windows in which to display and manipulate MIDI data:

- Edit window
- MIDI Edit window
- MIDI Event list
- Score Editor window

In the Edit window, MIDI data shows up on a track in a familiar piano roll–style display. This track can be resized and magnified much like any audio or Aux track, along with having the ability to save and display selected playlists. You can set a MIDI or virtual Instrument track view to display the following types of MIDI information:

- Blocks
- Clips
- Notes
- Velocity
- Volume
- Mute
- Pan
- Pitch Bend
- Mono Aftertouch
- Program Change
- Sysex
- Continuous Controller information

The MIDI Edit window opens as an expanded view of one (or several) MIDI or Instrument tracks, and has many more options for viewing and manipulating MIDI data.

Fig. 3-44

To open a MIDI Edit window:

- Choose Window > MIDI Editor
- Press Control + "="
- In the Edit window, Right-click a MIDI Clip or Track Name, then select Open in MIDI Editor from the pop-up list.
- If the MIDI preferences are set to allow it, you can double-click a MIDI clip to open that clip in a MIDI Edit window.

CHAPTER 3 REVIEW

1. When should you consider bit rate and sample rate for your sessions?
   a. When buying your Pro Tools system
   b. During pre-production
   c. When building a new Pro Tools session
   d. All of the above

2. True or False: Pro Tools now allows you to mix audio files with different bit and sample rates within the same session. _____

3. When creating a new session, you must choose between the following audio file formats for your session: _____ or _____.

4. To commence playback from the current cursor location, click the Play button on the Transport window, or simply press the keyboard _____ or the _____ key on the numeric keypad.

5. The Transport window can show _____ different counter displays.

6. The following MIDI controls can also be accessed from the transport: _____, _____, MIDI Merge mode, and _____, which is also called the Tempo Ruler Enable button.

7. When would you need to put Pro Tools into Online Synchronization mode? Whenever Pro Tools needs to sync to _____.

8. True or False: Clips erased or recorded using Destructive Record mode can be restored by using the Undo command. _____

9. The key command for initiating half-speed playback is _____ + _____. You can also Shift-click on the Play button in the Transport window.

10. Loop Play mode is accessible by Right-clicking on the Play button to expose a menu of playback options, or by pressing _____ + _____ on the Play button to toggle through the playback modes until Loop mode is reached.

11. Several recording modes are accessible by Right-clicking the Record button. These modes are:
   a. Normal
   b. Record
   c. Loop Record
   d. Destructive Record
   e. QuickPunch

12. Loop Record mode creates a new _____ for each recorded audio or MIDI pass.

13. With _____ enabled, new audio and/or MIDI is stored in a buffer from the point at which playback begins.

Building and Managing Your Virtual Studio

4

Just about every recording session is configured differently, so this chapter will walk you through the steps to create your own sessions with custom settings that match your exact needs. These can be simple or complex, but it's worth your time to explore the options using these building blocks.

Once you're familiar with these features, you can easily customize your own Pro Tools mixer to fit your project. As discussed in the previous chapter, you can even create your own templates to use for your next session.

Here, then, are the components for creating your custom virtual studio.

CONFIGURING A VIRTUAL MIXER IN PRO TOOLS

Building a custom mixer in Pro Tools allows you to completely sidestep the pitfalls of traditional analog or physical digital consoles. Pro Tools mixers are limited only by the capacity of your particular system and I/O hardware.

If you grew up on analog recording consoles, you got used to the fact that there were *always* limitations. Either there weren't enough inputs, or you had to sub-mix channels in order to get sufficient outputs, or there weren't enough sends; you get the idea. One of the first reasons to fall in love with Pro Tools is the ability to create *exactly* the right console you need to work on each and every song. Since the modules are virtual, you can grow or shrink the console to meet the immediate needs of your project.

Tracks

Each recorded audio channel should have its own track, as should Aux returns, sub-masters, MIDI tracks, and virtual instruments. This way you can balance, monitor, and meter each instrument independently of the other audio tracks.

Fig. 4-1

Level Control Fader

The volume level of each track, Aux send/return, instrument, and Master Fader can be adjusted by using a virtual volume control fader. In the Mix window, simply grab a fader with your mouse and move it up or down to change the apparent volume of the audio or MIDI track associated with it.

In the Edit window, you can click on the volume pane in the track I/O section to reveal a pop-up fader, or click on the small Fader icon in the I/O output assignment pane to open a window containing a condensed single-channel version of the Mix window view. This window contains a volume fader as well as Mute and Solo buttons, signal routing options, pan pots, and a meter. You can also access automation modes for that track and various status indicators.

Panning

Stereo Panning is the function of balancing a mono or stereo sound source between two physical outputs. Pro Tools provides a pan adjustment for every audio or MIDI track, usually in the form of a rotary pot or encoder.

A mono track will have one fader and one pan pot. A stereo track will have one fader and two pan pots, one per audio channel.

Stereo Pan Depth

Pro Tools now lets you select the amount of attenuation applied to signals panned to the center in a stereo mix. To access this setting from the Session Setup window, choose Setup > Session (Command + 2 on the numeric keypad). Select the Format tab, then click on the Pan Depth drop-down menu. You can choose from four different levels of attenuation:

Fig. 4-2   **Fig. 4-3**

- **-2.5 dB:** This is the only available setting for Pro Tools versions 8.x
- and below.
- **-3 dB:** This is the standard for many mixing consoles, and is the default setting for Pro Tools 8.1 and above.
- **-4.5 dB:** This is the standard center attenuation setting for SSL analog consoles.
- **-6 dB:** This is the standard for complete mono compatibility. Some US–made analog consoles offer the option of -3 dB or -6 dB center pan attenuation.

Fig. 4-4

Adjusting these settings will result in a subtle change in the way sounds are perceived when panned across the center. A greater degree of pan attenuation will result in more subtle level changes as signal is panned from side to side. Experiment to see if your mixes translate differently using the various settings.

Groups

When using several microphones to record an instrument, you can combine their tracks into groups, allowing you to control level, volume, pan, mute, solo, and record enable, and edit functions of each member track with a single command.

When recording a piano in stereo, for example, you would record each microphone onto its own mono track (instead of a single stereo track). This allows you to adjust level and pan, mute, and solo independently of the other track. You can still group the two tracks to enable joint control and editing capabilities. Recording drums would be another example of an opportunity to use groups during a tracking session. Each group can have its own attributes or follow global edit commands. Grouped tracks maintain their own independent output assignments.

Fig. 4-5

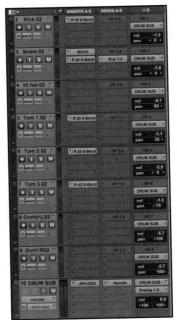

Fig. 4-6

Sub-Masters

Sub-masters differ from groups, in that tracks feeding sub-masters can retain their parameter control independent of a group. Tracks feeding a sub-master are summed together into an Auxiliary Input track, the output of which is fed to the main output Master Mix bus.

Aux Sends/Returns

An Aux send is a parallel output from a track or tracks, which can be used to feed a sub-master (as above) or provide input to an effect device/plug-in. An aux has a level control, which can send signal pre-fader (independent of track volume control) or post-fader (subject to track volume control).

Pre-fader sends are used for headphone mixes, where you usually don't want the volume of individual tracks changing in the headphones while you adjust or solo tracks in your control room mix. Another use for a pre-fader send would be to maintain a constant level of effect send on a track regardless of the track volume. An example of this would be setting up a chromatic tuner plug-in for monitoring guitar tuning. (If using RTAS plug-ins, those plugs will not remain active on a record-enabled track.)

Post-fader sends are used for reverb, delay, and other effect sends where you would like the send level to follow the track volume control. Example: if you turn down the level of a vocal in a mix, you may want the Reverb send level to get quieter in relation.

You will find that your effects sound more balanced and natural when the send level scales up and down in relation to the track level.

Inserts

Pro Tools gives you 10 inserts per track in two banks of five each: A–E and F–J. These can either be software plug-in inserts, hardware inserts, or instrument plug-ins. With plug-ins and hardware inserts, the track signal is routed through your effect, then returned to the fader input on the same track. Inserts are pre-fader on audio, Auxiliary, and Instrument tracks; inserts are always post-fader on Master Faders.

Fig. 4-7

You can bypass individual inserts by Command-clicking on the Insert button on a track in the Edit and Mix windows, or by clicking the Bypass button on the plug-in window itself.

Fig. 4-8

Repeat the command to toggle the in/out state. Note: You can bypass the plug-ins in the "A" slot of every track by Option-clicking on the Bypass button in any "A" slot plug-in window.

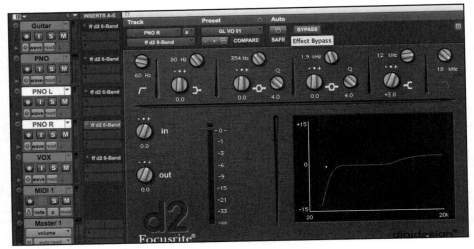

Fig. 4-9

Likewise for plug-ins in the "B" slots, "C" slots, and so on. Repeat the command to toggle the bypass state.

Making an insert inactive will save system resources and voices. You can make an insert inactive by pressing Control + Command + Click on the Insert button. Repeat to toggle state.

Note: You can make all of the "A" slot plug-ins inactive by pressing Control + Option + Command + Click on the "A" slot insert pane. (The Control + Option + Command key combination is also known as "the claw.") Repeat command to toggle.

Right-clicking on a Track Insert button will bring up a menu listing various insert options, such as Bypass, Make Inactive, and Automation Safe, and a sub-menu for Automation Dialog.

Insert Status Display

Fig. 4-10

There are a number of display conditions indicating the current status of the insert:

- **Active, unmuted; plug-in window open:** The Insert button is white with black text.
- **Active, unmuted:** The Insert button is light gray with black text.
- **Active, muted; window open:** The Insert button is light blue with white text.
- **Active, muted:** The Insert button is blue with white text.
- **Clipped:** Regardless of mute state, text is red, plug-in meter shows red clip indicator.
- **Inactive:** The Insert button assumes track color, with black text in italics. When opened, the plug-in window will display the message "Plug-in Inactive."

Clear Clip Indicator

To clear the clip indicator, click on a red clip indicator, or press Option + C to clear all clips.

Insert Order

Inserts process in series, so think carefully about the order in which you add your plug- ins. Each plug-in you introduce will have an effect on every other plug-in downstream. While there is no *best* way, there is a *commonsense* way to order your plug-ins. Let's have a look at this example of insert order for processing vocals:

- **Insert A:** EQ 3 1-Band
- **Insert B:** Compressor/Limiter Dyn 3
- **Insert C:** EQ 3 7-Band

As always, your mileage may vary, and here are the processing steps in order of function:

1. Filter unwanted frequency content *first*. That way your compressor doesn't have to respond to popped *p*'s or an overabundance of breath noise.
2. Compress the vocal a moderate amount in order to control its place in the mix balance, dynamically speaking.
3. Perform your EQ shaping after the dynamics have been tamed, and you will have a more consistent sound to work with. Plus, you won't accidentally be tripping the compressor with the +12 dB @ 16 kHz that you added to get the singer to sound breathy.

You will notice that no delay or reverb plug-ins have been inserted directly into the vocal track. Using time-based effects directly on a track makes it much harder to control the level of the track in the mix, and to control the balance of effect to dry vocal as well. It also increases latency dramatically for that track. Instead, take a moment to create an Aux bus to use delay and reverb as parallel-processed effects rather than series-processed. You will have more control over the effect, and your vocals will sound much more distinct using this technique.

An additional benefit of using Pro Tools Aux busses to administer effects is the obvious saving of CPU cycles. If you have 48 tracks of audio—each with its own reverb plug-in—you will be using much too much computer processing power to achieve your mixing goals. If one reverb isn't enough, create two, or four, or even 10 Aux busses to fulfill your reverb-drenched sonic fantasies. Better *10* than *48*. It's much easier to manage settings for a few reverbs than it is for a few *dozen*.

I hope this clarifies insert use and gives you solid techniques for maximizing your resources while striving for the best possible sound in your mixes.

Insert Output Format

Plug-ins can be configured in mono or stereo, but remember that because insert processing is done in series, inserting a stereo plug-in after a mono plug-in automatically makes all downstream inserts into stereo. You do not have the option of inserting a mono plug-in after a stereo plug-in.

There are three channel formats for plug-ins:

- mono-in/mono-out
- mono-in/stereo-out
- stereo-in/stereo-out

Note: Some plug-ins come in multi-mono versions rather than stereo or multi-channel; they will behave as stereo devices in your insert chain.

Moving Inserts

Simply drag the plug-in from the Insert pane on one track to the Insert pane on another track to move the inserted plug-in. All plug-in parameters will move along with the insert.

Copying Inserts

Option + drag the assigned insert to another Insert pane, whether on the same track or another. This is the fastest way to duplicate settings on an insert or plug-in.

Deleting Inserts

Click on the Insert pane you wish to delete or clear. The first choice in the drop-down menu will be "no insert." Click on this command to delete the insert and its settings from that Insert slot.

Note: You cannot undo this operation. Save your session before deleting anything you may change your mind about later.

Using Hardware Inserts

If you have favorite pieces of signal processing equipment that you would like to use in the Pro Tools environment, you can use hardware inserts to connect your gear on individual tracks or sub-mixes. You must use corresponding inputs and outputs on your I/O to send and receive using the hardware inserts. For example, if you are sending signal out of the Pro Tools hardware inserts on output channels 3 and 4, you must return the processed signal to input channels 3 and 4.

CAN I ACCESS DELAY COMPENSATION
IF I USE HARDWARE INSERTS?

Absolutely. Delay Compensation can be applied to hardware inserts using the H/W Insert Delay page in I/O Setup. Here's how you do it:

- Access the Setup menu and select I/O.
- Click on the H/W Insert Delay tab.
- Type the delay value (in milliseconds) into the input field where you have connected your hardware insert.

CALCULATING DELAY WHEN USING HARDWARE INSERTS

Check the user's manual for the device you are about to connect; there may be a processing delay value listed in the specs. If that info is not available, you can use Pro Tools to determine your hardware delay. This is a bit of a process but well worth the time invested. Follow these steps:

- **Step 1:** Enable ADC.
- **Step 2:** Set the Timeline Scale to measure minutes/seconds.
- **Step 3:** Create two mono audio tracks.
- **Step 4:** On the first track, create a short burst of tone using an oscillator plug-in. Alternately, use an audio file with an obvious visible transient peak, such as a snare drum hit.
- **Step 5:** Use a hardware insert on track 2.
- **Step 6:** Bus the track 1 output to the input of track 2, and arm track 2 for recording.
- **Step 7:** Record the test tone or other audio from track 1 onto track 2.
- **Step 8:** Zoom in and measure the distance between the beginning of the audio on track 1 and the beginning of the audio on track 2, using your Cursor tool to highlight the region.

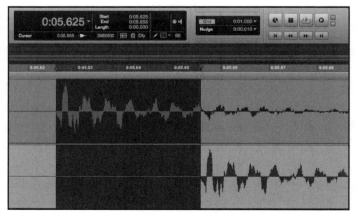

Fig. 4-11

The resulting region length is equivalent to the round-trip delay time of your external processor. This is also the value you will enter into the H/W Insert Delay page.

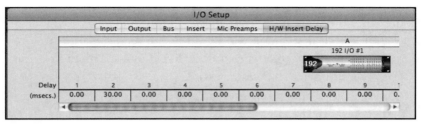

Fig. 4-12

Remember, any added external processing will use additional voices and introduce latency.

Sends

- Pro Tools gives you 10 sends per track in two banks of five each, A–E and F–J. These can be accessed from either the Edit or Mix windows, or from the send's own pop-up window.
- Sends are available in mono, stereo, or multi-channel on all audio tracks, Auxiliary Inputs, and Instrument tracks.
- Pro Tools sends can be configured pre- or post-fader, much like an analog console.
- Sends are used for parallel processing; returns are audible in addition to the un- effected audio.
- Note: A send must return to the mixer via an active audio track, Auxiliary Input, or Instrument track in order to be audible in Pro Tools.

Send level, pan, and mute can be set to follow group assignments. In other words, if you change the send parameters for one member of a group, all members' sends will change in relation.

Common Uses for Sends

These include:

- Sending audio to a real-time effect plug-in or hardware insert for processing—reverb or delay, for example.
- Creating a separate mix or sub-mix. Drum or vocal sub-mixes would be examples of sub-mixes you would use regularly.
- Creating one or more headphone mixes that are separate from the main monitor mix.
- Sending audio to a plug-in key input.

Assigning a Send to a Track

1. Enable Sends View in the Edit or Mix windows. For example, choose View > Edit Window Views > Inserts A–E.
2. Click the Sends A–E pane of the track on which you would like to add the send. Select which output or bus destination you would like to send signal to. You may assign a send to a mono or stereo bus or output. Send level can be adjusted from the send level fader that pops up when you click on a send.

Send View Options

- The default view for sends is by bank (A–E and F–J). The number of sends displayed is related to the height of the track being viewed.
- You can set your Send View options to display one send at a time (instead of five at a time) with send meter and all send controls visible all the time. To display Send A in the track send column, choose View > Sends A–E.
- From the Send A pane, you can choose to view other sends from the drop-down menu.
- To return to all-sends view, simply choose View > Sends A–E > Assignments; or View > Sends F–J > Assignments as desired.

Fig. 4-13

Send Status Display

There are a number of display conditions, indicating the current status of the send:

- **Active, unmuted; window open:** The Send button is white with black text.
- **Active, unmuted:** The Send button is light gray with black text.
- **Active, muted; window open:** The Send button is light blue with white text.
- **Active, muted:** The Send button is dark blue with white text.
- **Inactive:** The Send button assumes track color, with black text in italics. When opened, all controls in the Send window will be grayed out.

Fig. 4-14

- **Clipped:** Regardless of state, text is red, Send meter shows red clip indicator.

To clear the clip indicator, click on a red clip indicator, or press Option + C to clear all clips.

Opening Multiple Send Windows

Pro Tools normally allows you to have one Send window open at a time. It may be convenient for you to have more than one Send window open at once, in which case you can Shift-click on the Send button to open a Send window and keep it open on the desktop. Use the same technique to open more Send windows. You can also click the red Target button on open Send windows to keep them open. To close these windows, click on the red Close button in the upper-left corner of the Send window.

Create and Assign a New Track from a Send Pane

Using this feature, you can create and define a new send, create and define a new destination, and name the track, all in a single operation. Here's how to do it:
- From any active track, click on a send, and scroll down to the option named "new track…"
- The "new track…" pop-up dialog window offers you the option to select send width (from mono and stereo through 7.1), select the type of destination (Aux Input, audio track, or Instrument track), choose samples/ticks, and name the destination track.
- If you click the button marked Create next to Current Track, then click Create, your new destination track will show up in the track list immediately below the track in which you selected the send.
- This is a big time-saver over the old multi-step process, but know that you can still assign sends and create destinations in separate steps if you prefer.

Master Faders

Whether or not you create a Master Fader on your virtual console, it *is* present, and the main output of your mix goes through it. Adding a Master Fader gives you a knob and the ability to make quick and easy adjustments to the final gain stage.

Note: Adding a Master Fader does not change the resolution of your mix, even on fades—if it's a 24-bit session it will remain a 24-bit mix all the way down to infinity on the fader.

MASTER FADERS DO NOT USE EXCESSIVE DSP RESOURCES

A Master Fader track gives you an opportunity to meter and control your mix *post-fader*, so you know whether or not you're clipping the mixer output.

CREATING A MASTER FADER FOR
STEREO MASTER VOLUME CONTROL:
1. Using the Create New Track dialog (Shift + Command + N), create a new stereo
   Master Fader using the pull-down menus.

Fig. 4-15

2. Set the output for each track to the main audio output path, usually outputs 1 and 2
   from your main hardware I/O interface.
3. Set the output of the Master Fader to the main output path.

CREATING A MASTER FADER FOR SUB-MASTER INPUT TRIM:
• Using the Create New Track dialog (Shift + Command + N), create a new stereo
  Auxiliary Input track.
• Bus the output of the desired tracks to the input of the Auxiliary Input track.
• Create a stereo Master Fader; assign the output to the same bus that feeds the Aux In
  track.

INSERTING PLUG-INS ON THE MASTER FADER
This is the same operation as inserting a send on a track. Click the Send window, and select
from the drop-down menu.

USES FOR A MASTER FADER:
• Control and process output mixes.
• Monitor/meter outputs, busses, or hardware outputs.
• Control sub-mix levels.
• Control effects send levels.
• Control the level of bussed tracks (sub-masters).
• Apply dither and other effects to entire mixes.

Pro Tools Signal Flow

One of the more interesting topics of debate among Pro Tools users is the question of signal
flow. Where is the pan in relation to the inserts? Are the meters on the Master Fader pre-
or post-fader? Thanks to Andy Hagerman, AVID Training Partner Manager for the Asia/
Pacific region, we now have a definitive answer for these questions and more...

SIGNAL FLOW IN AUDIO TRACKS

WITH PRE-FADER METERING	WITH POST-FADER METERING
Audio from Hard Drive	Audio from Hard Drive
⇓	⇓
Clip-Based Gain	Clip-Based Gain
⇓	⇓
Inserts	Inserts
⇓	⇓
Pre-Fader Sends	Pre-Fader Sends
⇓	⇓
Metering	Main Fader
⇓	⇓
Main Fader	Metering
⇓	⇓
Post-Fader Sends	Post-Fader Sends
⇓	⇓
Pan	Pan
⇓	⇓
Output	Output

SIGNAL FLOW IN AUX AND INSTRUMENT TRACKS

WITH PRE-FADER METERING	WITH POST-FADER METERING
Input	Input
⇓	⇓
Inserts	Inserts
⇓	⇓
Pre-Fader Sends	Pre-Fader Sends
⇓	⇓
Metering	Main Fader
⇓	⇓
Main Fader	Metering
⇓	⇓
Post-Fader Sends	Post-Fader Sends
⇓	⇓

Pan	Pan
⇓	⇓
Output	Output

SIGNAL FLOW IN MASTER FADER TRACKS

METERING IS POST-FADER ON MASTER FADER TRACKS
Main Fader
⇓
Inserts
⇓
Metering
⇓
Output

CLEARING CLIPPED SIGNAL INDICATORS

- You can clear a signal clip indicator on a visible individual track meter by clicking the red clip indicator.
- Clear all clip indicators by pressing Option + C.

DITHER

Whenever you convert from 24-bit to 16-bit audio, there is a likelihood of introducing digital distortion at very low volume levels. This distortion is not usually audible at normal signal levels, but can become audible on fade-outs or reverb tails or in quiet passages.

Dithering is the process of adding low-level random noise to digital signal, essentially in the last bit. This serves to mitigate distortion, which is potentially more audible than the noise introduced. This has become a common practice when mixing for CD or another 16-bit audio destination format.

Pro Tools comes with two dithering plug-ins for use on your Master Fader: Dither and POWr Dither.

NOISE SHAPING

Noise shaping is part of bit reduction/dithering, and refers to the process of moving the resulting noise to a higher frequency range (above 4 kHz) where the human ear is less likely to detect it.

Maxim is a dynamic maximizer plug-in that features a noise-shaping component, as well as parallel processing and dithering—a nice feature set for use during mixing or mastering.

TURNING UP THE HEAT—HARMONICALLY ENHANCED ALGORITHM TECHNOLOGY

This is a new analog emulation software add-on for Pro Tools HD users. Designed by Dave Hill (of Summit Audio and Crane Song fame), this software is activated across every channel of your mix to bring the sound of multi-channel analog audio processing to your DAW (for those of us who don't own a Neve console and can't afford a Fairchild compressor).

It's worth watching the YouTube video of Dave explaining the analog recording and mixing process to understand what this software does, but activating and playing with it in your mix is the best way to experience the effect.

The controls are very simple: two knobs, Drive and Tone. There is a Master Bypass button as well as individual Channel Bypass buttons. The master section also has an on/off switch to free up DSP resources. A PRE button on each channel allows you to select pre- or post-insert processing.

Drive Control

This relates to the amount of distortion derived from overdriving the circuits of an analog mixing console. In the default 12 o'clock position, there is no HEAT processing active. Turn the Drive knob to the left to add analog console emulation and even-order harmonics. Turn the knob to the right to add the sound of tape saturation and odd-order harmonics.

Tone Control

Does what it says, pretty much. Turn the knob to the left to emphasize lower harmonics; turn the knob to the right to emphasize upper harmonics.

HEAT Meter

The channel meters at the top of each channel strip display how much HEAT processing is being applied at that moment. The brighter the meter, the more effect being added. The Master HEAT meter displays the amount of process being applied to the entire mix.

PRE Button

This places the HEAT process pre-inserts when lit, post-inserts when unlit. Experiment with pre/post positioning to hear how the final sound is influenced.

Note: HEAT can only be used on audio tracks. Aux busses and Instrument tracks will need to be printed to audio files in order to process with HEAT.

Another note: HEAT uses a healthy amount of DSP, so you should be aware that you may run out of system resources much more quickly when using HEAT on your mix. Opening a session with insufficient DSP resources may result in HEAT being deactivated or TDM plug-ins deactivated. (HEAT processing takes precedence over TDM plug-ins in the processing hierarchy.)

Tip: Keep your System Usage meters running during mixing to measure your use of system resources.

Mixing with HEAT

Since the controls are deceptively simple, you may not be aware that the complex harmonic processing going on behind the scenes is impacted by subtle changes in frequency content, dynamics, overall amplitude, and the number of active channels being processed ... kinda like a real console.

The best results will be achieved by getting your mix to sound the best it can *before* you add HEAT processing. Then activate HEAT and compare with the un-effected mix frequently to determine if the net results are in line with your vision for the mix.

Note: Be aware that adding HEAT to each song in your collection of mixes may result in a slightly different sound quality for each. As I mentioned previously, this is a very dynamic process, and it will respond differently to different program material.

There are no pre-sets to store or recall, but you can import HEAT switch settings via the Import Session Data command (Shift + Option + I). You will need to rely on your own ears to be sure you're using the appropriate amount of HEAT in each of your mixes.

After some experimentation, I felt that HEAT had a positive effect on some mixes and that I would definitely like to hear what HEAT sounded like in a mastering session where the focus was on subtlety and overarching tonal qualities.

HEAT, According to Its Designer

I *loved* the results of using HEAT in my mixing tests but couldn't figure out a way to effectively convey to you how it does what it does. So I called Dave Hill, who developed this ingenious software.

In response, Dave asked, "How do you describe a color, or distortion? HEAT works because you can't describe it—the more complex the function, the harder it is to describe. HEAT uses a complex algorithm to accomplish intensive calculations. But it only has two control knobs. It's an extremely complex thing made easy so that anyone can use it." He continued:

HEAT started out four years ago at a NAMM show as a way to bring analog sounds into the digital recording process. It got complicated very quickly, because the analog recording chain introduces some weird processes, from the single-ended, even-order harmonic distortion of analog consoles, to the hyped record/playback equalization curves of analog tape machines and the +6 dB-per-octave rise in high frequencies associated with multi-track head gap.

HEAT is written for TDM because it needs massive computing power in order to work across 48 tracks. TDM provides dedicated processing and is expandable to accommodate higher track counts.

Dave's suggested starting place: activate HEAT right away, turn it up two clicks, *then* build your mix.

Personally, I found HEAT to affect mixes differently depending on the program material and how many tracks were active in the session. It is hard to describe, but what a great *color* to bring to the mix.

ORGANIZING YOUR TRACKS

Track layout in Pro Tools is mainly based on traditional music production techniques developed for use with analog multi-track tape on analog mixing consoles. A common method is to order your tracks in the Edit window from top to bottom beginning with the drums, then bass, followed by chordal instruments (keys, guitars, and so forth), vocals, and ending at the bottom with effects returns and finally the Master Fader.

If you think ahead to the mix, you can begin to organize and structure the tracks in your session to make it easier for you to move into the mixing process once all of the tracks have been recorded and edited. In the Mix window, the tracks should appear from left to right, beginning with drums, bass, chordal instruments, vocals, and effects return tracks. This emulates an analog console layout and places the vocal tracks closest to the Master section of the console. The theory is that you'll be spending more time mixing the vocal tracks, and keeping them in the center of the console also puts you consistently in the parallax of the speakers.

You will develop your own scheme for laying out virtual console tracks, based on your workflow, the type of project, and your experience with template layouts.

Edit Window Layout

TRACK INFO DISPLAY

You can customize the information displayed in the Edit window by selecting from the drop-down menu at the top of the screen (View > Edit Window Views). From here you can choose which of the following to display:

- Comments
- Mic Preamps
- Instruments
- Inserts A–E
- Inserts F–J
- Sends A–E
- Sends F–J
- I/O
- Real-Time Properties
- Track Color

Note: These selections are also available from a drop-down menu located on the top left of the Edit window, just below the Rulers display. You can also Right-click one of the displays—the Sends A–E view, for example—to show the drop-down menu options.

To hide one or more of the displays, Option-click on the display title, Sends A–E, for example.

DISPLAYING RULERS

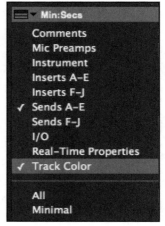

Depending on the timebase and editing style of choice, you can select the rulers best suited for your editing operation. You can also display Markers, Tempo, Meter, and other song-specific parameters in the Ruler display. To access these options, select the drop-down menu: View > Rulers.

GROUP ASSIGNMENTS

At the lower-left corner of the Mix window, you will find an area titled Groups. The default setting includes just one group—All—which, when highlighted, ties all tracks together for editing commands. When the All group is highlighted, any commands you assign to the global group will affect all tracks. You can add up to 104 groups of tracks (four banks of 26) of your choosing by selecting the Name field for each

Fig. 4-16

track and typing Command + G, then naming the group. It will then be added to the list of groups, and can be turned on or off by toggling the state within the Groups window.

You should create a new group for every instrument that occupies more than one track. In a typical rock band recording, you might have a group for each instrument with more than one track, which will make mixing an easier task. For example:

- Drums
- Bass
- Guitars (GTR)
- Keyboards
- Background Vocals (BGV)
- Main Vocal (VOX)

Having a group assignment for each species of tracks will make it much easier to balance levels between instruments, perform edits, and engage automation functions. All members of the group will respond to a parameter change on one member track.

Fig. 4-17

Note: The Group function can be temporarily suspended for an individual track simply by pressing the Control key and adjusting the parameter you wish to change. Releasing the Control key returns parameter adjustments to their group state.

VIEW TRACKS

The Tracks View pane lives on the left-hand side of the Edit window and shows/hides tracks in the Edit and Mix windows based on selection or type. There is a drop-down menu in the Tracks pane to allow access to these selections, as well as sorting options.

The Tracks pane can be shown or hidden by accessing the drop-down menu: View > Other Displays > Track List.

You can number the tracks in the Tracks pane as well, which is really handy for finding your way among a mix containing 96 tracks. Select from the drop-down menu: View > Track Number.

Fig. 4-18

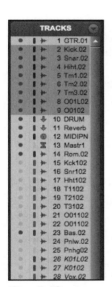

Fig. 4-19

HIDING TRACKS

If you have chosen to view the Tracks window on the left-hand side of the Edit window page, you now have the option to modify the number of tracks viewed in the Edit window at any time. Simply click the Dot icon next to a Track Name to alternately hide or make it visible.

This is a handy function if you have a number of input tracks you are not currently using. Or if you have recorded alternate takes or solos and don't need the info in your Edit or Mix windows, you may remove them from view. Keep in mind: hidden tracks will still play and utilize output voices. If you truly want a track to be silent, you should mute all clips within the track, make the track inactive, or delete the track from the sequence. If you choose the latter method, be sure to make a copy of your session and rename it so you don't lose any track info permanently.

Note: Group commands still apply to hidden tracks, whether or not you can see them. Don't be surprised when that muted scratch vocal track makes a mysterious and

Fig. 4-20

unwanted reappearance after you un-mute a visible track in the group. When in doubt, make a track inactive first, then hide it. For hiding multiple tracks, there is a Hide Inactive Tracks command within the Tracks column drop-down menu.

Grid Settings

If the song you are recording lends itself to a consistent tempo, try recording to a click track. Pro Tools will generate a click track when you simply select the "Create click track" command from the Track window. Then type a tempo into the Transport window, or tap the tempo using the "T" key.

It's supereasy to have all of your editing commands conform to precise bar and beat lines in Grid mode. Find the Grid pane at the top of the Edit window, and click the arrow. This allows you to access and modify grid settings. Typically, you will resolve the grid to quarter notes when in Bar/Beat mode, though this will depend on the tempo of the song and complexity of the edit you are performing. Set your Edit mode to Grid or Relative Grid so that everything you edit or move will snap to the designated beat.

If your song was not recorded with a click track, you can still use Grid mode, but it will not relate to the tempo of your song unless you create a tempo map manually. In this case, I would suggest setting the grid resolution to minutes/seconds and using it for elapsed time reference only. Use Slip mode for editing.

Suggestion: You can guesstimate tempo using the Tap Tempo mode in the metronome pane of your Transport window by turning the Conductor track off, highlighting the BPM rate, then tapping the "T" key in time with the music.

Nudge Settings

As in the description of Grid settings above, go to the Nudge settings pane in the Edit window and click the arrow. This gives you access to the nudge resolution. Again, if you have recorded your song to a click, then using Bar/Beat mode in the Nudge settings window will allow you to move clips or notes in beats or fractions of a beat. This can be really handy for editing MIDI performances.

Whether recorded to a click track or not, I leave my Nudge mode set on minutes/seconds and use 10 ms as the base nudge resolution. I have found that adjusting timing on performance recorded as audio tracks requires much finer resolution, and may only need to be moved 10 or 20 ms in order to rectify a late hit or a missed downbeat.

The following keys access nudge commands:

- The Comma key (,) moves the selected clip or note one increment earlier. The Period key (.) moves the selected clip or note one increment later. The "M" key (m) moves the selected clip or note 10 increments earlier. The Forward Slash key (/) moves the selected clip or note 10 increments later.

- If your Nudge resolution value is set to 10 ms, then the comma and period keys move in 10 ms increments, and the "M" and Forward Slash keys move in 100 ms increments.

Color Palette

Changing the color assignments on elements of your screen layout will help you quickly locate and identify tracks, clips, markers, or groups of tracks. Sometimes the drums just look cooler in green. Either way, the Color Palette gives you the option to organize by color.

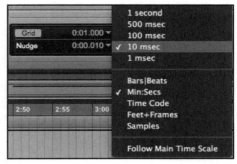

- Double-click in the color bar area left of **Fig. 4-21** the Track Name in the Edit window, also at the very top of the channel strip in the Mix window. (Or select Window > Color Palette.) This will bring up the Color Palette window, which allows you to choose colors for tracks, clips, groups, and markers. Note: If the Marker option is grayed out, you will need to go to the Preferences window, click on the Display tab, then click the Always Display Marker Colors button.
- Select the track(s), clips, group, or marker you'd like to modify. The currently selected color will be indicated by a highlighted swatch in the Color Palette window. You can select a new color by clicking the desired color swatch.
- The Undo command (Command + Z) gets you back to the previously selected color. You can also click the Default button in the Color Palette window to return to the factory setting for the selected item.

Memory Locations/Markers

Memory Location markers are a great way to identify and navigate quickly to positions within your session. This will be a huge time-saver when working on specific sections of a song during overdubs. Use markers to identify the beginning of a take, a section of a song, or an event within a song that you'll need to locate again easily. Markers are numbered sequentially as you add them. To display the Markers ruler, select from the View menu: View > Rulers > Markers.

Memory Locations Window

The Memory Locations window allows you to see all of the markers you've added to the session, edit the data stored in each, and view them in order of creation or numerical sequence.

CREATING A NEW MARKER

As you create a new marker, the New Memory Location window will reveal a number of options, including typing a marker name, changing the marker number, selecting Time Properties, and setting General Properties.

Marker Memory Location relates to a particular point in the timeline.

Selection Memory Location relates to a user-designated edit selection in the timeline.

- Select or highlight a region in the timeline.
- Create a Memory Location, then hit Enter to add marker.
- Click the Selection button, then click OK.
- The region selection is stored along with the other memory location parameters.

General Properties Memory Location relates to a set of session settings that can be stored and recalled.

- Storing or recalling General Properties data can include screen views, zoom settings, pre and post roll times, track show/hide status, track height, and enabled Edit/Mix groups. This does not necessarily require location information.
- This can be handy when viewing the drum kit or vocals during editing, or for recalling your Master Fader metering layout during the mixdown process.

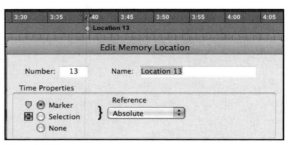

Fig. 4-22

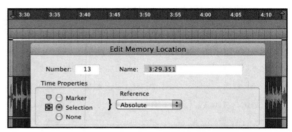

Fig. 4-23

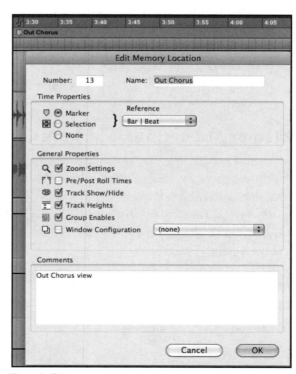

Fig. 4-24

- To store these details, set up the screen view to your satisfaction, then check the boxes corresponding to the information you wish to save.
- See the section below on Window Configurations to set up specific window layouts and views, which can then be recalled in the General Properties pane.

Each session can store up to 999 Memory Locations. These are stored and displayed in the Memory Locations window, accessed by typing Command + 5 on the main keyboard or by selecting the Window > Memory Locations window. Memory Locations can also be recalled, created, edited, and deleted from this window.

- Command-click to add a new marker.
- Option-click to delete a marker.
- You can sort, edit, and re-number markers in this window as well.

To locate a specific marker, type its number on the numeric keypad in this sequence: decimal point, number, decimal point. Locating to marker 2 looks like this: .2.

You can also click on the Marker icon in the Marker ruler of the Edit window, or in the Memory Locations window. You will find a list of your markers in the Memory Locations window.

Markers can be moved by grabbing the Marker icon in the Marker ruler and dragging it to the desired location.

Note: Markers will snap to Grid settings if moved while Grid mode is selected.

Common section marker names include:

- Intro
- Verse (or Verse 1, Verse 2, and so forth)
- Chorus (or Chorus 1, Chorus 2, and so forth)
- Solo
- Bridge
- Breakdown
- Modulation
- Outchorus
- Coda

You can type any other section names that might apply to the piece you are working on.

Audio post-production work uses marker terms such as:

- Spot 1, or :30 TV—when working on commercial projects.
- Bars, Tones, 2 pop—for use with short- or long-form video projects.
- Reel 1, Academy Leader, 2 pop—for working with film.

Note: Use the Enter key on the numeric keypad to drop markers at the beginning of each new section while recording. You can go back and name the markers/sections later, as well as adjust their precise location. Having these rough markers placed will be a tremendous time-saver when trying to locate sections within a project.

Another note: It's efficient (not to mention impressive) when a client asks to hear the bass line in the second chorus, and you can locate that section immediately, because you had the forethought to drop a marker there during the recording of basic tracks.

Yet another note: I like to add a marker at the very beginning and the very end of the project as well; this helps to easily identify the length of the entire piece when it comes time to bounce the mix to disk.

There are at least three ways to bring up the New Memory Location dialog. First, locate to the desired point in the timeline, or highlight a region. Then do one of the following:

- Press the Enter key on the numeric keypad.
- Control-click in the Markers ruler near the top of the Edit window.

- In the Memory Locations window, Command-click. Click on the "+" sign in the Markers ruler.

Fig. 4-25

Fig. 4-26

TO DELETE A MARKER:
- In the Marker ruler, drag the Marker icon down until it turns into a Trash Can icon. When you release the Mouse button, the Marker will be deleted.
- In the Memory Locations window, Option-click on a marker to delete it from the list.

These operations can be undone (Command + Z).

Window Configurations

This window allows you to create and store up to 99 custom window views per session for instant recall. This can be superhandy when editing and mixing, because you can instantly focus your attention (and screen real estate) on just the tracks you are editing and hide the remainder until you need them again. These configurations can be stored as Memory Locations as well, giving you nearly instant access to single or multiple track views.

HOW TO CREATE A WINDOW CONFIGURATION

Open the Window Configurations window by locating the drop-down menu Windows > Configurations > Window Configurations List, or pressing Command + Option + J.

Start by making a new Window Configuration setting named "Default" with your basic window layout of choice. You can add comments for your reference in the field provided. When you click OK, it will be saved to position 1 in your Window Configurations list. Use this as the main layout for editing or mixing.

Now let's make a new window layout featuring just the drum tracks:

1. Open the Clip Menu and open the Strip Silence window (Command + U).

Fig. 4-27

2. Open the New Configuration menu from the main Windows menu (Windows > Configurations > New Configuration …) or from the drop-down menu in the Window Configurations window.

3. Select Window Layout, and type the name "Drum Kit View" into the Name field. Press OK, and this will be saved to Window Configuration 2.

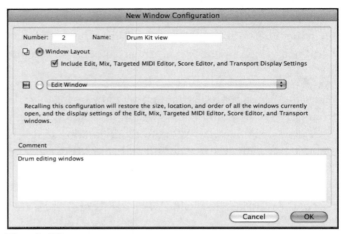

Fig. 4-28

Now we'll test the system; recall your Default Window Configuration by typing Period (.) one (1) Asterisk (*): .1* This should recall your original default window layout. Next, type: .2* This should restore your "Drum Kit View" layout.

Note: If you have selected Auto-Update Active Configuration from either drop-down menu, changes to the active view will be saved with the Window Configuration. The number of the currently selected Window Configuration will be displayed in parentheses next to the Window menu at the top of the screen.

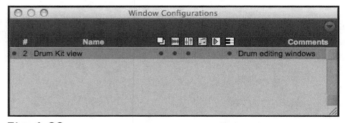

Fig. 4-29

I suggest leaving this item un-checked unless you need to modify your view, or you may accidentally overwrite your configurations. There is no Undo function for this operation.

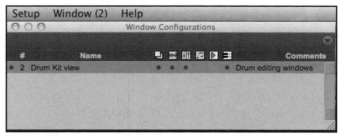

Fig. 4-30

To delete a Window Configuration, select the subject configuration from the Window Configuration page and choose "Delete (name of configuration)" from the drop-down menu. Another way to delete the setting is to Option-click on the subject configuration in the Window Configuration menu. It will then be permanently deleted.

Your Window Configuration settings will be saved with your session. Window Configuration settings can be imported from other sessions using the Import Window Configurations command in the Import Session Data > Import Options dialog.

Fig. 4-31

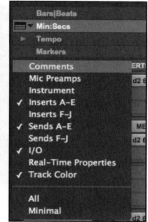

Fig. 4-32

Mix Window Layout Menus

Many of the functions and views in the Mix window are also available in the Edit window, and are accessible from the same menus.

Transport Window

Fig. 4-33

The Transport Window shows basic transport controls (Return to Zero [RTZ], Rewind, Fast Forward, Go to End [GTE], Stop, Play, and Record buttons), counters, and some MIDI controls. It can also be configured to show Pre/Post Roll, Count-off, Tempo, and Metronome settings, as well as enabling the Tempo Ruler (or Conductor Track).

While these commands can always be accessed at the top of the Edit and Mix windows, the Transport window can be a floating window as well. This allows you to position it on your monitor screen wherever you may need it. The quick access key command is Command + 1 on the numeric keypad. See more info on the Transport window in a separate chapter of this book.

SUMMARY OF KEY COMMANDS

OPERATION	KEY COMMAND
Session Setup menu	Command + 2 (numeric keypad)
Bypass Insert	Command + Clicking an Insert button

Bypass all "A" Inserts	Option + Clicking the "A" Insert button (or B, C, etc.)
Make Insert Inactive	Control + Command + Clicking an Insert button
Make all "A" Inserts Inactive	Control + Option + Command + Clicking the "A" Insert button
Clear Clip Indicator	Option + C
Copy Insert	Option + Drag to new insert slot
Keep Send Window Open	Shift + Clicking the Send button
Create New Track	Shift + Command + N
Import Session Data	Shift + Option + I
Import Audio	Shift + Command + I
Tap Tempo	T
Add Group	Select tracks, then Command + G
Undo	Command + Z
New Memory Location	Enter (numeric keypad), Control + Clicking the Marker ruler, or Command + Clicking the Memory Locations window
Memory Location Window	Command + 5 (main keyboard)
Delete Memory Location	Option + Clicking a Marker
Go To Memory Location	.number. (e.g., .2. for Marker 2) on the numeric keypad
Window Configurations	Command + Option + J
Delete Window Configuration	Option + Clicking on Window Configuration to be deleted
Strip Silence	Command + U
Transport	Command + 1 (numeric keypad)
Save	Command + S
Duplicate Track	Shift + Option + D
Heal Separation	Command + H
Separate Region	B, or Command + E
Cut	X, or Command + X
Copy	C, or Command + C
Paste	V, or Command + V
Mute Clip	Command + M
Nudge Left	, (comma)
Nudge Right	. (period)
Nudge Left x10	M
Nudge Right x10	/ (forward slash)

CHAPTER 4 REVIEW

1. Pro Tools now offers four levels of pan depth for varying degrees of stereo image accuracy when panning across the center position. These are _____, _____, _____, and _____.

2. An Aux send is used to send a parallel _____ from a track to a bus for _____ to effects or outputs.

3. _____ -fader sends are used for headphone mixes, while _____ sends are used for effects sends.

4. Pro Tools allows you to use either software _____ or hardware inserts on each track. A hardware insert requires physical inputs and outputs on your audio _____ in order to connect _____ hardware.

5. Hardware inserts use additional _____ allocation and introduce _____.

6. _____ plug-ins are usually added to aux inputs, and_____ are routed from the tracks to the reverb plug-in. This conserves processing horsepower.

7. Copying an insert or a send from one track to another is easily accomplished by using the _____ + _____ command to copy the insert or send with all settings intact.

8. Calculating hardware _____ in Pro Tools involves recording a short piece of audio through a _____ send/return path and comparing it with the un-delayed sample.

9. Pro Tools gives you _____ sends and _____ inserts per track.

10. Creating a _____ gives you a control with which to vary the output level of your mix.

11. You can clear clip indicators by pressing the _____ + _____ key command.

12. To manipulate more than one track at once, create a _____ by selecting the desired members, then pressing the _____ + G keys.

13. Tap in a desired _____ using the "T" key.

14. You can access all of the basic session navigation controls, including Record and Play, using the _____ window.

15. Hiding tracks from within the Tracks window will remove them from the_____ and _____ window views, but they will still be audible as long as they are active.

16. You can create very accurate edits using the Grid and Nudge settings. The Nudge key commands are the ___, ___, ___, and ___ keys, and they usually correspond to -10 x, -1 x, +1 x, and +10 x the nudge settings.

17. Use the _____ key on the numeric keypad to create a new marker. Each session can store up to _____ memory markers.

18. You can save your session by typing the key command _____ + ___.

19. The Pro Tools function used to remove sections of low-amplitude signal from within a clip is called _____.

20. Heavily edited clips can be combined to create a new file on disk using the _____ command from the File menu.

Playback and Recording

PLAYBACK MODES

Right-clicking the Play button (or Control-clicking the Play button when the transport is stopped) brings up a menu of playback options, including:

Half-Speed

Selecting this option immediately initiates half-speed playback from the current cursor location. Key command: Shift + spacebar, or Shift-clicking the Play button.

Prime for Playback

This command pre-loads audio into the playback buffer in order to initiate immediate playback when the Play button is pressed. It is possible for Pro Tools playback to lag the Playback command a bit, particularly when your session contains a large number of tracks. This command allows you to lock playback to timecode more quickly as well. Key command: Option-click the Play button. The Stop button will light, and the Play button will flash. Initiating the Play command will commence immediate playback.

Loop Play

This command will repeat playback of the selected region until the transport is stopped. To activate Loop Play, highlight a region, then Right-click the Transport play button and select Loop. Alternately, Control-click the Play button to toggle between normal play and Loop Play modes.

Fig. 5-1

Begin playback by pressing the spacebar, pressing "0" on the numeric keypad, or clicking the Play button in the transport. To stop playback, click the Stop button, press the spacebar, or press "0" on the numeric keypad.

Fig. 5-2

Dynamic Transport Mode

This command decouples the playback start location from the timeline region selection, allowing you to begin playback from any point on the timeline without losing your timeline region or edit selection.

Another playback modifier function is the Timeline Insertion/ Play Start Marker Follows Playback command.

This is a long-winded name for the option of having the cursor

Fig. 5-3

locate to the place where playback stopped, or return to the original starting position on the timeline. The key command is accessed by typing the letter "N" on the keyboard. I use this frequently when editing tracks. Note: It is possible to record over previously recorded or edited clips if this setting is not selected during recording. Hit the Play command twice to observe the playback start position if you are unsure of the setting.

RECORDING MODES

Right-clicking the Record button (or Control-clicking the Record button when the transport is stopped) brings up a menu of recording mode options, including:

- **Normal:** The Pro Tools default setting is Normal recording mode; when you use a record command, you will begin recording at the same time and position in the timeline at which you commence playback. Prior to recording, you may also designate a range in the timeline in which to record audio. If you define a range, the new recording will occupy only that range. (See Auto-Punch.) Pre-roll and post-roll are available in Normal recording mode, but otherwise Pro Tools cannot begin recording if the track is already playing. Normal recording is nondestructive, meaning that all successive passes on the same region will be named sequentially, displayed in the Clip list, and saved to disk.

Fig. 5-4

- **Loop:** In this mode, when you define a range in the timeline, you will be able to record multiple nondestructive passes one after another, while the section repeats until you stop the playback. The takes are numbered sequentially and placed into the Clip list. Clips can easily be placed in the timeline to audition takes.

Fig. 5-5

Note: There is an extremely useful variation of this technique when used in conjunction with playlists. In the Preferences menu, click the Operation tab, and check the box marked Automatically Create New Playlists When Loop Recording, under the Record section of the menu. Now when you use Loop Record, you will automatically create a new playlist in the stack for each pass recorded. Auditioning and comping tracks can be managed with ease using this technique.

- **Destructive:** In this mode, you will be permanently deleting and replacing the audio in any clip you happen to record over. While this does save on disk space, the chance of erasing something important is a very real possibility when using destructive recording mode. I would suggest you disable this mode and not ever use it. Disk space is cheap, and performances can be once-in-a-lifetime events. Save everything.

Fig. 5-6

- **QuickPunch:** QuickPunch mode allows you to instantly punch in and out manually during playback on a record-enabled track. Pro Tools creates a new file from the moment you begin playback, and this clip is stored in the Clip list when you punch in on a track. You may punch in and out up to two hundred times in a single pass.

The truly brilliant thing about QuickPunch is that it actually records audio from the point at which you start playback, not just when you hit the Record button. Why is this so great? Let's say that you started playback four bars before the punch, but your

Fig. 5-7

manual punch-in was a half-second late. Using QuickPunch mode, all you have to do is expand the beginning of the new audio clip to reveal the missing half-second. Brilliant! This has saved my bacon innumerable times, particularly when a performer does something really wonderful just before the planned punch-in. When I am rehearsing a performance on a record-enabled track and hear something worth keeping, all I need to do is hit record before I stop playback, and Pro Tools has captured the entire take. Love it!

Note: You should consider always using Pro Tools in QuickPunch mode so that you never miss an opportunity to record a pass.

Disclaimer: Once you stop playback, the QuickPunch buffer is emptied. In order to capture audio or MIDI in QuickPunch mode, you must have assigned a live input source to a record-enabled track *and* hit the Record button *before* stopping playback.

Additional Modes for HD Users

- **TrackPunch (Pro Tools HD only):** With TrackPunch enabled, you can enable/ disable record-arming, and punch in and out on any track or combination of tracks without interrupting recording or playback.

Fig. 5-8

- **DestructivePunch (Pro Tools HD only):** This is a destructive recording mode that allows you to punch in or out on a record-enabled track, thereby deleting that portion of the existing audio on the hard drive, and creating a new contiguous file combining new and old audio as recorded on the track.

Note: Unless you have a specific reason to do otherwise, I would disable DestructivePunch mode and work nondestructively as much as possible. I have worked with Pro Tools for well over a decade and have rarely used any of the destructive recording modes. I'd rather have the option to review and revise edited tracks at a later time.

Fig. 5-9

Additional Recording Tools

AUTO-PUNCH

When you define a region in the timeline, you can set up an automated punch-in to record in a selected range. Just highlight a range in the timeline or Edit window of the session, then start recording. The new recording will only occupy the predefined region of the track. You can add pre-roll or post-roll playback by clicking the appropriate button in the Transport window.

Fig. 5-10

Another Auto-Punch technique uses Dynamic Transport: From the Transport window, Right-click the Play button, then select Dynamic Transport; or type Command + Control + P. Now define a recording range by dragging the Timeline Selection Start and Timeline Selection End indicators in the Main Timebase Ruler to encompass the range you wish to record. (Note that these normally blue arrow indicators turn red when a track is record-enabled.)

Then, drag the blue Play Start marker triangle in the same ruler to the point at which you desire playback to begin, effectively

Fig. 5-11

using manual pre-roll. (Make sure the Play indicator is located earlier than the start of the recording range.) You can also click in that ruler or use the Rewind or Fast Forward keys to move the Play Start marker. When you click Play, you will audition the recording range with manual pre-roll. When you click Record, you will record that range with pre-roll.

Note: This is unlike QuickPunch, in the sense that Pro Tools does not record audio from the point playback has begun; therefore, you cannot extend the beginning of a recorded clip to reveal pre-roll audio.

LOOP RECORD MODE

In Loop Record mode, you will be able to record multiple passes of audio on successive takes, as the play command continues to cycle recording of the selected region until stopped. Use this command with the auto-playlist option to create a stack of takes on successive playlists.

DOUBLE-TRACKING

This refers to recording the same part twice, as identically as possible. To add depth to a performance or to create a wider stereo spectrum spread, try double-tracking a part or parts, then panning them opposite one another. This can be done with vocals, background vocals, guitars, horns, or just about anything.

RECORDING AT HALF-SPEED

Little-known fact: with Pro Tools it is possible to record at half-speed, which doubles the speed of the recorded part on normal playback. Click the Record button, then Right-click the Play button and select Half-Speed. The track will play back at half-speed, and the recording will capture at this speed, thereby doubling the speed at normal playback. Key command: Command + Shift + spacebar. Not quite sure how often you would use this trick, since you can easily accomplish the same results by using the Time Compression/Expansion Audio Suite plug-in, but it's fun to find new ways to mess with audio! Google "Les Paul," and listen to his recording of "Lover (When You're Near Me)" for an early example of this technique.

THE RECORDING PROCESS

Like life, the recording process unfolds as a series of events. If you've prepared well for your session, the natural order will appear self-evident. Let's examine the sequence in which a recording session with live musicians will typically progress.

Basic Tracks

Capturing live performances to hard drive (or other storage media) using multiple tracks of audio, one for each microphone or sound source.

Punch-ins

If the overall performance of a basic track is good, there still may be minor timing or other performance issues that need to be fixed. This is most easily accomplished by doing a punch-in (or spot record) on the track in question. Example: If a bass part is good except for a wrong note in the chorus, the bass player will replay just that portion of the track by punching-in, or recording a section of short duration, on the original performance track. This is best done when the performer is still set up for the tracking session, so you don't have to re-create the equipment settings and energy level of the original performance at a later point in time. Pro Tools gives you a number of options for handling punch-ins easily, which we will explore in greater detail later in this book.

Overdubs

Once your basic tracks are recorded, any new parts/tracks that you record on that song will be known as *overdubs*. This is because you are recording new parts or layers in addition to the existing basic tracks. Some songs will require no overdubbing, some will require many layers of overdubs. Some songs are created entirely by overdubbing one track at a time.

Editing

This is the process of selecting keeper takes, fixing timing or tuning errors, editing the content of the performances you've recorded, and otherwise choosing that which will or will not make it to the final mix of the song.

Mixing

Mixing means combining all of the tracks in your recording to make a stereo (or surround) mix, suitable for listening on standard consumer playback systems. This is the step in which you balance volume levels between instruments and vocals to achieve the best-sounding final product.

Mastering

This is the final step in the recording process before distribution, and one in which EQ and compression are applied to your mixes, to optimize volume and dynamics and make each song in your project sound like it belongs to the same sonic family as the others. A mastering engineer will also smooth out any fade-ins or fade-outs, remove count-offs or dead air from the beginning or end of mixes, and put songs in their proper order with appropriate space between cuts for a CD or vinyl album release.

Some engineers may choose to skip or combine steps; some projects may not require every step; each project is different and has to be considered on its own merits; but these are the basic building blocks of a typical multi-track recording session. Examine these steps, and consider how they might apply to the music you are about to record.

PREPARING FOR A SESSION

Pre-Production

I firmly believe that an hour of pre-pro can save you 10 hours in editing/mixing, potentially even more than that. In the earlier discussion about what makes a recording sound good or bad, we covered the idea of using a pre-session technical checklist to be sure your equipment is in proper working order. Since every session is different, you should develop a detailed pre-production checklist to help you avoid potential pitfalls when the time comes to hit the red button and start recording. The list will be longer and more detailed when recording a group of musicians as opposed to recording a single performer, but a checklist is valuable all the same. Some of the questions may seem obvious, but if following a pre-op checklist helps surgeons to be more efficient and make fewer mistakes, then we engineers can do it too.

Recording a Band

- What is the style of music?
- How many members are in the band?
- What is the instrumentation? What is the budget?
- Does the budget include expenses such as hiring additional musicians, mastering, duplication, or anything else?
- When does the project need to be finished?
- Is the same engineer recording/editing/mixing/mastering?
- Will the musicians be playing all at once or individually?
- Does the artist have demos of the songs you can listen to?
- What is the desired sonic outcome, for the band and for individual instruments? Is there a musical reference?
- What bit/sample rate will you be using?
- Who is providing the hard drives for this project, and who will ultimately be responsible for the data?
- What data settings will you be using?

We could do a chapter on each of these questions, but for now, answering the questions on this list will help shape the session and inform you about possible red flags before the band enters the studio.

Recording an Individual Performer

- What is the style of music?
- What is the instrumentation? What is the budget?
- Does the budget include expenses such as hiring additional musicians, mastering, duplication, or anything else?
- When does the project need to be finished? Is the same engineer recording/editing/mixing/mastering? Will the performer be working with loops, beats, or pre-recorded tracks? Does the artist have demos of the songs you can listen to? What is the desired sonic outcome; is there a musical reference?
- Who is providing the hard drives for this project, and who will ultimately be responsible for the data?
- What data settings will you be using?

The answers to these questions will shape the session and dictate the workflow. The more info you can get in advance of the session, the more efficiently you'll be able to work and the smoother your session will proceed.

Session Basics

You will need to determine some important session settings before you can start recording. You can start a new Pro Tools session by choosing New Session from the File menu, or by typing Command + N. You will then see a dialog box asking you to select a series of settings for the session.

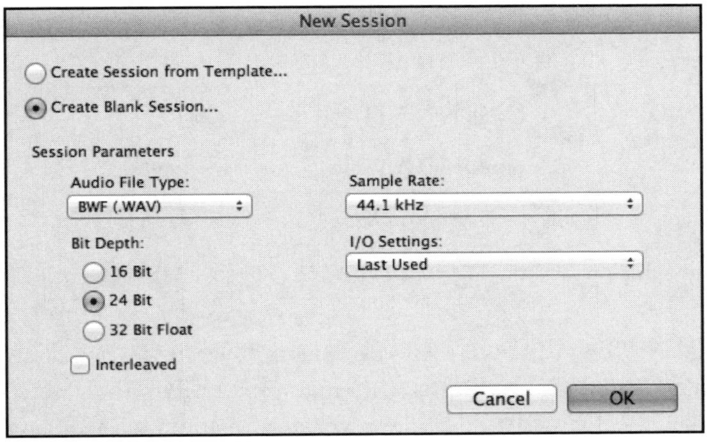

Fig. 5-12

Let's walk through the options for building your Pro Tools session:

SAMPLE RATES	BIT DEPTHS	FILE FORMATS
44.1kHz	16 -bits	BWF (.WAV)
48 kHz	24 -bits	AIFF
88.2 kHz	32 -bit FP	
96 kHz		
176.4 kHz		
192 kHz		

While you should always try to work at the highest-quality settings, it's not always possible or appropriate to work at 24-bit/192 kHz sample rate. For example, if you're working on audio for a game or a TV program, your ultimate delivery format may be 16-bit/44.1kHz WAV or 16-bit/48kHz AIFF, respectively. While you can always convert your mix to a different standard while bouncing, you may find it more efficient from a workflow standpoint to build your session to the specifications of the final delivery format. Also, working at higher bit/sample rates will increase the amount of hard drive space required to store the session data, will limit track counts within Pro Tools, and may affect system performance, depending on the capability of your machine. Here are some common delivery formats:

MEDIUM	AUDIO FILE FORMAT
Audio CD	16-bit/44.1 kHz AIFF
Audio DVD (DVD-A)	24-bit/96 kHz AIFF
Video DVD (DVD)	16-bit/48 kHz AIFF
TV	16-bit/48 kHz AIFF
Game authoring	16-bit/44.1 kHz .WAV
Online music distribution	16-bit/44.1 kHz AIFF, 128–320 kbps MP3, 128–256 kbps AAC

Note: While Pro Tools can import and export MP3 files, it will not allow you to record/edit/mix in that format. Conversion is a separate process. Pro Tools does not import or export AAC files. Pro Tools 10 now allows you to use audio with different bit, sample, format, and interleave settings within the same session. All recorded and imported stereo audio will be saved and used as interleaved files unless otherwise specified by the user. You can always choose to have your stereo files converted to multiple-mono files having the same bit rate, sample rate, and format as your session settings.

Using Session Templates for a Live Tracking Session

When you build a new session in Pro Tools, you can choose from a number of pre-built session templates, which can save a lot of time in building a session from scratch, particularly if you are tracking a band with many inputs. You can also build your own templates based on previous sessions or your own particular workflow. To explore the session templates when starting a new session, choose New Session from the File menu, or type Command + N to bring up the New Session dialog. From here, you will be offered the option to choose templates from a drop-down menu to aid in building your new session. When recording live musicians, select a template from the Record + Mix category, based on the number of tracks you'll need. For example, the 24 + FX Returns template features a pre-built session with 24 mono audio tracks with pre-assigned headphone, reverb, delay, and chorus Auxiliary sends, as well as Aux returns for the above. It also includes a Master Fader and a click track to complete the picture. If the session is MIDI based, choose from the Music or Songwriter categories for an array of pre-built options.

The template selection window gives you the ability to select audio file type (AIFF or BWF/WAV), sample rate, and bit-depth. Clicking OK will bring up the Save As destination window, prompting you to name the session and hard drive location for saving.

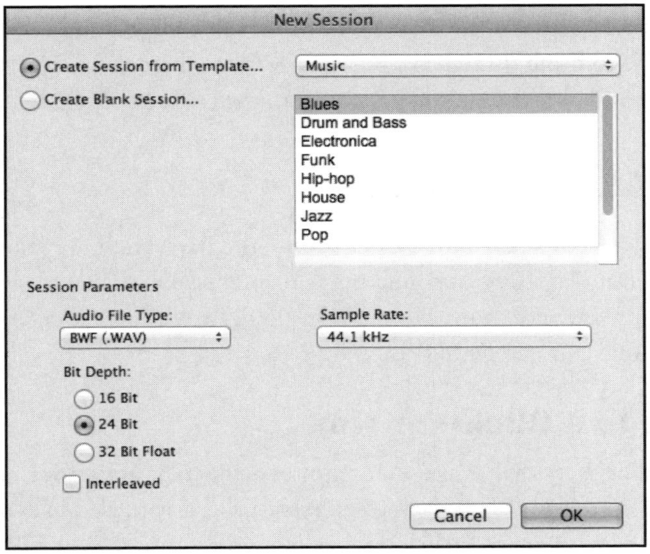

Fig. 5-13

Note: Saving a new session created from a template does not overwrite the template. Template data, once written, cannot be altered. Deleted yes, altered no. If you come up with a session format that you think you'll be using again, save it as a template using the "Save As Template…" selection from the File menu. This will prompt you to choose a name and location for the new session template, and whether or not any recorded media should be included in the template. (I can't think of a situation in which you would choose to save audio media in a music session template, but for post-production sessions, we will save test tones, 2-pops, and beep series for use in film/TV ADR and mix sessions.)

Building a Tracking Session from Scratch

Sometimes it's just easier/faster to build your session from the ground up. If you are using mainly stereo inputs, or if you have complex routing tasks, it may behoove you to create a session from jump street. Use the Shift + Command + N key combination to bring up the New Track dialog, or simply select "Track > New…" from the main menu. This allows you to choose the number, type, and format of sample-based (audio) or tick-based (MIDI) tracks to add to your session.

Naming Tracks

Please, please, *please* name your tracks something other than the default "Audio 1" before you record anything, particularly if you are handing your session off to another engineer to edit or mix. It will save you a great deal of time if you can identify a track or clip named "Guitar Solo" rather than "Audio 1-0_157." Just double-click in the Track Name pane of the Track window to bring up the naming dialog. From there you can name the track, add comments, and easily navigate to the previous or next track to continue the naming task.

PRACTICAL PRO TOOLS

This is the nuts and bolts part of the discussion—the part where we take all of the things we've learned about Pro Tools and put them to practical use in a session. All recording sessions require the engineer to make decisions; let's break down some of those decisions into understandable and manageable bits.

Recording to a Click—or Not

If you are recording a style of music that requires a constant and unwavering beat, then it makes sense for you to use a click track when recording basic tracks. In addition to working well with MIDI performances, a click track allows you to use the bar/beat boundaries and Grid mode in Pro Tools for precise timing and quantizing parts.

This can be very handy when it comes to editing or replacing parts, as the consistent tempo of the original performance will make Cut/Copy/Paste Edit alignment much easier than with constantly varying tempi. Loop-based music, urban, electronic, pop, rock, and country music are often cut to a click track.

Music with complex time signature or tempo changes can be programmed in advance, and the basic tracks can then be performed to the custom click track. This type of programming is often employed when recording music for film and TV, or any other visual medium requiring precise synchronization to image.

Some songs simply will not work with a click, and some musicians may find it difficult to play when confined to the inflexible pulse of the metronome. Jazz and classical music may not translate well when performed in time with a click track. As usual, it depends on the song and the musicians performing the piece.

Note: Music that is performed without a click track can still be conformed to a tempo grid after the fact using the Pro Tools Beat Detective function. Likewise, the tempo can be determined after the performance by using the Identify Beat command to create a tempo map.

CREATING A CLICK TRACK IN PRO TOOLS

The easiest way to create a click track is to select Track > Create Click Track. This creates a new mono Auxiliary track with the DigiRack Click plug-in installed in the Insert pane. From there you may choose different preset click sounds from a drop-down menu in the Click plug-in window, or you may customize a sound based on your needs.

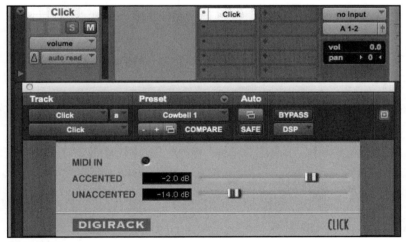

Fig. 5-14

Alternately, you may use the TL Metro plug-in (included with Pro Tools 10) as a source for your click sound. For more click options, you can install an instrument plug-in (such as Xpand2) on the click track insert, or even choose an external MIDI device by selecting the path of your connected MIDI device in the Track Input selector.

Next, you will need to enable the click track in order to be heard during recording or playback. Via the Options menu, select Options > Click. Alternately, at the top of the Transport window, click the drop-down menu triangle to reveal display options for the MIDI controls and the counters.

Fig. 5-15

Click the Metronome button in the Transport window to activate the click.

Fig. 5-16

Pressing the "7" key on the numeric keypad also toggles the metronome state.

CONFIGURING CLICK OPTIONS

You can quickly enable/disable the click in the Transport window as explained above. In some cases, it can be helpful for performers to hear the click track for a bar or two before the recording begins, in order to prepare for the passage to be performed and to play in time more accurately. To hear a click count-off before the recording or playback is to begin, click the Count Off button to highlight it. From there, double-click the bar count to select the desired number of bars to count off before recording or playback.

Fig. 5-17

When you need access to more options, you can open the Click/Count off Options dialog by choosing Setup > Click/Count off, or by double-clicking the Metronome button in the Transport window.

Fig. 5-18

In this window, you can select when you'll hear the click:

- During play and record
- Only during record
- Only during count-off

You can determine the number of bars of count-off, from 1 to 99, and whether you would like the count-off every time you hit Play/Record or only during recording. This window also gives you access to the MIDI note number, velocity, and duration for both accented and unaccented beats while using an external MIDI source for your click sound. There is a drop-down menu that allows you to choose between connected external MIDI sources.

Note: A click track should usually be used only when the performer or performers are wearing headphones. Playing a click track through speakers will cause it to be picked up by any and every live microphone in the room. If a performer's headphones are fairly loud, the sound of the click may still bleed into nearby mics. To prevent click contamination, always test the click in the headphones to be sure the sound isn't being picked up by adjacent microphones.

USING THE CLICK TRACK AS A WEAPON

In nearly every tracking session involving a click track and a drum set, I have found that the drummer will invariably want to hear the click approximately 10 times louder than anyone else in the band. Not a problem if you have the ability to give each musician a customized cue mix, but it can be a tremendous headache (literally) for anyone having to share a mix with the drummer. You can use this lopsided headphone mix to get even with a narcissistic singer, but in the long run, it will wear on the nerves of anyone having to listen to the incessant clacking of the metronome and result in migraine-like symptoms. Not to mention the potential for click leaking from the headphones into the sensitive microphones on the acoustic guitar and piano. The click track can be a mighty production tool ... or a formidable weapon. Create at least two discrete cue mixes for your group tracking session if possible, and avoid going to war.

The Headphone Mix

The click track discussion makes a nifty segue into the topic of headphone (or "cue") mixes. Cue mixes are beneficial for tracking musicians, in the sense that they can have a good-sounding mix that allows them to hear exactly what they need to hear to perform to the best of their abilities. The simplest way to build a cue mix is to send the musicians the same main mix that you hear in the control room. This works well for many situations, but when you need to solo or mute a track while musicians are playing during the tracking session, it will affect their mix as well, which may be disorienting or cause them to stop playing. Having a second set of physical outputs on your audio I/O will allow you to create a separate cue mix for the band, freeing you to solo/mute tracks or change the volume levels of tracks in your monitor mix without changing anything in the headphones. The more outputs you have available on your I/O device, the more cue mixes you can create for the performers. Using an 8-channel I/O device gives you the option to have a main stereo mix for the control room and up to three other stereo mixes for the performers. I would suggest using one cue mix for the drummer, one for the singer, and one for the remaining musicians.

There are headphone mixer systems, such as those from Aviom and Hear Technologies, which allow you to provide discrete mixes for each performer via a mixer that each controls him- or herself. Imagine the time saved and arguments averted by allowing the drummer to crank the click as much as he or she wants without subjecting the rest of the band to that torture! This is also a quick cure for the "more me" syndrome. Suffice it to say that I am a huge fan of individual headphone mixer systems.

Here's how to set up a dedicated cue mix in Pro Tools, assuming you are using an audio I/O device with at least two sets of stereo outputs:

- **Create a Headphone Aux Send on Each Track:** Holding the Option key, click on the Send A pane on the first track in your session (in either the Mix or Edit windows) and select "new track…" In the resulting New Track dialog window, build a stereo Auxiliary Input using Sample Timebase, and name it "Headphones." When you click the Create button, you will have created a headphone mix send in the Send A slot on each track in your session except for the Master Fader.

- **Designate a Hardware Output:** Locate the headphones auxiliary sub-master, then assign the output to the second (or other desired) set of physical outputs on your audio I/O device. We have already established that the more outputs you have available, the more cue mixes you can create. If you connect multiple audio I/O devices, you can increase the number of cue mixes as well. Note: You will need to use some sort of headphone amplifier, as the output of your I/O is not sufficiently powerful to drive headphones. Only the AVID HD Omni has its own headphone amplifier that can be used to drive headphones.

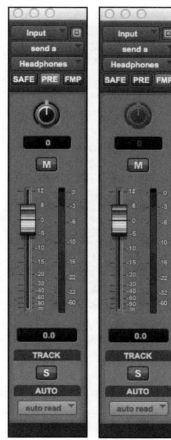

- **Set Cue Mix Levels:** Click on the Headphones send on any desired track. A small individual Aux send fader will display, allowing you to adjust the level of that particular track in the headphone mix. If you select the Pre button in this window, it becomes a pre-fader send, which maintains the level of that send as set by that fader. The level of this send will not change when the track fader is moved, muted, or soloed. This is the usual operating mode for cue mixes. If you wish the Headphones send level to mirror changes on the track fader level, leave the Pre button unchecked, making this a post-fader send.

- You can pan these sends independently of the main mix, or you can have the send pan control linked to the main pan control. To do this, check the FMP (Follow Main Pan) button on the Send page.

Fig. 5-19   **Fig. 5-20**

Note: Holding the Option key when clicking on the FMP or Pre boxes turns it into a global command, applying the change to all tracks/sends.

- **Copy Main Mix Levels to Cue Mix (For Pro Tools HD and Pro Tools CPTK users only):** Select a track by clicking the Track Name field to highlight. Type Command + A to select all tracks. From the top menu, choose Edit > Automation > Copy to

Send…, or type Option + Command + H to open the Copy to Send window. Tick the Current Value box in the "Copy:" field, then tick the Volume box in the "From:" field.

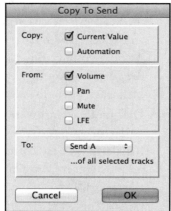

In the "To:" field, select Send A, then click OK. You have now copied all of the main Track fader levels to the Headphones send on every track, which gives your performers the same mix balance you are hearing in the control room. Control overall cue mix level by adjusting the Headphones sub-Master Fader.

- **Display Headphones Mix Levels:** From here you can make volume adjustments to suit the needs of the performers. To get a visual display of the individual

Fig. 5-21

track cue send levels, go to the View menu at the top of the main page, and select View > Sends A–E > Send A. This will display an expanded view of the Send A controls for each track, and allow you to easily see the cue mix balance and make adjustments quickly.

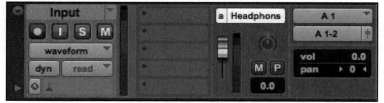

Fig. 5-22

Note: A number of these steps have been incorporated into the Record + Mix templates. Big time-saver!

Not all band recording sessions will require a cue mix. I recently tracked a group of bluegrass musicians for whom headphones were a distraction and actually made their performance less confident. They had been accustomed to rehearsing and performing without headphones for years, and found that they could balance and control their own levels much better without them. Solo performers may also choose to record without the benefit of a cue mix. If the performers are not using headphones, you will still need to find a way to communicate with them if you are in the control room and they are in a studio live room. Most studios will have a talkback monitor in the live room for just this purpose. You can send your control room talkback mic signal to the studio monitor speakers in lieu of making the performers wear headphones.

Metering

As you already know, DAW systems record digital audio with a wide dynamic range, especially at 24-bit resolution. It's important to remember that there is a limit to the amount of signal you can effectively record without distorting the signal. This is called full-scale, 100 percent modulation—or 0 dB headroom—and the way you know you've hit that ceiling is when the clip indicator (the red light at the top of the meter) is lit. In terms of signal flow, the meter can exist either pre- or post-fader. Pre-fader metering is the default setting in Pro Tools, and it's probably a good idea to leave it that way so you'll know when anything in the signal path on that track is clipping. Yes, a clipped plug-in will glow red as well, but it's much easier to notice the clip indicator on the track meter. Using post-fader metering can lull you into a false sense of security if the fader is pulled down to a lower level, because the clip indicator on the meter may not illuminate even if every plug-in in the chain is clipping. Remember: in digital audio, clipping is *bad*, and you should always avoid it. The meters are set to warn you if just a few consecutive samples are clipped, so if you do encounter some clipping, check the spot on the track that trips the clip indicator light. Solo that spot and listen carefully. If you do not actually *hear* distortion, you're probably okay. Then you must determine if your plug-ins are adding gain to drive the level into the red. Manage your gain structure so that you avoid clipping all along the signal path.

Pro Tools employs peak level meters that respond quickly to audio transients. If you are accustomed to setting levels on VU meters, be aware that you do not need to hit the top of the meter in Pro Tools. The equivalent of 0 dB on a VU meter is actually around -14 dB on a peak meter.

Setting Levels

It's a good idea to set levels on every microphone before you begin recording. Take the time necessary to listen to every mic on each drum, vocal, and instrument individually. This allows you to concentrate on getting your signal path straight and your levels accurately adjusted, and gives you the opportunity to carefully listen to the sound quality of each microphone to be sure you are getting what you really need to hear. We will briefly discuss the selection and placement of microphones later in this book.

If you are recording at 24-bit resolution, then you have plenty of leeway to allow for headroom when setting recording levels. Based on the ballistics of the peak meter as described above, your goal should be to set your recording level at an average of -14 dB with peaks of -6 maximum. Be particularly careful when recording drums, percussion, or any signal with highly transient peaks. Always use your ears to determine if you hear distortion in your recording. While you may have just the right amount of signal from the drum kit when setting levels, remember that a dynamic drummer may give you 6 dB more level when actually recording the song.

The Pro Tools default track size is fairly small; hence, the meter can be too small to read accurately. If you are having a hard time reading the meter, expand the track height by selecting the desired height from a drop-down list to the immediate left of the Track Name. Alternately, you can hover the cursor over the bottom edge of the track beneath the Track Name, then click and drag the edge higher or lower to shrink or expand the track manually. Option-clicking on either of these makes the change appear globally. If you claw click (Control + Option + Command) on the meter, it will toggle between normal and wide display, which may make it easier to see and set levels.

Recording with Dynamics Processing

At which point in the recording process do you need to control dynamics: before or after tracking? This is a sticky question, as some engineers prefer to record everything without compression and some choose to compress every mic they record. Personally, I prefer to record drums, bass, piano, strings, and electric guitar without compression. I will record vocals and acoustic guitar with light compression (no more than -4 dB of Gain Reduction) in order to control dynamics and avoid digital clipping. Use your ears and your best judgment to find out what works best for you. Just remember that any recorded processing will be there forever; you can't undo compression or other effects on your recorded tracks.

Recording with EQ

If you have selected and positioned your mics carefully, you shouldn't need to equalize very much, if at all, when recording. You may encounter low-frequency rumble with some microphones due to ambient noise, tapping feet, or other artifacts. This can be easily remedied by using a high-pass filter to remove low-frequency information below 60 Hz. Occasionally you may encounter a snare drum with a pronounced peak in the 1 to 2 kHz range, which can be diminished by using a notch filter or peak EQ tuned to the resonant frequency of the drum. The same axiom applies to equalization as to compression: you can't undo EQ on a recorded track. Be judicious in your use of signal processing on the way into your DAW.

RECORDING INSTRUMENTS

As discussed earlier in this book, recording engineers have two critical choices to make when recording live instruments: selecting the right microphone and putting that microphone in the right place. In this chapter, we will break down the miking process one instrument at a time. The techniques listed here are suggestions to get you started.

Drums

It's not always about the drums. Except in rock music. Or country, hip hop, electronic, pop, jazz, and some classical tunes. So let's get the drums recorded right, and the rest of our project will go much more smoothly.

While some classic records feature drums recorded with one or two microphones for the entire kit, I'm going to suggest that you use no less than eight for a standard drum kit consisting of a kick, snare, three toms, plus cymbals. You can always mute tracks to get back to the old-school sound. Here's the basic layout:

- **Kick:** For a more aggressive sound, use a large-diaphragm dynamic mic inside the drum pointed at the beater. For a better-rounded tone, use a large-diaphragm condenser mic outside the drum pointed at the front head, or on the beater side facing the head.

- **Snare:** A small-diaphragm dynamic mic positioned at a 45-degree angle to the top head looking toward the center of the drum will provide a great overview of the sonic information coming from the top head of the snare drum. You can supplement this with a small-diaphragm condenser mic on the bottom head to add more of the high-end snap of the snare strainer. If you do use two mics, experience dictates that you be prepared to flip phase on one of the snare mics. This can be done in post with an EQ plug-in.

- **Hi-Hat:** A small-diaphragm condenser mic positioned 4 inches above the outside edge of the hi-hat will give you a full-range picture of the hats. The position of the mic is critical here, in that the mic should not see the snare drum if possible. The snare is so loud that it may obscure the hi-hat on its own microphone.

- **Tom-Toms:** Dynamic mics work well if the drummer plays hard. If the parts are more subtle, you can try small- or large-diaphragm condensers. Remember that you will need to keep them a bit further from the drum heads, and those mics will pick up the rest of the drum kit. It's a delicate dance, but with a little practice, you'll find the right combination for your recording.

- **Overheads:** A spaced pair of large-diaphragm condensers or an X/Y pair of small-diaphragm condensers will do nicely. If you want to try something a little more exotic, use a pair of PZMs (boundary mics) mounted on the wall on either side of the kit to get a roomier sound from your overheads.

- **Room Mics:** If you have the capacity to record the extra tracks, I strongly advise that you record a stereo pair of room mics. Usually small- or large-diaphragm condensers will work well for this purpose. You can add these tracks in the mix to create a small amount of ambience or a huge amount of garage to the sound.

If you select and position your mics properly, there should be little need for compression or EQ during the recording.

Naturally, each mic gets its own track in the Pro Tools session. You should create a group assignment for all of the drum mics so that they can be muted or level-adjusted as a group. Highlight the Track Names of all drum tracks, and type Command + G to bring up the Create Group dialog. Label the group "DRUMS," and click OK to create the group.

Electric Bass

Use a direct box to interface the output of the bass with your mic pre-amp, and close-mic the speaker of the bass amp if applicable. The bass amp will typically provide a more aggressive, slightly distorted sound than the DI. You should be able to adjust between the two during mixdown to achieve a good balance of transparent direct sound and the grit of the bass amp.

Observe headroom carefully on your bass tracks. Dynamic range control might be advisable if the bass player is using slapping/popping techniques. The resulting transients can very easily send a track into clipping.

Acoustic Bass

An acoustic bass generates a lot of sound. Because of its size, the sound comes from all over the instrument, making it hard to capture accurately with just one microphone. If you need to record with one mic, select a large-diaphragm condenser and place it about 4 to 6 inches above the bridge.

With two mics, use a large-diaphragm condenser mic 4 inches away from the treble F-hole, and a ribbon mic aligned with the fingerboard and positioned 4 to 6 inches above the strings at the octave.

My preferred method is to use two mics plus a D/I. If a bass player has a pickup installed, it's usually a contact pickup affixed to the bridge. This will provide mid-range frequency content, plus more of the transient attack derived from plucking the strings near the bridge. These three tracks can be mixed together to deliver the best and most realistic sound from the bass.

Electric Guitar

The range of tones available from an electric guitar/amplifier can be very broad, encompassing everything from super clean and bright country sounds to blazing heavy metal distortion and everything in between. Nowadays, most guitar players have evolved their own signature sounds, and rely on an array of processing pedals (stomp boxes and other outboard processors) to create those sounds. This is an instance in which it is preferable to record an instrument with signal processing on the track. If there is any question about whether or not to record with a particular effect—flanging, for example—record without the effect, then add it in the mix.

When recording a guitar amp, you have many choices for microphone selection and placement, and just about anything goes if it sounds good in the track. The basic two-mic setup is a dynamic (or ribbon) mic close to the speaker cone, and a large-diaphragm condenser mic 4 feet away from the speaker cabinet. Though the tracks can be panned hard-left and hard-right, this is not really a *stereo* miking technique, so record each of these mics on its own track. That gives you the option to process, pan, and mix these tracks independently.

Acoustic Guitar

The function of the acoustic guitar in a song will determine how it should be recorded. If it's playing a strummed rhythm part, use a small-diaphragm condenser positioned near the 15th fret. A finger-picked part or melody line should be miked nearer the sound hole, preferably on the treble side of the instrument.

Piano

There are three basic techniques I use for stereo-miking a piano:

- **Close Miking:** Using a matched pair of large-diaphragm condenser mics, position them 4 inches above the hammers and about 2 feet apart. Lid may be open or closed. Good for rock, pop, and country recordings.
- **Mid-Distance Miking:** Using an X/Y stereo bar, mount a pair of small- or large-diaphragm condenser mics in an X/Y configuration at the bend in the piano (lid open), approximately a foot above the rim of the piano, parallel to the floor, and pointing into the open piano lid. Great for jazz, solo piano, and classical recordings.
- **Distant Miking:** Using a pair of large-diaphragm condenser mics, you can utilize a spaced pair, Blumlein, or X/Y stereo configuration. This technique requires a large, good-sounding room free from external noises. This is a useful solo or classical miking technique.

Organ

Assuming you have a Leslie cabinet attached to your organ, use a stereo pair of small-diaphragm condenser mics on the upper rotating horn, and a single large-diaphragm condenser mic on the lower drum.

Keyboards

Use two active D/I boxes when possible. When miking an amplifier or speaker cabinet, use a dynamic close-mic on a single speaker or two mics on a stereo amp.

Percussion

A stereo pair of small-diaphragm condenser mics positioned as overheads in an X/Y or spaced pair configuration will pick up a wide range of hand percussion, conga, bongos, and timbales. If you're just miking conga or similar instruments, close-mic them as you would toms on a drum kit.

Other Stringed Instruments

- **Violin, Viola:** Use small-diaphragm condenser mics above and pointing at the faces of the instruments.
- **Cello:** Use a large-diaphragm condenser mic pointed at the F-hole.
- **Mandolin, Dobro, Banjo, Ukulele, Oud, Shamisen, Balalaika, and Diddley Bow:** Usually a single small-diaphragm condenser mic, pointed in the general direction of the sound hole, resonator, or other source of the widest range of frequencies, will be the best bet.

Brass Instruments

If you are recording solo brass, try a large-diaphragm condenser mic at a distance of 1 to 2 feet. In a group, you can still use individual condenser mics, but you may have better luck with dynamics at a closer range. Be aware that you may need a pop-filter. If you're recording in a large room, use a pair of stereo room mics.

Wind Instruments

If you are recording solo woodwinds, use a small-diaphragm condenser mic at a distance of 1 to 2 feet and pointed at the middle of the horn. You might have success using a second small-diaphragm condenser mic at a distance of 4 to 8 feet from the instrument. In a group, lessen the distance from mic to instrument. If you're recording in a large room, use a pair of stereo room mics here as well.

Recording Unfamiliar Instruments

Position the performer in an open area of your recording space, then walk around the instrument as it's being played. If it's louder than a piano, try a dynamic microphone. If it's quieter, use a condenser mic. Aim for the source of the widest range of frequencies.

As with any of these suggestions, use your ears to determine the best mic selection and placement to capture the best sound. When in doubt, try to make the recorded sound of the instrument match as closely as possible the sound you heard in the room.

ADVANCED TECHNIQUES

Re-Amping

Take an existing recorded track and run it through a secondary process, such as an amplifier emulator plug-in, to add another texture to your sound. You can also use an additional Pro Tools I/O output to send the signal to a guitar amplifier, Leslie rotating speaker, or other external signal processor, then set up a mic and re-record that sound to a new track into your sequence.

This technique is not limited to guitars; you can use this with vocals, drums, or anything, really. Get creative!

Using Multiple Tracks for Guitars

Not to be confused with re-amping, the double-tracking technique described earlier can be used to beef up guitar parts. Then try playing an electric guitar part exactly the same way but on an acoustic guitar. Try playing a heavily distorted guitar part using a clean sound, or with a different guitar or amplifier, or through a wah pedal depressed halfway. Use half-speed recording mode to give your tracks an otherworldly sound you can't get any other way. Anything goes; this is your opportunity to evolve your own palette of sounds and techniques.

Using a Tuner in Pro Tools

If you are running Pro Tools HD and have installed a TDM instrument tuner plug-in on a track, you can use it in real-time on any available insert slot. Pro Tools|HD9 comes with the TL InTune or BF Essential tuner plug-ins, which give you a variety of display and resolution options. If you are running a host-based system, the process is essentially the same, except you will be using the RTAS plug-in as opposed to the TDM version of the plug.

Note: The process is a bit more complicated if you are running an HD system and want to use an RTAS tuner (or other RTAS plug-in). Since you cannot have an RTAS as the only active plug-in on a channel that is record-enabled or in input monitor mode, you have two options:

1. You can use the tuner plug-in on an Aux bus and route instruments to that bus for tuning.

Fig. 5-23

There is an advantage in this method, in that using the tuner as an Aux bus plug-in does not negatively impact latency on the input track. This is key to accuracy in timing when performing a live overdub.

2. You can insert any TDM plug-in on an insert before the RTAS plug-in, and it will work. Even if the TDM plug-in is bypassed. Not inactive, just bypassed. Try something small and efficient, such as a gain plug-in, which will use fewer system resources. Yes, I know, this is crazy, but it works. (It has to do with TDM bus priority, and will utilize additional voices.) I can imagine a scenario in which this would be useful, but #1 will always be preferable, IMHO.

HITTING THE RED BUTTON

Okay. You've built your session in Pro Tools, miked every instrument, patched in all your mic pre's and compressors, set your levels, and assigned everything to its proper place in your Pro Tools rig. Now it's time to record something. If you're working with a group of musicians, there's a good chance that they will want to rehearse a song once or twice (or for 12 hours) in order to get acclimated to the headphone mix and be sure they are hearing everything correctly. If they work with a click track, they will be adjusting the level and perhaps the tempo of the click track until it's just right. Don't overlook the opportunity to record these rehearsal takes. You never know when someone will play the golden solo or hit something exactly right. Especially when they think it's just a practice pass. When the pressure is off, people tend to play more openly. My advice: hard disk space is cheap; record everything.

Begin recording by clicking the Record button on the Transport, typing Command + spacebar, the F12 key, or the number "3" on the numeric keypad. Stop recording by pressing the spacebar or the number "0" on the numeric keypad.

If you are recording more than one song in a project, consider saving each song to its own Pro Tools session. This will make it easier to find and audition multiple takes of the same song.

RECORDING VOCALS

Capturing a great vocal performance can be an exhilarating experience or an exercise in frustration. This is an instance in which preparation can truly make a difference and result in a positive experience for all parties. Consider that this session is about more than just gear; it may be about the singer's health, physical ability, preparation, and attitude, as much as it is about your signal flow. The vocal session may be one of the most physically and emotionally demanding parts of a recording project. It can also be one the most rewarding.

Start with a Welcoming Creative Environment

It might seem like an obvious concept, but having the Pro Tools session built, the mic and signal path wired and tested, and the headphone mix up and running will go a long way toward making your singers (or other performers) feel like they are well cared for. If you are ready to rock when they walk in the door, you will earn more brownie points than by making them wait for half an hour while you suss out the buzz in the headphone system. I'm just sayin'.

If a singer is more comfortable singing in his or her living room, create that vibe by bringing in a comfy chair, a Persian rug, and some candles. If he or she thrives on playing in bars, turn the lights down low and hang Christmas lights around the room. I once had a singer who was an amazing club performer but nearly shut down entirely in the studio. She needed that club vibe to get comfy. What did we do? Set up tables around the live room and have the band sit at the tables. Then I had the singer hang onto a hand-held mic just under the expensive tube mic as she would have on stage. The pièce de résistance? She dangled an unlit cigarette from her lip. Voilà! She was transformed into the snarling, prowling stage denizen we hoped she would conjure for the performance. One pass, and done. The moral: do whatever it takes to get the take. (Subject to the laws of the realm and/or commonly accepted social behavior among consenting adults.)

Mic Selection

Every singer has his or her own sound, one reason why there are so many microphones on the market. If you only have one mic, use a large-diaphragm condenser mic with a pop-filter, positioned slightly above and about 6 to 10 inches away from the singer's mouth. Extra points if you have a tube or ribbon mic; now you can test a couple of different microphones to see which is best suited for the vocalist. Set up three (or more) mics, and record the singer singing a verse and chorus of the song in question. On playback, you should be able to jointly determine which mic sounds better. Experiment with distance from the mic and its angle of inclination toward the singer. Always use a pop-filter. If you end up recording a punk singer who insists on using a hand-held mic, put a foam pop-filter on the mic first. It's much easier to eliminate pops and sibilance by taking a preventative approach rather than trying to "fix it in the mix."

Headphones and the Art of Singing in Tune

The right headphone mix can be a blessing, especially with vocalists. But did you know that having your headphone volume cranked can affect your perception of pitch? That's right, the louder the cans, the more your pitch perception is skewed. In particular, the higher frequencies will sound sharper and the lower frequencies will sound flatter, so relying entirely on a pair of closed phones for accurate pitch reference can be dicey. There are three fairly common solutions to this problem:

1. Turn it down!
2. Use semi-open headphones. See AKG and Sennheiser, for example.
3. Take off one ear cup. Just rotate an ear cup toward the back of your head until that ear is free.

If you are able to hear yourself acoustically in the room, your pitch will be much more stable and true.

Vocalist Signal Chain

If you've settled on a suitable mic, the next step is to select a microphone pre-amplifier that will complement the mic and the singer's voice. This is based very much on personal preference, and I will not debate that in this forum. Instead, I will describe in general terms some options and leave it to you to determine what sounds best to your ears.

Mic pre's come in many flavors, but mainly those that are transparent and those that have a signature "sound." The latter can be really cool, if that's the sound you're after. Just remember that once you record a performance, you can't undo that "sound." My preference is usually toward a tube mic pre/channel strip such as the Avalon 737 SP or the like. It can be clean if you set it up that way, or it can impart a very distinctive tonal color to the signal.

Compression is often used in recording vocals, but sparingly. Knocking a dB or two off of the peaks is a fine thing, but leave the heavy compression for the mixdown, when you can exercise more precise control.

EQ is usually reserved for fixing signal problems on the way in, such as rolling off the low end with a high-pass filter to avoid foot-stomping noise and diminish popped *p*'s and such.

Vocalist Headphone Mix

Most singers like to hear their voices a few dB above the track, more than you would feel comfortable with in a normal mix. If you can't give them a mixer to create their own mix, then give them a custom mix that meets their needs. (See the earlier section on the headphone mix.)

Add a small amount of reverb to their mix so the vocal doesn't seem so exposed. On an Aux send, use a reverb plug-in that doesn't use a lot of signal processing power, such as D-Verb. Sample the presets to see if you can find one that suits the song. My default D-Verb setting on vocals is as follows:

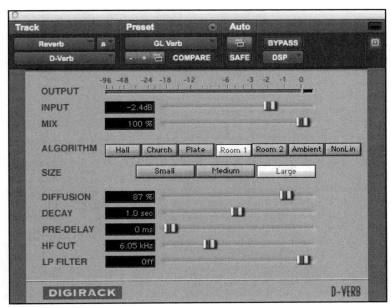

Fig. 5-24

- > -2 dB input level
- 100 percent wet mix
- Room 1, Large
- 87 percent diffusion
- 1 second decay time
- 0 ms pre-delay
- 6 kHz HF cut
- No LPF

Be sure to enable Solo Safe mode: Command-click the Solo button on the Aux master to keep the reverb return from being muted when you solo other tracks.

This will give you a starting point for a basic reverb sound. If you're working on a ballad, you may want to use a hall setting with a longer decay rather than a room setting.

Keeping Track of Vocal Takes and Keepers

Have a lyric sheet handy on which to pencil in notes on each take. Many top-level producers keep an Excel spreadsheet with check boxes per line of lyric so they can rate performances as they happen. I am somewhere in the middle, using a lyric sheet and a legal pad, and I will take notes on the legal pad as the singer performs. (Some things are still better analog.) Occasionally the takes come at you very quickly, and it may make sense to do the vocal comp edit on the fly. Figure out the best system for your workflow. Remember to save a new version before you commence editing takes.

Assembling and Editing Vocal Takes

Refer to the section on comping with playlists.

Double-Tracking

Double-tracking, or doubling, is simply recording the same vocal part twice in unison with oneself. This technique became popular in the 50s, as used on records by the greats Les Paul and Buddy Holly. This is sometimes referred to as manual double-tracking.

Automatic Double-Tracking, or ADT, is an electronic means of simulating the slightly random variations of recording a performance twice. Ken Townsend was the Beatles' engineer in 1966, and he developed this technique at the request of John Lennon. If you listen closely to early Beatles records, you will hear Lennon and McCartney doubling themselves manually. From *Revolver* on, you hear the ADT process, in most cases. ADT can be easily achieved after the fact using Pro Tools delay or chorus plug-in effects.

There are differences between and advantages to both techniques, so practice using both.

Using Multiple Tracks for Lead Vocals

Another technique for creating a more dramatic lead vocal sound involves duplicating a vocal part on two or more tracks, then processing them differently.

Use two vocal tracks, panning them opposite each other. Delay one track by 10 to 35 ms. This creates the illusion of 3D space, also called the Haas Effect.

Another trick: Use two or more vocal tracks. EQ the tracks differently, or modulate the pan setting of one track back and forth between the speakers, or flange one track, or all of the above at once. Use your imagination; this is your sandbox!

Self-Stacking Background Vocals

If you have a singer capable of doubling his or her existing tracks, it's easy to move to the next step—recording background vocals (BGV) by self-stacking parts. Once the lead vocals are recorded and edited, the vocalist can harmonize with existing parts or compose counterpoint and counter-rhythm BGV parts quite easily. Create a new track in Pro Tools for each BGV part to be added, then assign the vocal mic input to the new track and record the next part.

Another way to do this is by creating four new BGV tracks (or however many you will ultimately need). Record a new part on the first track, then drag the new audio clip into the next track. Repeat this until you have filled your BGV tracks.

Example: Enya is famous for stacking her vocals, in some cases more than 200 times in a song.

Group Background Vocals

This is a great way to build parts quickly and add new textures to your BGV sound. There are two ways to approach group vocals:

1. Use one or two small-diaphragm condenser microphones for the entire group. Adjust balance between singers by physically moving them closer to or farther from the mics. This works really well for large groups or choirs recording in large rooms.
2. Give each singer his or her own microphone, and record each mic on its own track. This technique results in the most powerful BGV sound, but is only practical for small groups unless you have access to a large studio with quantities of headphones and microphones sufficient for the size of your group.

Stacking these group vocals can add even more power and depth to the BGV sound. I often use three singers in a group, stacked two or three times to make a huge vocal sound. In the mix, these parts can be panned hard left and hard right to dramatic effect.

To Tune or Not to Tune

There is a strange phenomenon in music right now, a sort of Jungian mass hysteria surrounding the insatiable desire for all music to be perfectly in tune and on the beat. Artists can and will decide exactly how in tune they wish to appear on a recording. There are a few different schools of thought on the subject, ranging from "just tune the occasional bit" all the way to "set it on stun and let it roll." If you listen to the Beatles, you will quickly realize they were singing amazingly in tune. In fact, if you listen to anything produced before the 1980s, the performances were natural and un-effected, because the technology to modify tuning simply did not exist. Now we have to consciously make the choice of whether to tune vocals or not. Usually it ends up being another quality threshold set by the production team. For example, if a note is more than 20 cents out, it gets tuned. The tools do exist, and they can be used tastefully or experimentally depending on where you establish that threshold of quality.

Auto-Tune Versus Melodyne Versus Waves Tune

There are a number of tools used for tuning instruments or vocals, and while the results may be similar, the tools are applied differently.

Auto-Tune is a plug-in from Antares that is used to analyze and process single-note pitch correction in real-time. The technology allows you to establish parameters for processing, including key, scale selection, note inclusion/exclusion, sensitivity, and degree of effect. This processing is applied automatically in real-time. They have added a graphical editing mode that allows you to specify note correction on a per-note basis. This is a bridge to the other pitch-correction approach.

Melodyne is a product of the German company Celemony. Their approach is to first load the audio-to-be-tuned into their program, which is available as a stand-alone app with a plug-in bridge to port audio directly to and from the Pro Tools playlist or a direct editing plug-in page. From there, you can graphically edit each note's pitch, duration, formant content, amplitude, and pitch drift characteristics. Like the Antares plug-in, the processed audio is played back on the same Pro Tools track as the source, and can be written to disk with the real-time processing embedded. Melodyne recently announced their DNA (Direct Note Access) technology, which allows users to access and manipulate mono- and polyphonic content.

Waves Tune does basically what Melodyne does, but with a plug-in editing page only, no stand-alone app.

There are other plug-ins available that do essentially the same job, but these are the main proponents of the technology.

RECORDING MIDI

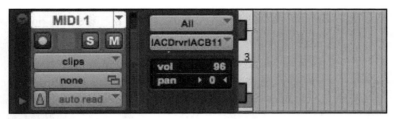

Fig. 5-25

Pro Tools makes recording MIDI information easy and very similar to recording audio. You can create MIDI and Instrument tracks right alongside your audio tracks, and edit them much as you do audio tracks. If you have configured your MIDI studio correctly, you should have instant access to your input devices and controllers from the Track control pane.

1. Select input source, whether All or Predefined.
2. If recording on a MIDI track, choose your Predefined output and patch setting.
3. If recording on an Instrument track, insert your virtual instrument of choice on a track insert. Select a patch setting.
4. Arm the MIDI or Instrument track by clicking the red Record button.
5. From the MIDI Controls menu, choose Wait for Note, or just hit the Record button. You will begin recording MIDI data as soon as you begin playing the keyboard or as soon as the transport begins playing back, depending on the selection you've made.

Each time you record a pass, you will be erasing any previously recorded MIDI data on the track—unless you select the MIDI Merge option in the MIDI Control menu, in which case you will be adding to previously recorded MIDI data. If you have enabled Loop Record and set your Operation preferences to Automatically Create New Playlists When Loop Recording, each successive looped pass recorded will generate a new playlist rather than erase the previous pass.

MIDI Real-Time Properties

In Pro Tools, you can modify MIDI data playback in the track without permanently altering the data recorded. By modifying Real-Time Properties, you can adjust the following parameters in real-time:

- Quantize
- Duration

Fig. 5-26

- Delay + or -
- Velocity

You can choose to view the Real-Time Properties information as a pop-up window by choosing Event > MIDI Real-Time Properties, or pressing Control + 4 on the numeric keypad.

Fig. 5-27

MIDI Real-Time Properties can also be displayed in a Tracks View pane by selecting Real-Time Properties from the Track View options menu.

You may choose to conform the Real-Time Properties modifications to a selected MIDI track by clicking the Write to Track button in the MIDI Real-Time Properties window.

CREATIVE EDITING AND ARRANGING

Editing = Making Choices

After recording a rock/pop/country record, you will likely have many more tracks than will actually make it to the final mix. There will come a time when you need to thin out parts that have been played throughout a song, editing them for content and to enhance the arrangement. You may ask yourself, "Do I really *need* to use all 14 of the guitar parts I recorded for this song?" A good rule of thumb is to listen to a rough mix of your song at a moderate to low volume. If you hear parts that conflict or compete for your attention, there's a good chance you may want to feature one part over another in the offending section. If a part cannot be heard in the mix, it may be due to a lack of level, or it may not fit in the song. Just because you recorded it does not mean it needs to be in the final mix! You do not have to use everything you record. Listen to some of the great hit songs, and you will hear sections where it might break down to just bass, drums, and vocal. This is the beauty of working in Pro Tools; you have the ability to test out arrangement ideas and save them as their own sessions for reference. You can easily create new song structures by moving sections around until you discover the perfect arrangement. You can just as easily undo edits to return to previous iterations in just a few seconds. Just remember: at some point you will actually have to make those choices and live with them.

Tracking a jazz group all at once might result in fewer edits than rock/pop/country, but you will have to make choices as to which solo to use, whether or not to edit a repetitive 64-

bar intro, or just how loud the three cowbells want to be during the chorus. (Don't laugh, it's happened.)

The trick to all this is determining when the song is actually done. Theoretically, that should be the point at which the song assumes its best and highest form. Is it the first mix or the twelfth? Is it the third take? Was it better in the demo recording? These are subjective decisions at which you will arrive when you feel you have exhausted all possibilities of adding more tracks, more harmonies, and more hard drives. In contrast, consider the maestro Leonardo da Vinci, who is quoted as having said, "Art is never finished, only abandoned." Consider making some of these choices as you go along rather than saving them all for the mix.

Recording Multiple Takes of a Song

If you spend enough time recording music, you may at some point experience the rare phenomenon of the "keeper first take." If this happens to you, make note of the details. This will likely become one of your better anecdotes.

More often than not, you will create a session for each song, record multiple takes of that song, then play these takes back for the band/artist, who will decide which version is the best. You will record each subsequent take after the previous take on the same timeline, so that you can see all takes in a linear and sequential order. Drop a marker at the beginning of each new take by typing the Enter key on the numeric keypad on your keyboard. You can name the marker "Take 1," for example, then add comments or information about that take in the comments field. This is a good navigation tool to help audition takes, and a great way to keep track of the takes per song or per session. It's easy to create other location markers in this manner on the keeper take, so create song section markers (verse, chorus, bridge, solo, and so forth) when you hear a new section begin.

Editing Multiple Takes into a Master Take

It is common for a producer or artist to prefer different portions of different takes rather than one continuous take, and to ask the engineer to assemble these portions into a master take. This master take becomes the foundation for all future overdubs and edits on this song. This is often called "comping"; comp is short for *composite,* a technique with which you assemble selections from different takes into a single composite take.

The solution to this task is rather involved, but quite manageable using standard Pro Tools editing functions. First, locate and mark the sections you wish to use from each take. For the sake of example, let's say that we will use:

- The intro section from take 1.
- The first verse from take 2.
- The first chorus from take 3.

- The outro/ending section of take 4. (Okay, so it's a short song.)

There are two ways to proceed from here:

1. When you have recorded with a click track, and

2. When you have not recorded with a click track.

If you recorded the song to a click track, enable Grid mode in bars/beats and resolve to 1-bar increments.

Then:

Fig. 5-28

1. Create a new marker a minute or so beyond the end of the last take, and label it "Edited Master Take." Make sure that your marker lies on the first beat of the nearest bar. This is where you will begin to assemble the new song. Turn on the All Groups function in the Groups window.

Fig. 5-29

2. Next, go to the intro section of the first take. Using the Cursor tool, drag a region that encompasses the entire intro, from the first beat of the first bar to the first beat of the bar following the intro. (Every track will be included if you enabled the All Groups function in the previous step.) Grid mode will ensure that your clip will conform exactly to the bar lines. Separate this clip by hitting the "B" key or Command + E, or by selecting from the main Edit menu: Edit > Separate Clip > On Grid. With this new clip selected, copy it by pressing the "C" key. Locate to the "Edited Master Take" marker and paste the intro by pressing the "V" key. The clip should appear beginning at the marker and extending to the end of the intro section. It should conform to the Bar/Beat grid as well.

3. Next, go to the verse section of the second take. Using the Cursor tool, highlight a region that encompasses the entire verse, from the first beat of the first bar to the first beat of the bar following the verse. (Every track will be included if you enabled the All Groups function in the previous step.) Separate this region by hitting the "B" key or Command + E, or by selecting from the main Edit menu: Edit > Separate Clip > On Grid. With this new region selected, copy it by pressing the "C" key.

4. Locate to the "Edited Master Take" marker, and click in the timeline at the end of the intro you just pasted. Your cursor should be blinking there. Now, paste the verse

by pressing the "V" key. The verse region will appear right after the intro and should extend to the end of the verse section.

5. Repeat this procedure for the remaining sections and any other sections you may wish to add. Voilà! You have just built the perfect take from the best parts of all the raw takes.

If you did not record using a click track:

1. As above, create a new marker a minute or so beyond the end of the last take, and label it "Edited Master Take." Make sure that your marker lies on or near the beginning of a full minute (e.g., 14:00.00). This is where you will begin to assemble the new song.

2. Go to the intro section of the first take. We will learn to use a new tool to find the precise beginning of the first beat by using the Tab to Transients function to drive the cursor to the beginning of the first audio transient. Click on the Tab to Transients button below the Tool Selector section at the top of the timeline in the Edit window. With this button enabled, you will be able to locate the next audio transient, as seen in the waveform display in the timeline.

3. Click on a drum track, then hit the Tab key. The cursor should advance to a position just before the next audio transient.

4. Drop a marker at this position labeled "Intro." Locate the end of the intro section, use the Tab to Transient function to locate the first beat of the next section, and drop a marker labeled "Verse." Turn on the All Groups function in the Groups window.

5. Locate to the "Intro" marker, then Shift-click on the "Verse" marker to select the entire intro region. Separate the intro region by hitting the "B" key or typing Command + E. With this new region selected, copy it by pressing the "C" key.

6. Locate to the "Edited Master Take" marker, and paste the intro by pressing the "V" key. The region should appear beginning at the marker and extending to the end of the intro section. While you're there, drop a new marker labeled "VERSE."

7. Go to the verse section of the second take. Repeat the steps described in the intro step to isolate the entire first verse. Copy the verse section.

8. Locate to the "VERSE" marker, and paste the verse by pressing the "V" key. The verse region will appear right after the intro and should extend to the end of the verse section.

9. Repeat this procedure for the remaining sections and any other sections you may wish to add. Even without the grid, you have just built the perfect take from the best parts of all the raw takes.

Now take a short break; you've earned it.

Note: You can disengage the All Groups function and fine-tune the transitions between sections track by track. You may need to adjust the clip borders one way or the other in order to accommodate slight timing differences between the end of one section and the beginning of another. Use your ears to determine if there are timing issues; use your eyes to identify where waveforms don't match up correctly.

USING PRO TOOLS PLAYLISTS

When you create a new track in a Pro Tools session, it is essentially an empty playlist waiting for you to record onto it or drag/ import audio into it. Playlists can be managed by accessing the Playlist Selector, which enables you to create a new empty playlist, duplicate an existing playlist, delete a playlist, or select other existing playlists.

Fig. 5-30

Using playlists to record a single (or multiple) track overdub gives you the ability to create alternate versions within an existing song in the timeline. Let's look at a practical example of how to use the Pro Tools playlist function.

Here's a common group tracking session occurrence: One musician performs his or her part correctly on an early take, while other musicians are still dialing in their parts. This can present a logistical challenge when the band wants to keep the drums from take 3, then overdub the remainder of the basic tracks on top of the take 3 drum track.

In this scenario, you would first duplicate the drum tracks playlist; next, create new playlists for the other instruments. This allows you to keep the drums intact on the timeline and add new parts from the other performers, who will be playing along with the drums and essentially overdubbing their parts. The complete original take will still exist in the playlist stack, so you can always go backward in time to that version if you need to.

If you engage the All Groups function, you can create or duplicate playlists globally merely by creating or duplicating a playlist on any track. This is another way to capture multiple takes, but in a vertical stack rather than in linear/sequential order.

Note: Anything you do to modify a duplicate playlist will be confined to that playlist. Edits, deletions, additions, and so forth will not affect the original playlist. Just remember to duplicate the playlist before editing. Take good notes in order to identify which playlist was the original version and avoid confusion.

Comping with Playlists

Previously we discussed comping takes in a linear session. Pro Tools has one of the slickest playlist comping interfaces of any DAW on the market. It's fast, easy, and great for the visually oriented engineer. Let's use a single-track overdub for this vocal comping example, and establish that the singer has performed the song from top to bottom four times on a track labeled "Vocal," with each pass on a new playlist. Our job is to assemble (or comp) a keeper vocal track from these four takes.

After each take, create a new playlist by clicking on the Triangle icon next to the Track Name. Select "New . . . ," and click to create a new empty playlist.

The default naming convention for a new or duplicated playlist is to retain the original playlist name and add ".01" as a suffix. Unless the name is otherwise modified, the suffix of each new playlist will increment. In this case, our four playlists will be labeled:

- First pass: "Vocal"
- Second pass: "Vocal.01"
- Third pass: "Vocal.02"
- Fourth pass: "Vocal.03"

In the Track View Selector, select Playlists.

Fig. 5-31

Assuming each vocal pass was recorded on a new playlist, there should now be four playlists visible.

Create a new playlist labeled "Vocal Comp." This new empty playlist should appear at the top of the playlist stack in the Vocal Track window.

Highlight and listen to phrases in sections of roughly 5 to 10 seconds in duration, beginning with the earliest pass (the "Vocal" playlist). If your transport is in Loop Play mode, you will be free to listen and switch between takes without having to constantly stop and start playback.

On the left side of the playlist lane, you will see the playlist name, a Solo button, and an Arrow button that performs the Copy Selection to Main Playlist function. Audition each phrase from within its playlist by clicking the Solo button to hear it in context with the rest of the mix.

Repeat this audition process for each playlist. When you have selected the best performance of the phrase, click the Copy Selection to Main Playlist button to promote that phrase to the main "Vocal Comp" playlist.

Do this one phrase at a time to assemble a seamless vocal comp track.

In the Track View Selector, select Waveform view to hide the playlists and return to the normal single-track view.

RECORDING OVERDUBS AND PUNCH-INS

When adding new parts to existing tracks, prepare for the session by making sure that:

- Delay compensation is turned off, and you are using minimal plug-ins directly on tracks.
- QuickPunch mode is turned on.
- There is a count-off accessible and ready for the performer to hear.
- You have marked the sections of the song to make them easier to locate.

It's generally a good idea to use new playlists to record overdubbed performances; that way you can easily keep track of select takes and assemble them into a comp track. Use a duplicated playlist for punch-ins so that you can easily go back to the previous unaltered version of a performance if necessary.

Using QuickPunch, you can do single-track or multi-track punch-ins in Pro Tools; just make sure that *only* the desired tracks are record-enabled, otherwise you may end up unintentionally overwriting audio or MIDI information.

TRACKING TIPS

Document everything. Take notes on mic selection and placement, signal path, and outboard gear settings.

Document everything. Keep your notes on individual takes in case you need to find them later while editing.

Document everything. Keep everything. Record everything. Roll a 2-track backup of the entire live session to CDR or DAT if you can. The singer might hit that impossible lick in between takes … when the multi-track recorder is not rolling. You can always go back to the 2-track and edit it into the session after the fact.

Eric Schilling is a Grammy®-and-Emmy®-award-winning engineer who records and mixes with Pro Tools HD using AVID ICON and EuCon control surfaces. When asked about tracking instruments, he talked about his method for recording multiple live performers, and shared a clever organizational system he uses to record groups of instruments or vocals. On tracking, Eric says,

I am dogmatic about labeling everything in Pro Tools before I hit Record. When I am actually recording live tracks with several musicians on the floor, I do not use multiple playlists but will record in linear order as I would on tape. This gives me a visual display of all my takes. I do use playlists when I get to individual players or vocalists.

Fig. 5-32

For large tracking dates, I will build a template for that session with all Track Names, routing, groups, etc., so as we move to record a new song, I can create a new session and import the tracks from the template and I am all ready to go.

In typically modest fashion, he describes his system for recording a group of performers that require doubling passes.

I guess one small thing I do that may be a little different is the following: When recording strings, horns, background vocals, or anything else where you double and triple, I always prepare a Pro Tools session setup for that recording date. Let's use strings as an example. Say I am doing three passes of strings. I make a group for every pass that will enable record and lock volumes for all tracks.

In system prefs, I make sure the Record button is not latching. So as I jump from pass to pass, it will disarm the pass I have just completed when I arm the next.

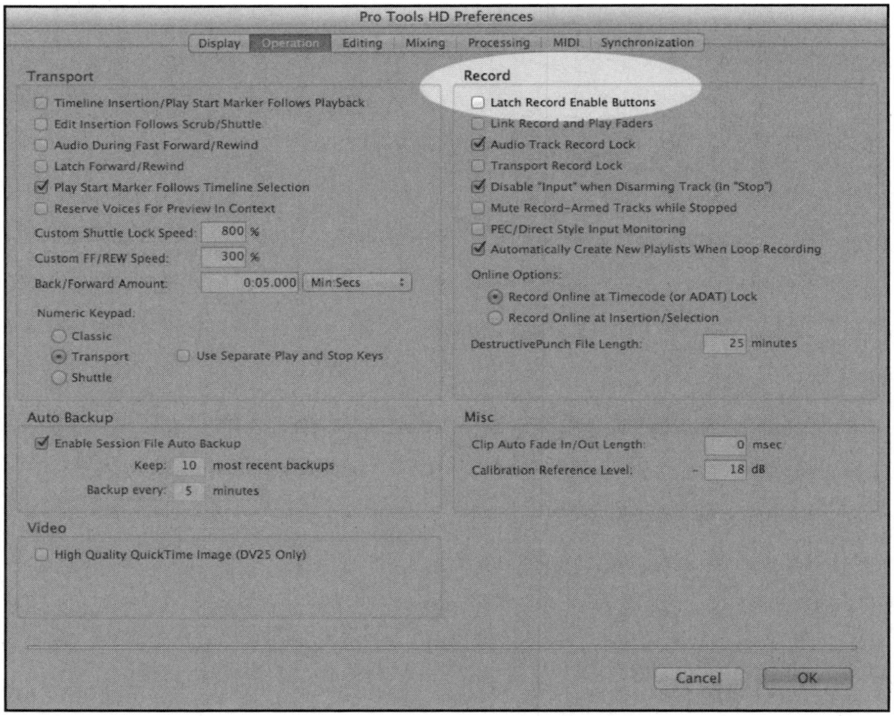

Fig. 5-33

Since tripling strings could take up 24 faders on a console, I route all passes out to the same faders (e.g., Violin L/R, Viola L/R, Cello L/R, Room L/R). In preferences, I make sure to uncheck the "Link Record and Play Faders" button.

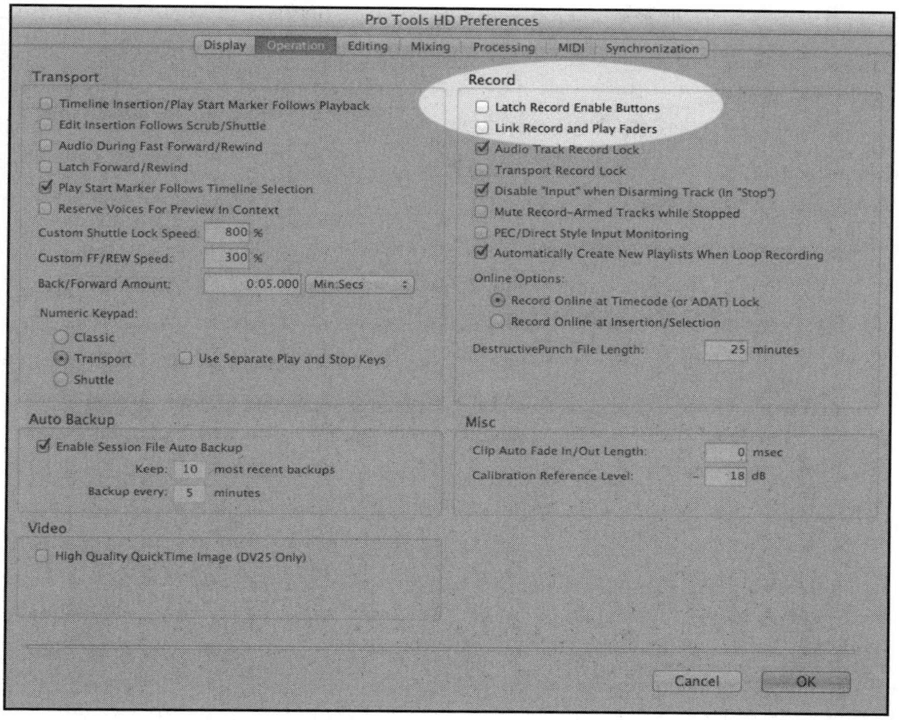

Fig. 5-34

With no string tracks armed, I set the volume of all string groups to -6 dB. As I arm each pass, I set the volume to 0 dB. So what happens? First, as I stack the strings, previous passes are played a little lower so I can feature the current pass I am recording. Second, this prevents buildup of volume as I stack passes.

At the end of your tracking day, back up everything on your hard drive to another hard drive just to be safe. You never know what can happen to digital data overnight. In the dark. When no one is looking. Sometimes it just … goes away. Hard drives are cheap, so create a backup. Better safe than sorry.

KEEPING TRACK OF SESSIONS AND FILES

Use the "Save As …" command to create a new version for every instrument you add or major edit you make to the song. I use a naming convention that starts with the song name, then the instrument or action, then any iterative numbers. For example, if I have already tracked a song and am about to add a piano overdub, I would name the session "SongName 01_PNO." A subsequent version with a second round of piano overdubs might be called "SongName 02_PNO." Unless you change the location when saving, all these Pro Tools sequence files will be stored in the session folder on your hard drive. This may seem like an unwieldy format for naming files, but in a list of 10 or more saved sequences, it's always easy for me to find the version I worked on last, or the version with the first vocal overdubs, or the version of "SongName 03_RoughMix" that had a corresponding audio file named "SongName03_RoughMix.aif." Here's a screen shot showing how this would look in a session folder:

Fig. 5-34

SUMMARY OF KEY COMMANDS

OPERATION	KEY COMMAND
Playback Options	Right-click Play, or Control + Clicking Play button when stopped
Half-Speed Playback	Shift + Spacebar, or Shift + Clicking Play button
Prime for Playback	Option + Clicking Play button
Loop Play	Control + Clicking Play button
Play	Click Play, Spacebar, 0 (numeric keypad)
Timeline Insertion/Play Start Marker Follows Playback	N
Recording Options	Right + Clicking Record button, or Control + Clicking Record button when stopped
Dynamic Transport	Command + Control + P
Half-Speed Recording	Command + Shift + Spacebar
New Session	Command + N
Select all tracks	Click Track Name, then Command + A
Copy to Send window	Option + Command + H
Create Group	Command + G

Record	Command + Spacebar, F12, or 3 (numeric keypad)
Cut	X
Copy	C
Paste	V
Separate Clip	Command + E, or B
Mute Clip	Command + M
Save	Command + S

CHAPTER 5 REVIEW

1. Command + Shift + spacebar enables _____ _____ recording.
2. You may use a number of methods to create a click track in Pro Tools. The fastest method is to select the _____ menu > Create Click Track. This creates a new Aux track and installs the AvidRack _____ plug-in automatically.
3. Pro Tools displays _____ type meters on every audio and Aux track.
4. One of the advantages of recording at 24-bit resolution is the wide_____ range.
5. What hardware is required in order to create a dedicated headphone mix out of Pro Tools? _____
6. Clicking the FMP button on a send fader enables that send to _____ settings.
7. The AVID _____ interface has its own built-in headphone amplifier.
8. The _____ command allows you to store and rename a new version of your session on your session hard drive.
9. Two of the most important choices a recording engineer must make involve mic _____ and _____.
10. True or False: The miking processes described in this chapter represent suggestions for a starting place only. _____
11. When recording an unfamiliar instrument, you should strive to make it sound like _____.
12. _____ requires re-recording a sound into your DAW using secondary processing.
13. True or False: Record-enabling a track in Pro Tools HD will bypass any RTAS plug-ins inserted on that track. _____
14. The Record key commands are _____ + _____, _____, or _____on the numeric keypad.

15. Excess headphone volume can alter your perception of _____.

16. Generally speaking, vocalists prefer to hear some _____ on their voice in the headphone mix.

17. _____ involves having a performer record his or her part again in perfect sync and in tune with the original performance.

18. _____ or _____ can be an effective way to make background vocal tracks sound fuller.

19. _____ vocals with AutoTune or Melodyne has become a regular part of the music production process.

20. The process of assembling multiple takes into a single master take is known as _____.

21. To easily edit sections of music recorded to a click track, enable _____ mode resolved to bars/beats, then turn on the All _____ function. You will be able to edit and move sections of a song with greater rhythmic accuracy.

22. The Pro Tools _____ function enables you to record multiple takes on a single track, then edit a keeper take without using additional tracks.

23. It's a good idea to record overdubs and punch-ins using _____ mode, so as not to risk missing a key portion of a performance by a late punch.

24. True or False: When finished with a project, there should be only one Pro Tools session file. _____

Editing Operations 6

Okay, now that we have some of the mechanics squared away, let's get down to editing the tracks. As we get into practical application of the tools and techniques presented here, you will quickly see that there are at least five different ways to do everything in Pro Tools. Or so it would seem. This is not designed to make you crazy but rather to give you options at every turn. If you know at least three ways to solve a problem, you will naturally choose the method that is fastest or most efficient. With some practice, you will find that a lot of these operations become muscle memory as a result of having used them so often. Saving, for instance. You should save your work often, and the fastest way to do this by far is to use the keyboard to type Command + S. Most DAW users can find that command in the dark, and you should too. Again: save everything all the time.

EDITING AUDIO

Playlists

If you have recorded tracks with alternate playlists, you should review them to be sure you're using the master take. View alternate playlists by clicking the Track View Selector button in the Edit window, then selecting playlists. This will open a playlist lane beneath each track showing you all takes for each track.

Fig. 6-1

You can also view a playlist by clicking the Track Name button and selecting the number of the playlist you wish to view.

Note: Playlist views subscribe to group assignments, so if you switch playlists on the drums group, for example, the view of all member tracks will switch as well. By activating All in the Groups pane, all tracks will switch their playlist views when one member's view is changed.

Fig. 6-2

Duplicating Tracks

You can duplicate tracks by selecting Track > Duplicate … (or Shift + Option + D), then completing the instructions and clicking OK.

Note: You cannot undo this operation. You will have to delete the track manually if you want it gone.

To delete a track: Highlight the Track Name to be deleted, select Track > Delete; a pop-up window will then ask you if you're sure, because there are active clips within the track. Click OK to delete. You cannot undo this operation either.

Cleaning Tracks

Whether you recorded every instrument yourself or inherited tracks from other engineers, you will find it necessary to edit portions of the tracks if you find them to be noisy or otherwise unusable. Pro Tools gives you a number of ways to deal with the job of cleanup.

STRIP SILENCE

Pro Tools has a handy function called Strip Silence that eliminates sections of a clip falling below a user-defined threshold level. If you select a clip and open Strip Silence (Command + U), you will see a dialog box giving you access to four adjustable parameters allowing you to define "silence." As you adjust the Strip Threshold, you will see the clip view divided up into smaller and more numerous sub-clips. Use this to determine the minimum amplitude at which a new clip will be created. The other parameters—Minimum Strip Duration, Clip Start Pad, and Clip End Pad—allow you to force durations onto the new clips to be created. In other words, you can add a few milliseconds of silence before the clip start time, set a minimum duration, or extend the endpoint of each clip. This is a great way to remove noise between tom hits, headphone leakage between vocal lines, or amp hum between guitar lines.

Click the Strip command button to complete the operation once your selections have been fine-tuned.

Note: You can always undo this operation later in the process by selecting all the stripped clips and pressing Command + H to heal the track, thereby restoring it to its original state before the Strip Silence operation was performed (as long as you didn't move the sub-clips or change the timing).

NOISE GATES

Another way to mute noisy tracks is to use a noise gate plug-in on the offending track. Noise gates can be set to automatically reduce track volume (or even be silenced completely) when signal falls below the gate threshold. Gate attack, release, and duration can be set to your specification in real-time, tailoring the ADSR of the gating function.

Frequency-dependent gates allow you to focus in on the part of the spectrum where, say, a snare drum lives, and use that specific part of the frequency spectrum to open the snare gate. Regardless of how hard the drummer is whacking the floor tom. This is also super handy for drums, horns, noisy amplifiers, audience mics, and so forth.

Gates can be "keyed" or triggered by audio from another track, giving you the option to have the kick drum control the opening of the gate on a bass guitar, for example.

Gates can also be used to trigger a reverb send or return for heightened dramatic effect, opening when the vocalist sings above a particular volume level.

The more you mess with gates, the more practical uses you will discover.

Manual Editing of Tracks

There will be times when using Strip Silence or a noise gate just doesn't give you the control you need to clean up your tracks. An example would be cleaning tom tom tracks on the recording of a drum kit. There's usually too much going on in a drum kit to use Strip Silence, since the background noise on tom tracks typically doesn't drop low enough to consistently differentiate a tom hit from a snare hit. A noise gate would suffer from the same false triggering issues, and is not smart enough to respond to an overlapping cymbal crash with a natural-sounding decay time. The solution is to clean your tracks manually using Pro Tools editing functions to separate and mute unwanted clips.

Once you have isolated a tom hit, separate the clip (B). Next, highlight the region before the tom hit, and cut (X), delete (Delete), or mute it (Command + M). Do this operation for every tom hit on the track(s).

Now you can fine-tune the duration of each tom hit clip and fade in or out as the context of the performance dictates—i.e., if tom hit 1 occurs without any cymbal bleed, you can draw a 500 ms fade after the wave form dissipates, and it'll sound pretty natural in the mix. If there is a cymbal crash concurrently with a tom hit, you may need to extend the end of the tom hit clip by 2 seconds, then draw a 1-second fade out. Do this with every tom hit on all tom tracks, and you should have a cleaner-sounding drum kit overall, as the toms usually contribute noise and tonal coloration that takes away from the sonic quality of the drum kit.

Mute Clip Versus Cut and Remove

Let's say you've decided to invest the time in editing your tracks manually. Do you delete the unwanted clips, or do you simply mute them? I do either or both, depending on the situation. If there is nothing but noise, hiss, or hum in the space between actual playing or singing, I will delete the unwanted bits. Likewise, if the track is silent for most of a take, I will truncate the clip(s) to include audible parts only.

If a performance is to be edited out—for content or for mistakes—I like to mute the clip rather than delete it. This grays out the clip but allows me to see if there are still waveforms present, and gives me the option to easily un-mute and bring those clips back into the mix if I want them. Especially useful if I've edited a tom track and temporarily lost a subtle fill.

Consolidating Clips

Once you have cleaned your tracks and made your final edits, you should consolidate a heavily edited track into a new contiguous region by using the Consolidate command from the Edit menu at the top of the page. This serves to make a single file out of many edited clips, thereby conserving CPU and disk load. It also makes it much easier to keep track of files when it comes time to back up your session.

Note: Consolidating a clip or clips writes a new audio file to disk much faster than real-time. However, the new file will not contain any of the underlying automation or any plug-in or insert processing. Capturing processing to an audio file requires a real-time bounce.

BEAT DETECTIVE

Depending on your point of view, Beat Detective is either the best or the worst thing ever to happen to recording. Best, because you can now quantize and time align rhythmically complex recordings, and save sub-standard performances from the cutting room floor. Worst, because you now have drummers who play through a song once and say, "You can just put that into Beat Detective and fix everything, right? I'm out." True story, but I'm not naming names.

Beat Detective was designed to correct and/or modify the timing of percussion performances. You can also use it to adjust loops and samples to match the tempo of your session.

This is a fairly deep and complex module within Pro Tools, and it takes a good amount of experimentation in order to finesse a drum track with competent results.

Beat Detective Quick-Start

Let's look at a simple operation using Beat Detective to slice up a loop into component beats and conform it to the tempo of your session.

1. Begin by selecting a track for analysis.
2. Open the Beat Detective operations menu by choosing Event > Beat Detective, or by pressing Command + 8 on the numeric keypad.
3. Select Clip Separation from among the options at the left side of the menu.
4. Ignore the Selection pane, proceed to the Detection pane, and select Normal from the drop-down menu.
5. For most broad-frequency loops, choose Enhanced Resolution from the Analysis menu, then click on the Analyze button.
6. You should see a number of brightly colored vertical lines—or triggers—in the clip, aligned with various beats. Adjust the Sensitivity slider until each of the vertical lines

corresponds with the beat or beat subdivision you wish to use as your edit resolution. This operation detects and defines audio trigger points. You can add, subtract, and move trigger points as well, using Control-click to add a trigger, Option-click to delete, and the Mover tool (Hand icon) to click and move a trigger.

7. Click the Separate button at the lower-right corner of the window. This separates the audio clip into individual clips containing the beats as defined by the audio trigger points.

8. In the Selection pane, define the length and location of the timeline area where you would like the loop to reside.

9. Use the Clip Conform button at the left to move the separated clips to their "quantized position in relation to the tempo ruler." This will snap the beginning of audio clips to the nearest beat or sub-beat, much like quantizing MIDI performance. Click the Conform button at the lower right to quantize and move the clips into place.

10. Choose Edit Smoothing to fill gaps between clips and cross-fade between overlapped clips as necessary to match the tempo of the song. Click Smooth to complete the operation.

The Beat Detective module can also be used in Collection mode to analyze and extract Groove Template information from existing performances that can be copied to a Groove Clipboard or saved to disk, and later apply it to other tracks using the Clip Conform operation within Beat Detective.

Because of the wide variation in drum track performances, you should expect to make lots of subtle changes to the Beat Detective settings in order to achieve the best results.

ELASTIC AUDIO

Elastic Audio is the highly-evolved cousin of Beat Detective, in that it uses sophisticated transient detection algorithms to analyze and define rhythmic subdivisions and pitch variations within a performance. You can then use integrated time compression/expansion tools, along with pitch change algorithms, to make dramatic changes in the timing and tuning of rhythmic and melodic performances. If Beat Detective is a deep river, then Elastic Audio offers a virtual ocean of creative options for modifying your tracks. Let's take a look at some of the options and their practical use.

Elastic Audio uses the analysis process to create Event marker points, which are just pointers to transient events in an audio clip. These Event markers can be quantized or conformed to current track tempo settings, or to user-defined settings. When Warp markers are added and moved, the Elastic Audio processing takes over and automatically expands or contracts audio files using time compression/expansion to fill the space. This yields a most believable result when applying tempo changes or adjustments to recorded tracks. I recently applied Elastic Audio to a recording of 10 drum tracks and made dramatic changes to timing and tempo throughout a 5-minute long song. The net result: we salvaged a once-in-a-lifetime performance that would otherwise not have been included on a commercially released album.

Depending on the Elastic Audio plug-in settings, you can choose the processing algorithm best suited to analyzing various types of audio source material:

- **Polyphonic:** For use with complex harmonic material, chordal instruments, full arrangements.

- **Rhythmic:** To be used with drums, percussion, or anything with obvious rhythmic transient peaks.

- **Monophonic:** Use this setting with voice, bass, brass, woodwinds, or other monophonic source material.

- **Varispeed:** Emulates the combination of speed and pitch change when slowing down or speeding up playback on a tape deck.

- **X-Form:** This algorithm takes a bit longer to analyze and process clips and is more accurate, but only works with rendered Elastic Audio processing.

- **Real-Time Processing Versus Rendered Processing:** Selecting Real-Time elastic processing allows you to hear tempo and pitch changes immediately, but it takes a great deal of computer processing resources to do so. If you are modifying a number of tracks at once or find that you are running low on system resources, you may choose to use the Rendered Processing option. This creates a new temporary audio file or files using the most recent elastic processing parameters. Playing back this file is less taxing on system resources, but it may take a few moments to render before the first playback.

Elastic Audio Quick-Start

Here is a quick-start tutorial for exploring the Elastic Audio process:

1. Create a new session, and set the main Timebase Ruler to bars/beats.
2. Using the DigiBase browser, search "loop," then select and drag a stereo drum loop into the session Track list on the left side of your Edit window.
3. As you import the loop, a pop-up dialog will ask if you want to "Import original tempo from file?" Click Import. Your loop will show up on a new track starting at the beginning of the timeline, and the session tempo should match the original loop tempo.
4. Click the Tick-based track selector.

5. Next to the Tick icon is a Warp icon. Click that icon to reveal the menu of options for Elastic Audio Plug-in settings. Select Rhythmic from the list of options.

6. In the Track View Selector, choose Warp. You should see a series of vertical lines superimposed over the waveform; these are the Event markers, which should correspond with transient peaks within the loop. (By selecting Analysis from the Track View Selector, you can adjust the location of these Event markers.)

Fig. 6-3

7. Press Play to begin playback of the loop. The loop will play back at the tempo ascribed to the timeline. Now if you change the tempo in the timeline, the loop will change speed to match the new tempo.

Note: If you keep the Track Timebase Selector set to Samples, the tempo of the clip playback will *not* change with Timeline tempo changes.

You can also import loops created at different tempi and use Elastic Audio to conform them to your session tempo. Using the session you created for the previous exercise, follow these steps:

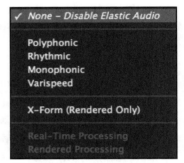

Fig. 6-4

1. Using the DigiBase browser, search "loop," then select a stereo drum loop with a tempo that differs from the session tempo. Drag this loop file into the session Track list.

2. Click the Tick-based track selector.

3. Next to the Tick icon is a Warp icon. Click that icon to reveal the options for Elastic Audio Plug-in settings. Select Rhythmic from the list of options.

4. Select the clip in the timeline. From the Clip menu, choose Clip > Conform to Tempo. This will change the timing of the clip to match the session tempo.

5. Press Play to begin playback. When you change the tempo in the timeline, the loop will change speed to match the new tempo.

Warp Markers

You can use Warp markers in a variety of ways to fine-tune the tempo changes in your Elastic Audio–enabled tracks.

1. Click the Track View selector on an Elastic Audio–enabled track.

2. Select Warp from the pop-up menu options.

This will display the vertical lines, or Event markers, representing the points at which TC/E will reference beats after analysis. From here you can adjust markers manually to fine-tune tempo variations in a performance, or you can drag markers to create interesting TC/E or Varispeed effects.

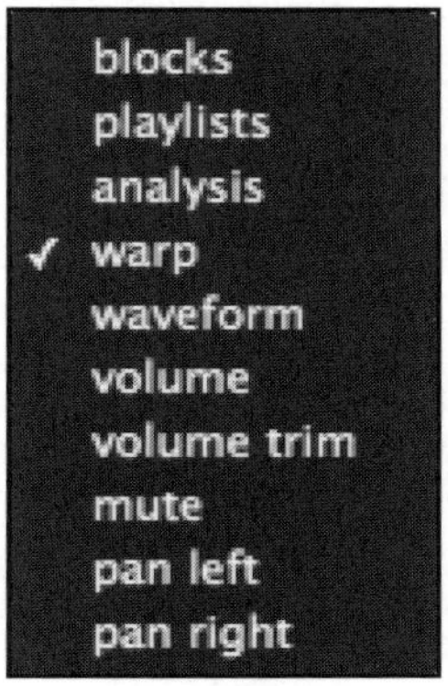

Dragging a Warp marker in the middle of the clip results in a Telescoping Warp, in which the overall length of the clip is expanded if dragged to the right in the timeline, or compressed if the Warp marker is dragged to the left in the timeline. This changes the tempo of the clip playback manually, and it will no longer be locked to the timeline tempo.

You can add or delete Warp markers in this view as well:

Fig. 6-5

- Control-click on an Event marker to add a Warp marker.
- Double-click on a Warp marker to delete it.
- Control + drag a Warp marker to change its position without warping the audio.
- Drag an Event marker between two Warp markers to warp the audio relative to the nearest Warp markers. Read that again, then continue.

Fig. 6-6

This is where it gets interesting. If you add one Warp marker in the middle of a clip and another Warp marker several beats later in the same clip, you can now manipulate the audio within the area bounded by the two Warp markers. To paraphrase the Pro Tools manual, think of the audio file as a rubber band and the Warp markers as two pins holding the rubber band to a table. The audio on either side of the "pins" can be manipulated without altering the tension of the rubber band between the pins. Likewise, the audio in between the pins can be manipulated without altering the tension of the rubber band outside of the pins. This allows you to make dramatic tempo changes within a defined area of a clip without affecting the rest of the audio clip. This is a good opportunity to experiment; Elastic Audio offers amazing creative possibilities once you dig into it.

More Elastic Features

- **Pitch Change:** If you select a clip in an Elastic Audio–enabled track, then choose Clip > Elastic Properties (or press Control + 5 on the numeric keypad), the Elastic

Properties menu will open, giving you the option to transpose the pitch of the clip up to +/- 2 octaves and +/- 100 cents.

- **Input Gain:** The input of the Elastic Audio plug-in can be adjusted from here; with trim of up to -6 dB available, this should be adjusted if your Elastic Audio processing causes the audio to clip or distort. How will you know if it clips? The data panes in this window will glow red if your audio is clipped.

- **Event Sensitivity:** This adjustment determines the threshold of sensitivity to transient peaks in the audio file and determines how many Event markers to assign to the clip. If you have too many Event markers in your clip, you can decrease the sensitivity setting to reduce the number of Event markers. This is called confidence level. The more clearly a transient is defined, the greater the confidence in the location of the Event marker. In other words, louder and more obvious transients will produce better pointers for Elastic Audio processing.

The Tempo adjustment fields here are available to change clip length and timing using direct numerical input, as an alternative to dragging the markers using Telescoping Warp.

Disabling Elastic Audio Processing

To disable Elastic Audio processing on a track, locate the track's Elastic Audio plug-in selector in the Track view window. Click the Warp icon, then select None—Disable Elastic Audio.

If there is any Elastic Audio processing on that track, a dialog box will prompt you to make one of three choices:

- **Revert:** Removes all Elastic Audio processing from the track and reverts all clips to their original state. This includes all playlists on the track as well.

- **Cancel:** This cancels the operation and leaves Elastic Audio processing enabled on the track.

- **Commit:** This command renders, or "commits," Elastic Audio processing to the clips in the track and writes new files to disk. Elastic Audio processing is then disabled on that track. The new files will contain any fades, plus additional :05 audio handles, if applicable. Note: You can undo the Commit operation.

Fig. 6-7

To remove Pitch Shift on an Elastic Audio–processed clip, choose Clip > Remove Pitch Shift.

Rendering Elastic Audio

Rendering is different from committing in that a rendered file is a temporary file made for playback purposes. The rendered files are kept in a Rendered Files folder in the session folder. Once you are satisfied with the final settings for your Elastic Audio processing, you should always commit those tracks by disabling the Elastic Audio processing on a track, then selecting Commit from the subsequent dialog window. You can also commit a clip by dragging it to a non–Elastic Audio–enabled track.

Note: Once you have committed your clips, new files are written to the Audio Files folder, and the temporary files in the Rendered Files folder are automatically deleted.

EDITING MIDI

Once you have recorded MIDI data, you can view it in the timeline as individual notes, clips, or blocks. In Notes view, MIDI data can be edited directly in the timeline.

You can also view and edit MIDI data in a MIDI Editor window (choose Window > MIDI Editor, or press Option + "="), Score Editor window (choose Window > Score Editor, or press Control + Option + =), or MIDI Event List window (choose Window > MIDI Event List, or press Control + "=").

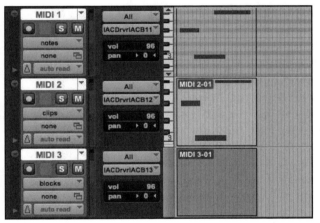

Fig. 6-8

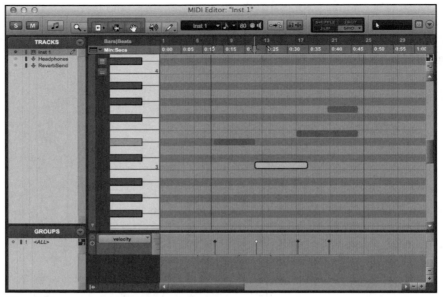

Fig. 6-9

Each of these editors opens in a new window.

The editing toolset used in editing audio clips can also be used to edit MIDI data in the timeline and the MIDI Editor window. The only real difference is that when using the Smart tool, the cursor turns into a crosshair in empty track space. This enables you to select notes that are not next to one another simply by holding the Shift key when clicking to make noncontiguous note selections.

MIDI notes and clips can be muted or unmuted by making a selection in the timeline, then pressing Command + M to mute or un-mute the selection.

You may change the properties of a MIDI note or group of notes by making a selection, then altering the characteristics of those events from the Event Operations menu (Event > Event Operations > Event Operations Window, or by pressing Control + 3 on the numeric keypad). This menu gives you access to the following operations:

- Quantize
- Change Velocity
- Change Duration
- Transpose
- Select/Split Notes
- Input Quantize
- Step Input
- Restore Performance
- Flatten Performance

In the event that you are using a MIDI device or devices with inherent processing delays, you can compensate for these delays using the MIDI Track Offsets window.

Choose Event > MIDI Track Offsets: The pop-up menu gives you the option of entering an offset in samples for each track, and an overall offset value in the Global MIDI Playback Offset field.

Fig. 6-10

SUMMARY OF KEY COMMANDS

OPERATION	KEY COMMAND
Save	Command + S
Duplicate Track	Shift + Option + D
Strip Silence	Command + U
Heal track edit	Command + H
Cut	X
Copy	C
Paste	V
Separate Clip	B, or Command + E
Mute Clip	Command + M
Fade	F
Beat Detective	Command + 8
Elastic Properties	Control + 5 (numeric keypad)
MIDI Editor window	Option =
MIDI Score Editor window	Control + Option + =
MIDI Event List window	Control =
MIDI Note Properties	Control + 3 (numeric keypad)

CHAPTER 6 REVIEW

1. For removing breaths and other noises from a recorded track, you can use the Pro Tools _____ function, which automatically cuts clip falling below a user-set threshold.

2. When finished cleaning a track, it's a good idea to _____ the clips into a single audio file, making them easier to track and archive.

3. The Pro Tools function dedicated to editing the _____ of audio tracks is called Beat Detective.

4. The action of aligning audio and MIDI clips to the grid is called _____.

5. When you want to quantize the separated clips in the Beat Detective window, you use the _____ command.

6. Whereas Beat Detective separates audio clips at transient peaks and moves them to conform to a grid, Elastic Audio uses _____ and Expansion to stretch audio in the timeline.

7. True or False: Elastic Audio can only match audio clips to the session tempo. _____

8. For Real-Time processing, Elastic Audio uses four optional algorithms to manipulate audio with best results. Those algorithms are:

   a. _____

   b. _____

   c. _____

   d. _____

9. In addition to changing the speed of audio file playback, Elastic Audio allows you to change the _____.

10. MIDI data can be edited directly in the timeline window. You can also edit MIDI in the following windows:

    a. _____

    b. _____

    c. _____

11. Pro Tools lets you compensate for MIDI processing delays using _____, accessible in the Event > _____ window.

Mixing Tools

7

In this section, we will look closely at ways to manipulate your recorded tracks, whether bouncing processed audio clips to disk or using real-time plug-ins.

AUDIO SUITE PLUG-INS

When used with clips selected in the sequence timeline, Audio Suite plug-ins create (or *bounce*) new files with plug-in settings. These new files replace the original clips in your timeline. Pro Tools 10 now bounces AudioSuite files with handles, meaning that you can include audio before and after the edit selection when your clip is processed. There is a window in the bottom-right corner of the AudioSuite plug-in windows that allows you to enter the amount of time to include as handles when bouncing files.

Audio Suite processing saves real-time processing power by permanently printing your effects.

Saving the session with the effects already printed gets you one step closer to having the session prepped for long-term archival or delivery.

WORKING WITH PLUG-IN INSERTS
RTAS—Real Time Audio Suite

These plug-ins employ host-based processing to affect signal in real-time during playback.

- AVIDRack Plug-Ins are the 70-plus free plug-ins that ship with Pro Tools software. Check the AVID website for the latest list of plug-ins shipping with Pro Tools.
- Most of the virtual instruments in Pro Tools use RTAS technology.

- Because of the architecture of Pro Tools software, there is a limit to the number of RTAS virtual instrument plug-ins you can use in a session.

Note: As of this writing, Pro Tools is a 32-bit program and will only access 2 GB of physical RAM for the actual application. This may limit the number of RTAS plug-ins, but will definitely limit the number of virtual instrument plug-ins you can use in real-time.

TDM—Time Division Multiplexing

This refers to the proprietary AVID HD PCIe cards, which use dedicated Digital Signal Processing (DSP) chips for real-time signal processing power, as opposed to using the host computer.

The TDM system provides the processing power necessary to record/overdub/play back with minimal latency. (Not to be confused with ADC, which merely compensates for system latency on playback by making everything…later.)

HDX—The Next Generation in Dedicated Processing

This is the newest and most powerful type of Pro Tools system, and requires a tower computer (or Thunderbolt expansion chassis) to accommodate the cards. The HDX cards are the replacement for HD Accel cards and have substantially increased processing capacity.

Note: You can run RTAS, AudioSuite, AAX, and TDM plug-ins on your system if you have the HDX processing cards. You can run RTAS and AAX plug-ins on any system, but you need the TDM or HDX hardware to run all four types.

AAX: The New and Improved Plug-in Format for Pro Tools 10

AAX is an acronym that stands for Avid Audio Extension, and is a host-based plug-in platform with higher performance than RTAS plug-ins. We expect that AAX may pave the way for the 64-bit plug-in architecture of the future.

AAX plug-ins also support AudioSuite non-real-time audio processing.

Inserting Plug-ins on Your Tracks

Pro Tools gives you 10 plug-in slots per track.

You are limited only by your computer's processing power and RAM allocation.

If you are working in the Edit window, click on the Triangle icon in the Insert window. This will bring up an alphabetized list of all the plug-ins you have installed on your system. Mouse over a category—EQ, for example. The list will expand to show all available EQ plug-ins by name. Mouse over and select one of the EQ plug-ins, and click. This will insert that plug-in on your track in the Insert slot that you selected.

To insert multiple plug-ins, select sequential slots and repeat the above procedure.

The inserted plug-in will open in your main window as a floating pop-up window. You can position this window anywhere on your screen, preferably someplace where it won't interfere with the other windows. Clicking on the plug-in name will close the plug-in window.

If you click on the name of another plug-in, the previous plug-in window will close, and the newly selected plug-in window will open.

Viewing Multiple Plug-in Windows

If the plug-in window is already open, click the red, square Target button to keep that particular window open. Then a new window will open for the next plug-in you select. You can leave any number of plug-in windows open while you work. Likewise, if you Shift-click on the plug-in name in the insert window, that plug-in will open and stay open until you close it manually.

Note: If you are working on a Pro Tools HD|TDM system, Pro Tools software will now let you assign TDM or RTAS plug-ins in any order. This is new for Pro Tools. You should be aware that inserting an RTAS plug-in between TDM plug-ins will use additional voices. This will only be an issue if you are working on a massive mixing session with many tracks, and may result in track muting if the total number of available voices is exceeded.

Plug-in Manipulation

Some plug-ins use a proprietary on/off button; most do not.

Bypass versus Make Inactive:

- Bypass simply turns off the plug-in effect.
- The bypassed plug-in still uses system resources.
- Inactive plug-ins retain their settings but do not use system resources.

Plug-ins use a series of mouse-adjustable controls to modify the various parameters displayed onscreen, which can be then be compared A/B style to default settings. Once you find a setting you like, the parameters can be saved for later recall by accessing the Plug-in Settings menu in the Plug-in window. This menu allows you to copy, paste, save, and import settings, as well as determine the destination for storing plug-in settings.

Fig. 7-1

Copying Plug-in Settings

If you really dig the EQ sound you got on your left overhead track and want to duplicate that on the right overhead track, you have a few options for matching settings.

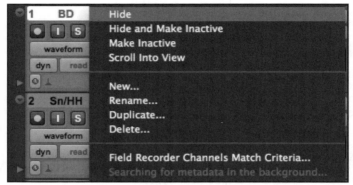

Fig. 7-2

- **Copy/Paste Settings:** In the plug-in window for the left overhead, locate the Preset menu, then select Copy Settings (Shift + Command + C). Insert the same plug-in on the right overhead track, locate the Preset menu, and select Paste Settings (Shift + Command + V).
- **Save the Setting:** If you found a sound you think you may use again and again, you can save it for easy future access. In the left overhead plug-in window, locate the Preset menu, then select "Save Settings As..." This gives you the option to name the setting and save it among the other presets for future use.
- **Option + Drag:** This may be the quickest way to duplicate a plug-in; just copy the entire plug-in with settings intact to the destination insert (Option + drag). Voilà!

The Secret of the Right Mouse-Click

The right mouse-click gives you access to hidden menu options depending on where you click. For example, Right-click on the Track Name to show a menu of track options.

Right-click on a plug-in name in the insert pane to show a menu of plug-in options. This is a handy shortcut in case you forget the secret keystroke combination.

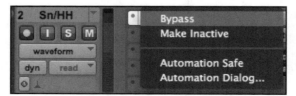

Fig. 7-3

Printing Tracks with Real-Time Plug-in Effects

If you're working on mixing a project that you may need to revisit in the future, you should consider printing your tracks with effects.

Note: This is particularly valuable if there's chance that the project will be opened on a system without the same plug-ins or on a different DAW platform.

This process differs from printing files using Audio Suite plug-ins, in that the process is done in real-time using Aux tracks and internal bus routing. Here is a standard method for bouncing individual or group tracks:

Step 1: Create a new mono or stereo Aux Input track. Click on the Output pane of the guitar source track and select "New Track…" Name the Aux track some variation of the source name—e.g., "Guitar SUBMIX."

Step 2: Select the bus named "Guitar SUBMIX" for the output destination of the track(s) you wish to print with effects.

Step 3: Create a new mono or stereo audio track (Shift + Command + N), and name it "Guitar Bounce."

Step 4: Select "Guitar SUBMIX" as the input for the "Guitar Bounce" track. Click the Record Enable button, and record a clip from the beginning of the song. This new clip will be named "Guitar Bounce_01," and assuming you have engaged ADC, it will be perfectly in sync with the other tracks.

Step 5: Deactivate the original source tracks for this bounce so that they no longer play back or use system resources.

The newly created Guitar Bounce track now contains the guitar clip you bounced with effects and will be the track you use while mixing.

The process will be the same whether you bounce one track or several, as long as you remember to route all of the source tracks to the Aux Input you create.

Side-Chain Effects

- **Kick and Bass Compression:** Tighten up the low end of your mix by using a kick drum–keyed compressor side chain input on your bass track to decrease the volume of the bass when the kick drum hits.

- **Kick Drum Augmentation Using an Oscillator:** Use the kick drum to key a noise gate open/close on an oscillator track generating a 20 Hz tone.

- **De-Essing:** A de-esser controls the volume of a narrow frequency band using a combination of EQ and compression. See instructions on building a de-esser later in this chapter. Note that side-chain processing with RTAS plug-ins uses additional voices.

PROCESSING TOOLS FOR YOUR TOOLKIT

There are loads of tools available for you to create pristine, raw, or downright crushed and mutilated mixes. These tools generally fall into one of four categories:

- Frequency tools
- Dynamic Range Control tools
- Pitch tools
- Time-Based tools

FREQUENCY TOOLS

EQ

Equalization (EQ)

Provides you with the means to increase or decrease the amplitude of a particular band of frequencies.

Parametric EQ

Gives you the ability to select a frequency center point, vary the bandwidth (or Q) of the effected frequencies, and make them louder or softer. Multi-band parametrics can be very powerful tools when combined to make notch filters.

Quasi-Parametric EQ

Pretty much like the parametric, but without the Q control. Used on many mid- and lower-priced mixing consoles.

Graphic EQ

Separates the frequency spectrum into fixed bands (typically 31), each with its own level control, which can then be made louder or softer independent of adjacent frequencies.

British Style EQ

Made popular on British recording consoles, consisting of four equalization bands:

- High Shelf
- Upper mid-band parametric
- Lower mid-band parametric
- Low shelf

EQs also include notch filters, bandpass filters, high-pass filters, and low-pass filters.

Pro Tools ships with three basic EQ plug-ins that are quite flexible, giving you the option of using a single band or up to seven bands of EQ that are user configurable. Think of the 7-band as a super-British EQ.

AVIDRACK EQ 3 PLUG-INS:
- 1-band equalizer, with six curve and filter profiles.
- 4-band equalizer, each band fully parametric.
- Low frequency, lower mid-band, higher mid-band, high-frequency bands.
- 7-band equalizer, adds a mid-frequency band and two dedicated filters.

Fig. 7-4

USING EQ TO FIX PROBLEMS

You may encounter a problem that can only be fixed by applying the right EQ. As an example, I once mixed a string quartet project in which the cello had a very *pronounced* low G note, which became even more prominent when trying to balance the string section. Everything else was fine: good tone, no buzzing or wacky noises. The solution came in the editing stage before mixing, where we tried a number of solutions to cure the loud notes. In the end, we doubled up two parametric EQ bands set to reduce amplitude by -16 dB each at the same center frequency, essentially creating a very narrow notch filter, which reduced the amplitude -32 dB at exactly 98 Hz. The mix was automated to bypass the EQ circuit *except* for when the offending G note was played. The result was amazing! The entire performance was in balance and sounded full, and no change in tone was discernible.

Yes, I could have used 1) a limiter set on *crush,* or 2) a narrow-band boost EQ keying a limiter to achieve the same effect (essentially, constructing a low-frequency version of a de-esser), but I wanted to accomplish this without using compression, due to the ballistics of a compressor and its inability to recover quickly after such dramatic Gain Reduction.

USING EQ TO ENHANCE SOUND

EQ can be used to emphasize frequencies that are not sufficiently present in a recording, such as the high end of cymbals or the low end of a kick drum.

There are two ways to apply EQ:

- **Subtractive EQ:** Making a selected frequency (or frequencies) quieter. For example, kick drum: subtracting -3 dB @ 400 Hz, medium Q with a parametric equalizer can make a kick drum fit better with a bass or guitar track.

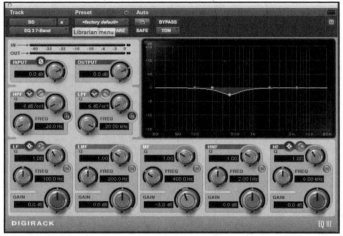

Fig. 7-5

- **Additive EQ:** Making a selected frequency (or frequencies) louder. For example, electric guitar: adding +3 dB @ 3 kHz with a peak EQ can make an electric guitar sound more dominant in a mix.

Make subtractive EQ changes before you start adding gain to your mix. Folks generally tend to reach for additive EQ right away—I strongly suggest you determine what your objective is first, then see which frequencies you can reduce in order to achieve the objective. (See the kick drum/bass guitar example.)

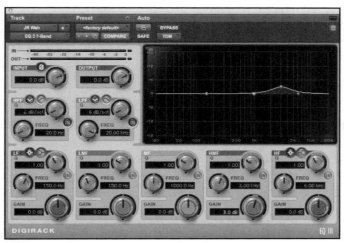

Fig. 7-6

Note: A well-recorded instrument may sound great alone but might not work with other instruments in a mix. For example, an acoustic guitar recording might sound full and have a wide frequency response but compete with other instruments in a mix. It may be necessary to thin out some of the low-end response of the acoustic guitar by reducing the low-frequency shelf EQ by -3 dB at 150 Hz. The resulting sound may not be the perfect solo acoustic guitar sound, but it will work better in context with other chordal instruments.

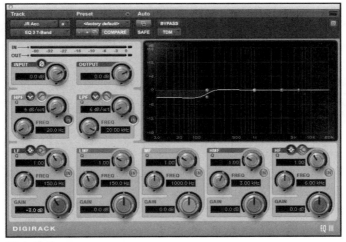

Fig. 7-7

Harmonic Enhancement

High-end and low-end enhancers, such as the Aphex Aural Exciter and Big Bottom, use a proprietary process that restores or adds to the perception of high- or low-frequency content without increasing level. A number of dance and electronic music artists use these processes on their mixes.

DYNAMIC RANGE CONTROL

Compression/Limiting

The compressor is perhaps the most misunderstood piece of gear in the studio, largely because it's difficult for the untrained ear to hear exactly what a compressor does. A good compressor well used may not even be discernible in a track. Here's a simple guide to comp/limiters.

A compressor or limiter is used to control the dynamic range of a performance.

What's the difference between a compressor and a limiter? The Gain Reduction ratio, as in:

< 10:1 = compression
> 10:1 = limiting

What does the ratio relate to? Input to output gain comparison. Look at it this way: assuming your ratio is set at 2:1, if your input signal increases 2 dB above the threshold, your output level will only increase by 1 dB.

At 4:1, for every increase of 4 dB above the input threshold, the output will increase 1 dB.

At 20:1, for every increase of 20 dB on the input, the output will increase 1 dB.

At infinity:1 … well, you can do the math.

There are two kinds of compressors in my opinion: units that are clean, clinical, and fairly transparent sonically; and units that are dirty and distorted and sound amazing if used/abused in the right manner. And of course, there are a few that can do both depending on how you set them up.

Fig. 7-8

While I don't generally believe in "one size fits all" solutions for equipment settings, there is a basic compressor setting that will get you started with just about any recording. This gives you clean dynamic range control without being terribly obvious. It looks like this: 2:1 ratio, 10 ms attack, 150 ms release, set threshold for no more than -6 dB Gain Reduction. Use it on a vocal track to get it to sit properly in a mix; use it on room mics to get a drum set to sound more aggressive; use it on just about anything to even out dynamics for mixing. Obviously, this won't work in every situation; you wouldn't use this setting on a stereo bus, for example.

Pro Tools comes with an AVIDRack Compressor/Limiter: Dynamics 3.

Multi-Band Compression

A multi-band compressor is an amalgam of a crossover, an EQ, and a compressor. This handy device allows you to select a frequency band(s) to compress independently of its neighboring frequencies. Used most often in mastering, it can also be used to add final polish to a vocal track, drum track, or anything with complex frequency content that needs to be managed.

One of the great features of multi-band compression is the ability to use different dynamic control settings on each band. You could use a quick attack, quick release setting with GR of -6 dB on the low frequency band; a fast-attack, slow-release setting with GR of -1.5 dB on the mid-range band; and a slow-attack, slow-release setting with -3 dB GR on the high band. By contrast, a single-band compressor uses one ratio, one attack time, one release time, and one threshold to process all frequencies that pass through the device.

Pro Tools does not include a multi-band compressor in the standard complement of plug-ins. There are a number of great third-party units out there; my personal preference is for the TC Electronics Master X3 (TDM) or the WAVES C6 (TDM/RTAS).

Expanders/Noise Gates

An expander (or downward expansion circuit) is a gentler form of noise gate and is the functional opposite of a compressor. An expander reduces the level of a signal below a threshold, whereas the compressor decreases the level of signal above a threshold.

An expansion ratio of 2:1 will result in a level reduction of 2 dB for every 1 dB below threshold. So a signal drop of 2 dB below threshold would result in a further reduction of 4 dB.

At a 4:1 ratio, the output level would drop -4 dB for every -1 dB below threshold. Hence, a -2 dB drop would result in level reduction of -8 dB on output.

At ratios of 10:1 or higher, the expander becomes a noise gate.

Pro Tools comes with an expander/gate that has an optional Look Ahead feature, the purpose of which is not actually to see into the future, but rather to assess the attack time required to preserve transients and to delay the output by that amount.

De-Essers

Ever notice that your vocal tracksss ssseem ttto have a lot of sssibilance? Use a de-esser plug-in to dynamically control the high-frequency saturation on a vocal track when *s*'s and *t*'s are emphatically and vigorously (sp)uttered.

In the absence of a de-esser plug-in, you can construct one using your EQ 3 plug-in and Dynamics 3 plug-in. Place the EQ first in the chain, followed by the compressor. Adjust the high-frequency shelf (or notch) to emphasize the problem frequency. (I know, sounds counterintuitive, but hang in there for a minute.) Then use the EQ plug-in to trigger the key input on the compressor. Varying the EQ frequency and amplitude boost, as well as the amount of Gain Reduction on the compressor, will yield a surprisingly effective method of controlling sibilance in a vocal track. Don't overdo it, or you'll end up with a lisping singer. Great fun at parties, though.

Pro Tools comes with a dedicated de-esser plug-in as part of the AVIDRack series. Insert this plug-in before you compress or EQ your vocal tracks, or your processing might make the job of de-essing much less effective.

Fig. 7-9

PITCH TOOLS

Pitch Change

A pitch change plug-in is a tool that manipulates samples in time in order to create pitch change, and can be automated to create a dynamic change in a performance. If a sax part has one note that is consistently out of tune, a pitch plug-in can be set to correct the intonation for each occurrence. The RTAS AVIDRack plug-in, Pitch, allows you to raise or lower pitch up to an octave, and works in real-time. This function is automatable.

Note: If you want to make the pitch change more permanent, these effects can also be applied using Audio Suite Pitch Shift processing to create new pitch-altered clips, thereby keeping the real-time host processing demands to a minimum. This can be a great deal of manual work, which brings us to the alternative.

Pitch Correction

Auto pitch-correction tools have gotten very sophisticated, and can take the automation task out of the hands of the engineer and place it in the realm of the computer and its ability to make lightning-fast calculations to analyze changes in pitch. Using a frequency counter function to determine the half-wave pitch of the note as performed, the plug-in determines the nearest note played, then calculates the pitch change necessary to bring that note into tune. This is a real-time operation and uses a great deal of processing power to accomplish. Examples of auto tuning plug-ins would be:

- **Antares Auto-Tune:** First designed as a stand-alone hardware pitch corrector, this has evolved into a versatile real-time pitch correction tool with numerous editable and automatable parameters. Set it to maximum for the infamous T Pain effect.

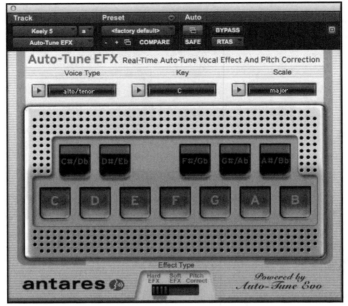

Fig. 7-10

- **Melodyne:** Perfected the art of offline performance editing, now including the ability to edit pitches within a polyphonic performance. This is a virtual laboratory of delights for the serious vocal producer.

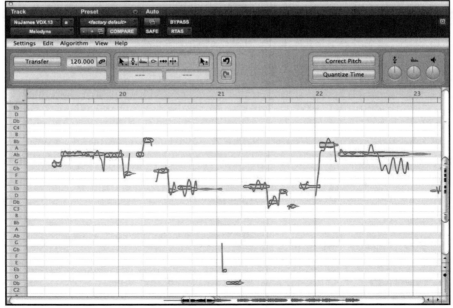

Fig. 7-11

Creative Use of Pitch Effects

Caution: Use subtly and sparingly. Overuse can cause nausea or motion sickness.

- **Chorus:** To make a chorus effect, take a stereo pitch-change plug-in and set the left-side pitch at +6 cents and the right side at -6 cents. Adjust the mix control to determine the amount of chorus effect. (Reference the Mike Stern school of clean guitar tone.)
- **Harmonies:** Use a mono pitch-change plug-in to add a higher octave to a bass guitar. Set mix control at 50 percent. This is particularly effective when used in a trio setting or sparsely orchestrated song. Try tuning it an octave below when used with a lead guitar part. (Think Prince, "When Doves Cry.") You can set it to other intervals as well for chord or harmony effects.

TIME-BASED EFFECTS

Phase-Reverse

Phase errors can occur when there are minute timing differences between two or more microphones capturing the same sound source. Phase errors are the bane of multi-track recording. Inserting a phase reverse plug-in (or activating the phase flip on an EQ or other plug-in) will shift the phase of that signal by 180 degrees, thereby reversing the phase error and eliminating a great deal of unwanted cancellation—or reinforcement—of frequencies when mixing.

To check phase on two tracks: Pan them mono, adjust levels equally. Then reverse the phase on one track. You may have a phase problem if:

- The signal drops in level.
- The signal increases in level.
- A portion of the frequency spectrum gets quieter.
- A portion of the frequency spectrum gets louder.
- The signal goes away completely.

If you encounter any of these problems, you are very likely hearing phase cancellation in the recording. Use the phase reversal function on a short-delay (or other) plug-in to determine the setting that most faithfully represents the sound of the original recorded instrument. Phase is particularly hard to control when recording/mixing a drum kit. Good miking practice when recording is just about the only solution to this problem. Prevention is the best cure, so remember the 3 to 1 rule when recording. (Two microphones must be three times farther from each other than the distance to the sound source when recording.) Most of the AVIDRack EQ and dynamics plug-ins incorporate a phase reverse button into their designs.

Reverb

Reverberation, or reverb for short, is the third temporal stage of sound, after direct sound and early reflection. Reverb is a complex series of delays that appear to be diffuse and indistinct to our ears, and which give space and depth to sound. Think about the sound you get while bouncing a basketball in a gymnasium. Big halls with long reverb decay times (> 3 seconds) are good for slow songs, vocals, sparse arrangements, or special effects. Rooms with medium decay times (1 to 3 seconds) are good for general use with all instruments. Plates or small rooms with short decay times (< 1.5 seconds) are good for percussive sounds, up-tempo songs, and creating post-production "room tone."

Don't forget that bastion of the '80s pop music, the gated nonlinear reverb, a.k.a. "the Phil Collins drum sound." Phil didn't invent it, but he sure did popularize it. It's still a valid tool, especially when trying to make a snare drum sound bigger in the mix. Just don't overdo it, or you may end up popping the collar of your polo shirt and craving *Miami Vice* reruns.

Reverb is usually applied as parallel processing in a send/return configuration using Aux tracks. You can use a dedicated reverb plug-in per track, but it will consume lots of CPU cycles by the time you instantiate a reverb plug-in on every track that requires 'verb. It's also easier to change settings on one or two plugs rather than duplicating settings across multiple instances of a reverb plug-in.

Pro Tools ships with a number of reverb plug-ins, including AIR Nonlinear Reverb, AIR Reverb, AIR Spring Reverb, and D-Verb.

Delay

Delay is a repeated sound that can be heard as a discrete echoed event occurring a short interval of time after the original event. Delay can consist of a single or multiple repeats.

- Short delays (< 100 ms) create a doubling effect.
- Medium delays (100 to 200 ms) are used for slapback delay and tape delay emulation. Think Rockabilly music or some of the classic Sun Records recordings of Elvis, Johnny Cash, Carl Perkins, and so on.
- Long delays (> 200 ms) appear as discrete echoes of the original sound and can be used to lengthen the apparent duration of a sound or performance.

Pro Tools delay plug-ins give you the option of setting delay times based on tempo and note durations, making it much easier to create musical delay settings without reaching for your calculator.

Pro Tools comes with the following delay plug-ins: AIR Dynamic Delay, AIR Multi Delay, Short Delay II, Slap Delay II, Medium Delay II, Long Delay II, Extra Long Delay II, and D-fx Legacy.

Modulation Effects

These are also time-based effects, but the pitch can be dynamically altered by a LFO to produce sweeping effects, such as flanging or chorus.

- Flanging occurs between 2 and 10 ms.
- Chorus effects occur between 10 and 50 ms.

Pro Tools ships with the following modulation effect plug-ins: AIR Chorus, AIR Ensemble, AIR Flanger, AIR Multi Chorus, AIR Phaser, and D-fx Legacy.

Time Compression/Expansion, or TC/E

Used for lengthening or shortening the duration of a file or clip. This can be applied as an Audio Suite process or as an editing function when the Time Compression/Expansion mode is selected for the Trimmer tool.

For obvious reasons, a new file is written when this effect is applied. It gets back to that "no seeing into the future" thing we covered earlier.

Fig. 7-12

Note: Technically speaking, pitch effects are also time based. For the purpose of this book, it is important to draw a distinction between pitch effects and delay effects.

OTHER EFFECTS

Distortion

In the world of audio, distortion occurs when signal processing changes the basic shape of an audio waveform. An example would be the over-modulated clipping of a sine wave resulting in a square wave—a distortion of the original waveform. Remember when I wrote about learning the rules so you could break them later? Okay, now's your big chance. We usually avoid all types of distortion when recording tracks, but yes, you can use distortion as an intentional effect in the mixing process. It serves multiple duties, because distortion can add harmonic richness, distinctive equalization, and dramatic compression effects, all using one plug-in properly applied. Pro Tools comes with a brilliant guitar amp emulator, called, simply, Eleven. (Google *This Is Spinal Tap.*) It sounds killer on guitar, of course, but it can also lend a dramatic sense of urgency to a variety of other instruments, including vocals.

There are two ways to use distortion effects in your mix:

- **Option 1:** Apply the Eleven plug-in as an insert on an aux input. This allows you to dynamically mix the effect to taste in the context of your mix. The send can also be easily automated.

• **Option 2:** Apply the Eleven plug-in directly onto a track insert, and tweak until you achieve the perfect amount of distortion for your track. The plug-in parameters can still be automated, but you will not be able to control the balance of un-effected track to effected track quite so easily. This method is good if you want the effect during the entire song and don't need to obsess over the subtleties. You can try to introduce distortion by overdriving one of your EQ or dynamics plug- ins, but do so cautiously or it may result in harsh digital clipping. (This is a whole other sonic animal than the pleasing low-order harmonic enhancing effects of a nice tube amp or distortion pedal.) Distortion can be very effective on drum sub-mixes as an enhancement. See *Nine Inch Nails* for reference examples. Trent Reznor is one of a handful of producers who effectively use distortion as a creative tool.

Other Tools and Plug-ins

BEAT DETECTIVE

Beat Detective was originally designed as an automated module to help edit and change the timing of drum parts, primarily. Before Beat Detective, this type of editing was done manually and was a slow and painstaking operation. Now it's easy to fix timing on sections of multiple tracks, change tempos, and change or apply groove characteristics to a live performance using this handy—but fairly complex—module.

The difference between Beat Detective and Elastic Audio is that Elastic Audio uses TC/E to achieve timing and tempo changes, whereas Beat Detective edits a track or tracks into tempo-delineated sub-clips and shifts the timing of those clips according to the current tempo and grid settings.

See chapter 6 for more information about Beat Detective.

ELASTIC AUDIO

Okay, AVID has found a way to see into the future. Not enough to get you tomorrow night's lotto numbers, but just enough to change the tempo of a recorded track without altering the pitch. And yes, it happens in real-time.

Elastic Audio changes tempos in real-time by using time compression/expansion (TCE) to achieve dynamic tempo changes.

See chapter 6 for more information about Elastic Audio.

VOCALIGN

This is a third-party software plug-in that compares two similar audio files and adjusts the timing of one audio file to match that of another. VocaALign uses TC/E to adjust the destination audio and writes a new file, replacing the destination clip in the timeline. As this is a third-party plug-in, it does *not* come with Pro Tools, but it is very useful with vocals, particularly in audio post-production.

STEREO PANNING

Panning is the term used to describe the distribution of signal in the stereo field between the left and right channels or speakers. In strategizing your mix beforehand, you probably thought about how to present it across the stereo spectrum. The most common practice in panning is to present the song as it might be heard in a live performance, with instruments panned roughly as they might appear onstage. There are plenty of opportunities to get creative with panning, including automating pan sweeps to tempo or using ping-pong delays to pan alternating delayed signals from side to side.

Each mono track has a single pan pot; a stereo track has two pan pots. This is true of Audio tracks, Aux tracks, and Instrument tracks. Use these to adjust the position of your signal in the stereo spectrum from full left pan (-100 percent) to full right pan (+100 percent) or anywhere in between. Don't be afraid to use the entire stereo field. You can pan things to the extremes and still be subtle, musical. Season to taste, and find the right effect for each song.

Note: Once you're happy with your stereo panning, it's important to check to the mix in mono just to be sure you haven't wiped out some important signal by accidentally (or intentionally) reversing the phase of your delay(s).

Pro Tools comes with more than 70 useful and creative plug-ins that should provide you with hours of entertainment. I have already described a number of the more common plug-ins. The remaining plugs range from metering devices to guitar amp emulators and virtual instruments. There are also lo-fi plug-ins for sound design applications or creative applications of audio distortion.

SUMMARY OF KEY COMMANDS

OPERATION	KEY COMMAND
Copy Plug-in Settings	Shift + Command + C
Paste Plug-in Settings	Shift + Command + V
Duplicate Plug-in	Option + Drag
Bypass Plug-in	Command + Clicking an Insert

CHAPTER 7 REVIEW

1. Audio Suite processing writes a new _____ with the _____ embedded into the clip.
2. RTAS stands for _____ and refers to the host-based plug-in set that comes with Pro Tools software.

3. TDM stands for _____ and refers to the dedicated DSP processing power of the Core and Processing PCIe cards installed in HD systems.

4. You can insert up to _____ plug-ins on each track.

5. In order to save system resources and free up voices, you may have to make plug-ins inactive by typing _____ + _____ + _____ on the Insert button associated with the plug-in you wish to deactivate.

6. The right mouse-click is a time-saver, providing extra menus accessible by clicking around the Edit and Mix windows. How do you access the Right-click menu with a one-button mouse? _____.

7. You can print tracks with effects using two methods. The first is by using _____ plug-ins, the second method is by using an _____ bus to route the output of a track with plug-in effects to another track for recording.

8. The three types of real-time plug-in processing available in Pro Tools are: _____, _____, and _____.

9. An _____ is a frequency-based tool that allows you to raise or lower the volume of a particular frequency or band of frequencies.

10. Pro Tools includes a powerful EQ plug-in called EQ 3, which has three different versions available: ___band, ___ band, and ___ band.

11. When using EQ on a track, you should try _____ EQ first before using _____ EQ.

12. A well-recorded track should never need EQ. True or False? _____

13. Compression versus limiting: A compression ratio of 8:1 indicates _____, while a ratio of 2:1 indicates _____.

14. A multi-band compressor is a combination of crossover, an EQ, and a compressor, and allows you to selectively compress_____.

15. An expander becomes a noise gate at ratios of _____ or higher.

16. The function of a de-esser is to reduce the _____ in a vocal performance.

17. To correct the pitch, or tuning, of a recorded performance, you can use a manual _____ plug-in for single notes, or an _____ tool, such as Antares Auto Tune or Melodyne.

18. _____ is used to correct recorded phase errors between two microphones.

19. Reverb is actually a complex series of _____, which our ears hear as diffuse space.

20. Name four of the Pro Tools delay plug-ins:

    a. _____

    b. _____

    c. _____

    d. _____

21. Chorus and flanging are two examples of modulated _____ effects.

22. Adding _____ to a vocal track can be a radical effect, but completely valid in the right context.

23. Panning is an important tool for distributing energy across the _____ field.

Understanding Automation

The automation capability of Pro Tools has always been one of the most convincing reasons to use it as an all-in-one recording and mixing platform. While you can mix from a manual mixing console into your DAW by recording your mix live into an audio track, the *real* power and glory in working with Pro Tools lies in the ability to have the computer memorize and repeat each and every parameter change and nuance of a mix. It is quite simple to edit and refine dynamic automation information in nearly infinite detail. Not to mention the ability to instantly recall the exact same mix—weeks, months, even years later—in order to make revisions.

The scope of this topic is very broad, so I am devoting an entire chapter to automation functions.

Note: Some advanced automation functions are available in Pro Tools HD and Pro Tools CPTK only. This will be noted in each occurrence.

QUICK-START GUIDE TO AUTOMATION

Getting started with automation is fairly simple; just follow these basic steps:

- **Step 1:** Using the Automation window (Window > Automation), enable the types of automation data you plan to record.

Fig. 8-1

Fig. 8-2

- **Step 2:** Select the Automation mode on the tracks you plan to automate.
- **Step 3:** Hit Play.

Any changes you make to the enabled controls will be written as automation data, which can be played back, edited, modified, or erased. Automation data is saved along with your session file.

AUTOMATING TRACK PARAMETERS

Audio Track Parameters

- Volume
- Volume Trim (Pro Tools HD and Pro Tools CPTK only)
- Pan
- Mute
- Send Level
- Send Level Trim (Pro Tools HD and Pro Tools CPTK only)
- Send Pan
- Send Mute
- Plug-in Parameters

Auxiliary Input Track Parameters

- Volume
- Volume Trim (Pro Tools HD and Pro Tools CPTK only)
- Pan
- Mute

Master Fader Parameters

- Volume
- Volume Trim (Pro Tools HD and Pro Tools CPTK only)

MIDI Track Parameters

- MIDI Volume
- MIDI Pan
- MIDI Mute
- Continuous Controller Events

Instrument Track Parameters

- Audio Volume
- Volume Trim (Pro Tools HD and Pro Tools CPT2 only)
- Audio Pan
- Audio Mute

RECORDING REAL-TIME AUTOMATION

Automation Modes

- **Off:** Turns off all automation parameters on the selected track.
- **Read:** Plays automation data written for the track.
- **Write:** Writes new automation data from the point at which playback is started. Overwrites existing automation data.
- **Touch:** Automation data is written only when a fader, switch, or knob is touched, and stops writing when released. Data before and after the touch is unaltered. Overwrites existing data while active.
- **Latch:** Starts writing automation when a fader, switch, or knob is touched, and continues writing until the transport is stopped or the automation mode is changed. Overwrites existing data while active.
- **Trim:** While other automation modes write *absolute* auto data, Trim mode writes *relative* automation data. In other words, when using Trim mode, all of your previously written automation moves remain intact but can be dynamically trimmed louder or softer. This is the perfect solution for raising vocal levels overall by +1 or 2 dB, for example.
- Note: Trim mode is available in Pro Tools HD and Pro Tools CPTK only.

Enabling Automation

Choose the automation control Window > Automation (Command + 4), then click the corresponding buttons to enable the parameters you wish to write to the automation playlists. From this window, you can also suspend all automation functions and activity, and control Manual Write commands. For Pro Tools HD and Pro Tools CPTK users: you also have access to Auto Join and Auto Match controls.

- **Auto Join:** If the transport is stopped in Write mode, Auto Join lets you automatically resume writing in Latch mode.

Fig. 8-3

- **Join:** If the transport is stopped in Write mode, Join lets you manually resume writing in Latch mode. This mode is only available with a supported control surface connected.
- **Auto Match:** When writing automation, use this button to immediately return all automation controls to their previous levels before that pass.
- **Preview Mode:** Allows you to audition changes to an automation pass for all write-enabled controls. The Preview button isolates the control and suspends writing data for that control. If you want to capture the changes, you can punch them in using the Down Arrow to the right of the Preview button. This gives you the opportunity to rehearse or fine-tune automation moves before committing them to an automation playlist.
- **Capture:** Highlighting a region or section of a song and then pressing the Capture button copies the current state of all automation parameters, often called an automation snapshot. Locating to another part of a song and then clicking the Down Arrow to the right of the Capture button transfers all of the automation settings in the Capture buffer to the current location. This is a very quick means of copy/pasting automation data within a song.

Performing an Automation Pass

When you activate the Write-Automation modes, you enable Pro Tools to capture automation data when the state of faders, buttons, or knobs are changed while playing the sequence.

Plug-in Automation

All plug-ins have automation capability, so you can automate nearly all plug-in parameters.

To enable plug-in controls:

- Open a plug-in window and click the Automation Enable button, or locate the track's Track View selector in the Edit window, and Control + Option + Command + Click on it. This will bring up a Plug-in Automation window, which will allow you to enable any or all plug-in parameters to be automated.
- Select the controls you wish to enable, click Add, then click OK to close the window. Repeat this step for each plug-in you wish to enable.

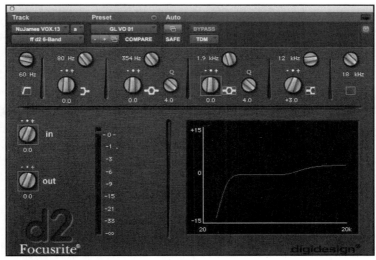

Fig. 8-4

The plug-in window will now show a colored highlight surrounding the parameters you have auto-enabled.

Whenever you roll the track and adjust one of these parameters, the data will be stored to an automation playlist.

Auto Safe Mode

Once you're satisfied with the plug-in automation pass you've captured, click the Auto Safe button to keep plug-in automation from being overwritten. Click it again to enable auto-writing.

Viewing and Editing Automation Data

Pro Tools stores automation data in a separate playlist for each track and parameter. This can be viewed and edited as a series of breakpoints, which can be added, deleted, or moved individually or in groups. The information can be viewed as an overlay on the track waveform display or in a separate lane. The automation lane can be activated by selecting from a drop-down list on the left side of each track.

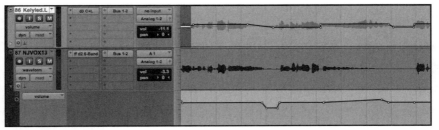

Fig. 8-5

You can view and edit automation data two ways in the Edit window:

1. Choose Track View Select, and click on the parameter you wish to view/edit. This displays one parameter at a time.
2. Click on the Lane View Selector in the track you wish to view. This adds a small, scalable lane below the audio track displaying an automation parameter. You can choose which parameter is displayed in the Lane View Selector drop-down menu. You can open as many of these automation lanes as you have parameters to view.

From either of these windows, you can view or edit automation data, which appears as a series of breakpoints connected by a line. Using the cursor and its various Pencil tools, you can edit, add, or delete any automation point you like. The Pencil tool allows you to draw automation data in a variety of shapes, either in free time or locked to the sequence grid settings. Experiment with these Pencil tool settings to create rhythmic panning effects, level effects, mute effects, or just about anything or any parameter you can think of creating.

You can also copy and paste automation data by region. Automation data can be deleted from these views by simply highlighting the desired region and hitting the Delete key.

Thinning Automation

When you write dynamic automation, Pro Tools captures the maximum density of automation data available. In a complex mix with many moves, sometimes the amount of data captured can significantly slow system performance on playback. In order to restore system performance while retaining the automation moves, it may be necessary or desirable to thin the automation written. This can be done automatically or manually.

- **Smooth and Thin Data After Pass:** This button, located in the Preferences > Mixing tab, gives you the option to automatically thin data after each pass (by selectable degrees) when the button is checked.
- **Thin, and Thin All Commands:** These manual commands allow you to select a track region and thin the displayed data parameter (Option + Command + T), or thin all automation parameters in the region (choose Edit > Automation > Thin All).
- **The Undo Command:** This command will return automation to its previous un-thinned state.

Suggestion: If you apply any of these automation edit commands, A/B the selection to make sure you haven't lost subtle moves vital to your mix.

Strategies for Automating Your Mix

- Once you have a good rough balance, make a basic pass through the song in Write mode, adjusting the general shape of the mix levels.

- Continue to refine your mix a section at a time, or a track (or group of tracks) at a time, using Touch mode.

- With plug-ins in place and adjusted, make dynamic changes as necessary or desired by enabling automation parameters on the plug-in page.

- If your computer gets sluggish or won't play back your automation, it's possible that you have generated a large amount of automation data by capturing dynamic changes. In which case, you should review and thin the data to make sure your computer can process the data effectively.

TRIM MODE

When you have arrived at a satisfactory mix, fine adjustments can be made using Trim mode. This data can be easily modified or deleted to reveal your original mix data. Use Trim mode for the last 1 percent of changes to your mix to create the perfect balance.

CLIP GAIN

While the dynamic automation process described above works with tracks and real-time track parameter information, you can use Clip gain adjustments to automate levels on individual clips in the timeline.

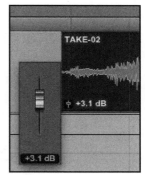

Clip gain can be adjusted by using the Clip Gain Fader icon at the lower-left corner of each clip. Clicking this fader will show a pop-up fader, allowing you to make adjustments from -infinity to +36 dB of gain. The clip waveform display will shrink or grow vertically to reflect the amount of gain change you have applied.

Clip gain can be nudged up or down by increments as specified in your Preferences. Choose Preferences > Editing > Clips to **Fig. 8-6** adjust the nudge increments in dB. Select the clip to be adjusted, then press Control + Shift + Up Arrow to boost Clip gain. Press Control + Shift + Down Arrow to attenuate gain. If you use a mouse or trackball with a scroll wheel function, you can scroll the Clip gain up or down by pressing Control + Shift and scrolling up or down.

Clip gain can be modified graphically within a clip by using break-point automation, similar to the break-point track volume automation with which you are already familiar. First, you must display the Clip gain line by choosing View > Clip > Clip Gain Line. Next, create break-points in the usual manner, by Command-clicking on the Clip gain line using the Grabber tool. These points can be added, moved, or deleted individually as required.

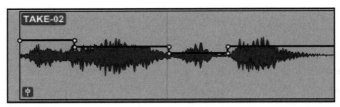

Fig. 8-7

Delete a Clip gain node by pressing Option-click on the desired node.

You can bypass Clip gain settings by choosing Clip > Clip Gain > Bypass Clip Gain.

Resetting the Clip gain is easy as well; just Option-click the Clip Gain fader on the clip you want to reset. This returns the Clip gain to 0 dB and deletes any gain change nodes or break-points you may have added.

This has completely changed my editing workflow, in that I can use Clip gain to compensate for gross level deficiencies and use track volume automation for fine-tuning. I use the Audio Suite Normalize plug-in much less frequently now, as I can now make Clip gain changes directly in the timeline. Big time-saving step there, as long as you're aware of the potential for

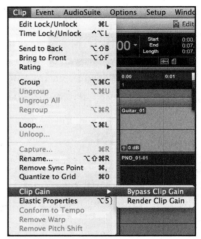

Fig. 8-8

clipping. (The Normalize function automatically analyzes your file to be sure you aren't clipping samples.) It's not mandatory that you render new files with gain change, but it's easy to do so. Just choose Clip > Clip Gain > Render Clip Gain to create a new file in the timeline with your gain changes embedded.

Converting Clip Gain to Track Volume Automation

When saving a Pro Tools 10 session to an earlier version (anything prior to Pro Tools 10), you must first convert any Clip gain settings to track volume automation, or the volume changes will be lost. In order to preserve this data, you should convert the Clip gain data using the following steps:

1. Select a clip or make an edit selection in the timeline containing the Clip gain settings you wish to convert.

2. From the menu at the top of the screen, choose Edit > Automation > Convert Clip Gain to Volume Automation.

The Clip gain change will be converted to track volume automation, and the Clip gain setting will be returned to 0 dB.

Note: This option is only available to Pro Tools HD or Pro Tools CPTK users.

NB: Any Clip gain changes above +12 dB will be lost when converted to track volume automation data.

Converting Track Volume Automation to Clip Gain

You can force track volume automation data onto a clip by converting that data to Clip gain settings.

1. Select a clip, or make an edit selection in the timeline containing the track volume automation data you wish to convert.
2. Choose Edit > Automation > Convert Volume Automation to Clip Gain.

Track volume automation will be converted to Clip gain settings, and the track volume settings will be returned to 0 dB.

Note: This option is only available to Pro Tools HD or Pro Tools CPTK users.

Coalescing Track Volume Automation to Clip Gain, and Vice-Versa

If you find yourself with a lot of track volume and Clip gain automation, you can coalesce, or merge, that data into either track volume automation or Clip gain settings.

1. Select a clip or make an edit selection in the timeline containing the track volume automation data and Clip gain you wish to coalesce.
2. Depending on the function you require, choose Edit > Automation > Coalesce Volume Automation to Clip Gain, or choose Edit > Automation > Clip Gain to Coalesce Volume Automation.

The source settings, whether Clip gain or track automation data, will be merged with the destination data. The source gain or volume settings will be reset to 0 dB.

Note: This option is only available to Pro Tools HD or Pro Tools CPTK users.

NB: Any Clip gain changes above +12 dB will be lost when converted to track volume automation data.

WORKING WITH CONTROL SURFACES

While each control surface is worthy of its own book, I will briefly discuss the merits of using these devices to extend the capabilities of Pro Tools by giving you immediate and simultaneous availability of many more parameters than you could possibly access using your mouse and keyboard alone.

Note: Control surfaces do not usually include I/O devices, so you will need to connect sufficient I/O for your session needs. There are a good number of compatible control surfaces available for use with Pro Tools.

For the purposes of this book, we will take a general look at two popular systems, the AVID C|24 and the Euphonics EuCon Artist Series.

AVID C|24

- The C|24 is a fixed-form (not expandable) control surface using 24 moving faders and a dedicated analog monitor section. This is a mid-level, self-contained console solution for engineers requiring many of the features of a traditional analog console, including multiple speaker selections, headphone outputs, talkback functions, multiple input monitoring, plus 16 built-in mic preamps/line/DI inputs. Each of the 24 virtual channels has dedicated buttons to control Mute, Solo, Record, Select, EQ, Dynamics, Insert, Send, and Automation functions.

- The touch-sensitive fader encoders make it easy to write or update automation passes by simply grabbing the motorized fader and making dynamic level changes in real-time.

- Even though there are 24 physical faders, the C|24 is capable of accessing any number of Pro Tools tracks by changing banks up or down. An LED scribble strip lets you know what's on each fader in that bank.

- The C|24 encoders are 10-bit resolution for accurate data capture, which is interpolated to 24-bits on playback.

EuCon

When AVID purchased console manufacturer Euphonics in 2010, they brought a wide range of consoles and control surface options to the massive Pro Tools install base. Almost immediately, AVID announced the Artist Series control surfaces, including the MC Control and MC Mix modular mixer components. I installed both the MC Control and an MC Mix module for the purpose of illustrating the benefits of mixing with a control surface.

Fig. 8-9

Setup of the modules requires the installation of EuControl software, which senses the availability and identity of EuCon modules when the system is booted. Once the system recognizes that the modules are powered up and connected (via Ethernet cables), you must set up Pro Tools to recognize the modules. In the Preferences pane, you will be able to access the Ethernet Controller page and activate the EuCon functionality with a single mouse-click.

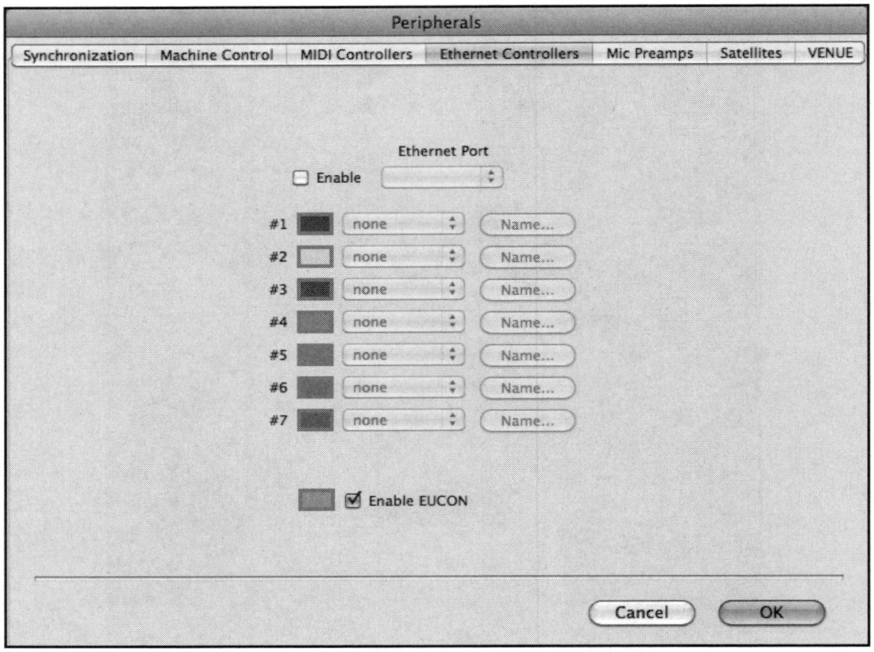

Fig. 8-10

The MC Control has four motorized faders with Function buttons and a dedicated transport control, as well as a plethora of soft button controls on a user-definable touch screen.

The MC Mix offers a bank of eight motorized faders with Function buttons, and an LED scribble strip for track identification.

A great thing about working with the Artist Series is the amount of parameter control you get in a relatively small footprint. In a space roughly 10 x 20 x 1.5 inches, you can control an infinite number of Pro Tools tracks (or other DAW software, video editing software, and so forth). By using bank commands from the control surface, you are able to control groups, VCA faders, or individual tracks at your fingertips—plus edit commands, disk commands, and more. And of course, it's expandable up to 36 faders.

The dedicated parameter encoders give you instant access to plug-in parameter control and are fully automatable.

- One of the most convenient aspects of using a control surface relates to writing automation. Growing up on an analog console gives me an appreciation for grabbing a handful of faders and feeling my way through a mix. With a control surface, you can perform a preliminary automation pass by feel, then go back and fine-tune your moves with unprecedented levels of precision.

- EuCon encoders use 12-bit resolution for a high degree of parameter capture/playback accuracy.

SUMMARY OF KEY COMMANDS

OPERATION	KEY COMMAND
Automation Control window	Command + 4
Plug-in Automation window	Control + Option + Command + Clicking an Insert button
Thin Automation Data	Option + Command + T
Boost Clip Gain	Control + Shift + Up Arrow
Attenuate Clip Gain	Control + Shift + Down Arrow
Reset Clip Gain	Option + Clicking a Clip Gain fader

CHAPTER 8 REVIEW

1. The main automatable audio track parameters include: _____, _____, _____, and _____.

2. The Automation modes are various ways to handle automation data. Four of the modes are: _____, _____, _____, and _____.

3. The Automation window allows you to enable multiple controls. This window can be accessed by using _____ + ___.

4. Nearly every plug-in parameter can be automated using the plug-ins _____ _____ menu. This menu can accessed by selecting it in the Plug-in window.

5. Auto Safe mode refers to the state of a plug-in protected from automation _____. This is enabled using the Safe button on the Plug-in window.

6. It can be advantageous to _____ Pro Tools automation data when automating a large or complex mix.

7. The two ways to view auto data in the Edit window are by using Track View Select and choosing the _____ parameter, and by activating one of the _____ _____ using the Lane View Selector below the audio track.

8. A good way to refine your mix automation is by using _____ mode to fine-tune your automation moves.

The Art and Science of the Mix

Let's take a look at some of the creative and technical decisions you'll be facing in the mixing process.

THE WEAKEST LINK—RECORDING QUALITY VERSUS FINAL RESULTS

Here's an axiom to consider carefully: Your mix will only sound as good as the original recording. If your original recording/performance quality is poor, chances are you won't get the greatest results in your mix. A common misconception is that you can "fix it in the mix." While a nifty rhyme, it's not a good philosophy for making great music. (Frank Zappa famously said, "We'll fix it in the shrinkwrap.") Taking a few extra minutes and a little more care in the recording process can literally save you hours in the mix. In other words: garbage in, garbage out. You can't polish a turd, etc.

MUSICAL STYLES/GENRES

Mixing a classical recording requires different tools and a different approach than mixing hip hop, so you should prepare for your session accordingly. Listen to well-known projects to familiarize yourself with the common palette of techniques used in mixing for that genre. Think about how hip hop mixers approach compression and EQ differently than rock or pop mixers. There are many engineer interviews available online via MixOnline.com and TapeOp.com. Study up on processing techniques, and then try new ideas in your own mixes. This is how you build your toolkit.

Note: Mixing a live recording usually requires a fair amount of setup and processing in order to get the best results.

EDITING FOR CONTENT

Editing for content falls more into the realm of producing, but there may be times when a song needs a little help with arranging the form or the groove. Mixing your own material gives you one last opportunity to examine the form of the song: Is it too long? Can the intro or solo be edited out? Does the second verse actually work better as a first verse? What about a breakdown to bass and vocal in the third chorus? This is a great time to get experimental to find out what a new perspective on the arrangement might bring to the music.

Note: As a mixer working on someone else's recording, you need to exercise some restraint before you chop the song into little pieces and reassemble it and add loops and a rap section. Develop a rapport with your client so you understand one another's needs and goals. Who knows, if you're good at it you could make a name for yourself as a re-mixer.

MIXING "IN THE BOX" VERSUS MIXING ON A CONSOLE

There are advantages to each method as well as disadvantages, but let's be sure we're considering the *real* pluses and minuses before declaring one method good and the other...not so much. Mixing "in the box" means handling all of your level changes, panning, and signal processing within the host application, using no external audio mixing console or processing gear.

The other option is mixing on a console, using Pro Tools as a playback device only. All leveling, panning, EQ, dynamics, and other processing would be done using the console and/or outboard gear.

You can employ a hybrid version of these methods by sub-mixing Pro Tools tracks to sub-masters, then mixing those sub-masters on a console. You can also use external compression, EQ, or other processing in a send/return configuration. This gives you the power of combining Pro Tools automation with the sonic integrity of your vintage outboard kit. You may find that different songs each require a different approach in order to achieve the desired results. Experiment; figure out which method works best for you.

DOCUMENTATION

If you've followed good mental hygiene and named all of your tracks during the session, then your job will be much easier at the mixing stage. There's nothing more frustrating than weeding through 72 tracks named "Audio 1," "Audio 96," and so forth. If a session comes to you for mixing that looks like this, take the time to decipher which track is which and name it accordingly. It'll make your life so much easier when you're looking for the right background vocal part among 50-plus takes across two dozen tracks.

Keep notes on important aspects of a recording, either in the Comments field in a Pro Tools track or in a separate text document, so you can identify cool things (or problems that may need attention) when it comes time to mix.

KEEPING TRACK OF MIX SESSIONS AND MIX FILES

Pro Tools allows you to keep many sequences within the session folder that also contains your audio files, fade files, video files, and sequence backups. It's important to keep all materials related to your session together in one place so you can re-create the session at a later date.

Keep track of your hard disk usage; if the disk becomes too full, you may not be able to write fade files or save sequences to the original session folder. In this case, you should consider copying the entire session folder to a new hard drive or partition with sufficient capacity to finish your work. This is accomplished by using the "Save copy in . . ." command in the File menu at the top of your screen.

NAMING CONVENTIONS

When recording, name tracks using the instrument or part first, then include other identifying info—for example, Vocal Lead, Vocal Verse, Vocal Chorus, and so forth. Or: Guitar Solo, Guitar Acoustic Rhythm, Guitar Squawking Noises, and so on. If you follow this method, all of your recorded clips will show up in the Clips list in alphabetical order, making it much easier to locate all of the guitar parts, then find the subset of takes you're searching for.

If you are given a session to mix that uses the default "Audio 1" naming scheme, you must decide whether or not to take the time to rename all clips, consolidate all regions on a track into one file with an appropriate name, or leave the clips alone and identify them by color and memory.

If tracks are clearly named, that may be sufficient for you to work with; however, locating an alternate background vocal or guitar take can be a challenge if the original engineer has spread takes across multiple shared tracks.

DATA MANAGEMENT

Save session versions that correspond with their mixed files. Since you can (and should) keep all of your sequence files in your session folder, it's important to be able to identify your session files as they relate to your mixes. I save a new version of a sequence every time I make a major change to the song or mix. There may be five or six versions of an edit before I even get to the first mix, but the name of the first mix file *always* corresponds to the name of the sequence. For example, if I've edited five versions of Song A and saved that version of the sequence as "Song A Edit 05," the mix resulting from that sequence will be titled "Song A Mix 05."

Why? Two reasons:

1. If my clients love the vocal mix on Version 05 but really want the edited guitar solo from Version 03, I need to be able to quickly locate and identify the sequence elements in order to give them the mix they want.
2. Text characters don't cost anything but the time it takes to type them. If you name your files sequentially, it will be way easier to keep track of everything and not have to rely on your memory when looking through files named "Good Mix" and "OK PNO" and "Sequence 13."

If you view your files alphabetically and use the binary numbering system (01, 02, . . 27, ... 99, and so forth), then your first version will always be at the top of the file stack, above Version 27 and Version 99.

Find a naming system that works for you, and stick to it.

KEEP AN EYE ON THE FINAL DELIVERY MEDIUM

Always consult with your mastering engineer to see which file types and formats he or she prefers to work with. Most engineers can accept any format in any configuration, but many have preferences that will make the process faster and simpler. Usually they will ask for the highest possible sample and bit rate, depending on your original session settings.

If you are delivering files for inclusion on a CD, your mix file format should be dithered 16-bit 44.1 kHz Stereo Interleaved AIFF.

Online distribution services have various delivery specifications; these change from time to time, so check with each outlet to determine current delivery specs. The iTunes standard file format is a 256 kbps AAC file, which is a fairly compressed format. This file, like MP3 files, uses data compression to make files smaller. While you have the option to make files that have a higher bit rate (and result in higher fidelity), it should be noted that all AAC, MP3, WMV, and AC3 files use data compression, thereby changing the sound of the original uncompressed, full bandwidth, linear PCM files that you created for your high-quality mix.

P&E DAW SESSION GUIDELINES DOCUMENT

The Recording Academy (a.k.a. the Grammy® people) has a special organization of members dedicated to the technical trade. This group is the Producers and Engineers Wing. Besides providing ongoing professional education and advocacy on behalf of all music makers, the

P&E Wing has developed a series of guidelines and recommendations documents designed to help standardize workflow for professional engineers and enthusiasts alike. Of particular interest to Pro Tools users is the *DAW Session Guidelines* document, which discusses standard ways to name tracks, files, and sessions, and includes many helpful tips for keeping your work organized.

Check it out at www.ProducersAndEngineers.com. Look for the link on the right labeled Guidelines and Recommendations.

While you're on the P&E website, download and read the Master Delivery Recommendations document as well. This will explain the official specs for delivering your final project to a record label or other Intellectual Property (IP) owner.

P&E Wing

And since you're already there, you should consider joining the Recording Academy! It's a great way to meet music makers, expand your professional network, and (if you qualify) vote on the Grammy Awards.

BASIC APPROACHES TO MIXING

It's good to have a strategy for mixing: an overarching view of what you plan to do and what your desired outcome will be. There are two basic ways to approach working on a mix: building a house and sculpting.

BUILDING A HOUSE (OF ROCK)

Start with the foundation. This method uses a layered approach to building a mix. Usually I start with the rhythmic instruments and other instruments that occupy the low-frequency register and work my way up through the arrangement, finally adding the vocals at the end to complete the picture. Let's take a look at this method for mixing rock/pop/jazz/ country music one instrument at a time.

Drums

It's not always about the drums. Except in popular music. Pat Metheny once expressed that if the drummer is having a good day, the whole band sounds better. I would paraphrase that to say: if the drums sound good the whole mix sounds better. If you're mixing rock or pop, country or hip hop, the drums (or beats) are the foundation on which the rest of the mix is built. Paying special attention to the drum sounds will improve the overall sound and feel of your mix.

Depending on the song, getting good drum sounds can be one of the bigger challenges to the quality of your mix. If you get the drums right, the rest of the musical puzzle pieces will fall into place much more easily.

Here is a detailed method for handling drum tracks in your mix. Line up your tracks in the Edit window like so:

Fig. 9-1

- Track 1: Kick
- Track 2: Snare
- Track 3: High Hat
- Tracks 4–6: Tom Toms
- Tracks 7–8: Overhead Mics
- Tracks 9–10: Room Mics

If you have additional kick, snare, or tom tracks, just put them in order and label them descriptively. (Kick Inside, Kick Outside, Snare Top, Snare Bottom, Tom 1, Tom 2; or Rack Tom, Floor Tom, and so forth.)

This track order lets you work on components of a drum kit in order of *groove priority* (my term). The drum tracks should appear at the top of the vertical stack in the Edit window and at the left-most side of the mixer in the Mix window. This becomes your foundation, and is easy to locate as you work progressively through the mix.

Fig. 9-2

This would be a good time to start thinking about using color-coding for your instruments and groups to make them easier to locate. When you double-click in the color bar area next to the highlighted Track Name(s), a color-option pop-up window will give you access to a series of color controls. You can set the color of one or more tracks, a track group, or clips in a track, along with other options, to modify the look of your Edit and Mix windows.

See the Color Palette section for more details.

Fig. 9-3

- **Step 1:** Get a general balance of the drum tracks so that you can hear all the tracks equally well.
- **Step 2:** Edit the individual tracks so that there is no additional noise at the beginning or end of the track. Take a few moments to edit out the count-off at the beginning and any other chat that happens at the end of the take.
- **Step 3:** Apply any EQ or compression as necessary to get the individual tracks to sound their best. Use other musical references to be sure you know what your goal is. Keep some reference tracks available for listening; you may even want to import tracks into your session to make direct comparisons to your mix.

- **Step 4:** Create a track group consisting of all the drum tracks. Highlight the Track Names, then type Command + G, then type the name "Drums." Exclude the room mics (if you have them) from this group, since they will likely be treated with different effects than the rest of the kit. This will make it easier to edit the tracks, adjust and automate levels, solo/mute the kit, and generally treat the entire drum kit as a single instrument. If you want to be color coordinated, double-click in the color field to the left of the Track Name, and choose a single color for this group of tracks. It will be easier to identify the drum tracks at a glance if you do. Plus it'll look hipper.

Fig. 9-4

- **Step 5a:** Create a new stereo Auxiliary track; this will become the destination for your DRUM SUBMIX bus. Here's how you do it: Click on the Output button on the last drum track in the group, mouse down to the "new track …" menu. From the Width drop-down menu, select Stereo; in the Type menu, select Aux Input; in the Timebase menu, select either Samples or Ticks, whichever is applicable to your session; and name the track "DRUM SUBMIX." (Why all caps? It'll be easier to find as you scroll through dozens of tracks titled in lowercase.) Tick the button labeled "Create next to current track," then click the Create button. Note: in Pro Tools, the input "DRUM SUBMIX" will already be selected when the new Aux track is created. Champion!

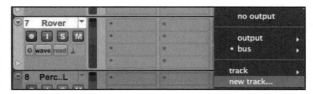

Fig. 9-5

- **Step 5b:** Select all the drum tracks by name, then press Shift + Option + Click on the Output pane of one of the tracks. Select the "DRUM SUBMIX" bus.

- **Step 6:** Select a compressor plug-in for the first insert slot on the "DRUM SUBMIX" track. For this exercise, let's use the BF76 Compressor plug-in. Adjust the controls to match those in the figure.

Fig. 9-6

Fig. 9-7

Editing Drum Tracks

You may find it necessary at some point to edit some of the drum tracks in order to fix timing issues or remove noises. Just be careful not to change the timing of one of the drum tracks without changing the others. See the example under "Manual Editing" for two different methods to clean up tom tom tracks.

Time Aligning Room Tracks

Since you have already located the Room Mic tracks just below the overhead tracks in the Edit window, it should be easy to zoom in and see if the waveforms are aligned. Chances are, the room mics were placed 10 or more feet from the drum kit and will result in the "flamming" of every hit when played back with the rest of the kit. This is because you hear every hit 10 to 30 ms later on the room tracks.

Here's a Pro Tools editing technique you can use to rectify the time alignment issues and add extra power and depth to your drum sounds.

- **Step 1:** Create a new stereo audio track (Shift + Command + N), and drag the two room mic clips into the new track, which you will then name "Room Mics Stereo." This allows you to access and edit both tracks as one, saving time and CPU cycles. (Note: This can also be helpful when working with other tracks that were recorded as mono tracks but need to be edited or processed as a single stereo track.)

- **Step 2:** Zoom in to see how far apart the waveform transients appear on the room tracks as compared to the overheads. Grab the room mic clip and slide it so that the transient edges match up with the overheads. You can also nudge the tracks into place by setting your nudge factor to 10 ms and using the comma (,) or period (.) keys to nudge left or right in 10 ms increments. Use a finer setting, such as 1 ms, to nudge clips more precisely. Remember, the "M" and "/" keys move clips 10 times the Nudge setting.

- **Step 3:** Mix to taste. You will get all of the live-sound goodness of the room mics, but now all the attacks will occur in the right places.

- **Step 4:** Optional—Insert an EQ on the Stereo Room Mics track to tailor the frequency response of those tracks. You might find it handy to diminish some of the mid-range frequency content around 400 Hz.

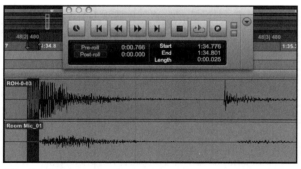

Fig. 9-8

- **Step 5:** Optional—Insert a compressor on the track to increase the intensity of the room effect. This is where you can get that trashy "garage" sound that really gives the drum track some energy. Not so much if it's a gentle ballad.

Adding a distortion plug-in or a guitar amplifier emulator such as Eleven or SansAmp could lead to interesting results. Experiment with different settings and plug-ins to get unique effects.

EQ on Drum Tracks

This is a pretty subjective area and really depends on how well the drums were recorded. Or not. The descriptions below assume that the drum tracks were well recorded to begin with. Always use your ears and your own sensibilities to determine if you need EQ and, if so, to what degree.

KICK DRUM EQ

It's important to reserve a portion of the low end of the frequency spectrum for the kick—separate from the bass track. Allowing those frequencies to overlap will make the low end sound muddy and indistinct.

Using the 5-band EQ 3, set up the low band for a narrow peak curve, set the amplitude for +3 dB, then sweep the low frequencies between 20 and 100 Hz to find the spot that most emphasizes the extreme low end of the kick drum sound. If you have mid-field speakers, you should hear the result clearly.

Note: The smaller the kick drum, the higher the frequency center, thereby pushing it up into the bass range. Be careful not to emphasize the same frequencies that make up the fundamental pitches of the bass track. This results in too much low-end energy and will force you to reduce the level of the EQ in that band later in the process.

Using the lower mid-band of the EQ 3 in wide peak mode, set the amplitude for +6 dB, and sweep the mids between 250 Hz and 1 kHz to find the hot spot. This frequency will sound remarkably louder than others when you reach it. (It sounds icky, like the box the drum came in.)

When you locate that frequency, use that as your target, then adjust the amplitude setting to -6 dB. You will notice a major change in the kick drum sound, and you will hear much more clarity in the instruments occupying the neighboring frequencies.

If you need more of the attack or better sound from the kick, you can sweep the upper mid-band of the EQ 3 as above to find the frequency that gives you more of that attack. It will typically be somewhere between 1 and 10 kHz.

I know that's a broad range, but no two kicks are alike, and I wasn't there when you recorded yours. I was there when the kick drum in this exercise was recorded, and I can tell you that it also depends on the mic used to capture the sound. This recording was made using an AKG D112, which has a bit of presence rise around 3 kHz and increased sensitivity below 100 Hz. You may find it unnecessary to increase the extreme low end very much, if at all. There is plenty there in the recording.

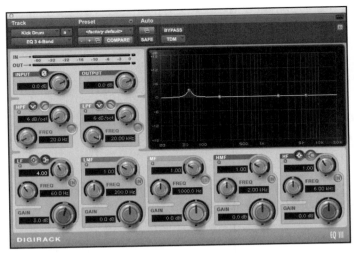

Fig. 9-9

SNARE EQ

Snare drums have energy all across the frequency spectrum, depending on the drum and the drummer. The key here is to get the snare to occupy a space in the mix that is well defined, yet stays out of the way of other instruments.

A good place to start is to insert a 5-band EQ 3 plug-in on the snare track, then ascertain the one or two frequencies at which a snare drum has the most impact without obscuring other tracks. Since snare drums are all about the initial attack, try to isolate and enhance the sound of the snare strainer wires. This is a high-frequency sound, probably in the vicinity of 4 kHz or above. Sometimes +6 dB of 10 kHz shelf EQ is just right. Listen in context with the other drums. Season to taste.

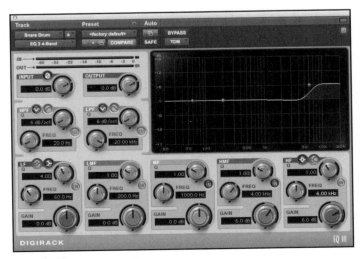

Fig. 9-10

Some drums, such as piccolo snares, have a sound that makes them easy to feature in a mix because they are so identifiable. Occasionally, this can work against you. For example, a 5-inch-deep snare drum with a tightly tuned head can sometimes generate a loud "honk" overtone at around 1 kHz. This might be cool for a grunge tune, but if it sticks out in a mix or if the pitch is too distinct, you may need to do some EQ surgery to get it to behave.

Try sweeping a notch filter across the spectrum until you find the frequency where the honk is diminished or goes away. Make sure the notch doesn't carve too much out of neighboring frequencies, or it may become hard to hear the snare in the mix when the other instruments are added.

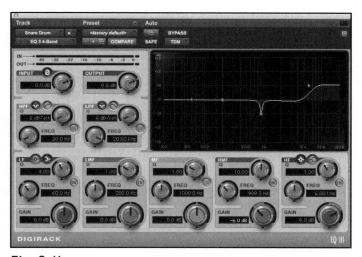

Fig. 9-11

Sometimes a snare will need some bottom end added in order to fill out the sound. Try using a peak EQ band on the EQ 3 to add +3 dB at 150 Hz. That should give more body to the snare sound without interfering with the kick drum.

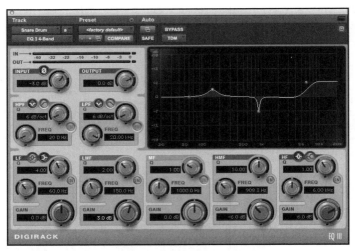

Fig. 9-12

DYNAMICS PROCESSING ON DRUM TRACKS

There are two main reasons to use dynamics processors on individual drum tracks: 1) to smooth out the dynamics of an uneven performance, and 2) to tighten up the sound of a kick or snare drum and make for a more energetic kick/snare relationship within the mix. The first example is easy to comprehend; the second scenario needs a bit of explanation.

How can controlling dynamics lead to a more energetic-sounding record? Seems counterintuitive at first. If you remember the exercise where we used a compressor on the room mic tracks, you will recall that the net result of compressing a recorded track is to limit the amplitude of the peak transients while increasing the amplitude of the quieter material between hits. Compressing the kick makes each hit roughly equal in volume, and compressing the snare brings up all of the quieter detail in the performance (all the stuff between the big backbeat hits). In addition, by compressing the initial transient, you get a drum sound that sustains longer than the hundred or so milliseconds of natural decay. Hence, you get bigger-, badder-sounding drums.

Using the Dynamics 3 plug-in will give you very clean dynamic range control without a lot of tonal coloration. If you want to hear tonal coloration, try the BF76 plug-in using the setting titled "All buttons in." Control the amount of limiting by increasing or decreasing the input volume, then compensate by adjusting the output control to get back to nominal output volume. You will hear the difference almost immediately.

Fig. 9-13

Bass

EDITING BASS PARTS

Depending on the accuracy of the original performance, you may wish to adjust the timing of certain bass notes to line up with the kick drum hits. This is entirely dependent on the type of music and the artistic goals of the artist and producer.

Timing can be adjusted using the same waveform comparison technique we used in adjusting the timing of the room mics in the previous exercise. In this instance, we will only be moving certain notes, most likely.

Drag the recorded bass track (or tracks) up underneath the kick drum tracks, and play through the song, listening for errors or timing issues. When you find something that sounds out of sync, zoom in (using the "T" key command) so that the bass note in question can be compared visually with the kick drum track. If you can hear an error, I guarantee you will see a difference.

Once the problem is located, you need to decide which part to correct. If it's the bass, no problem. Isolate the note using the Separate Region command (Command + E), then nudge or move the note until it lines up visually with the kick drum hit. Audition the edit by backing up a few seconds and playing across your edit. If the bass and kick sound better, then it worked. If not, move it back where it was (Undo) or use the Heal command (Command + H) to restore the clip to its original state.

If the problem lies with the drum performance, the process for fixing the timing is the same, but the operation is more complex, because you must select *all* of the drum tracks, including the room mics, before you perform the Separate/Move operation. One drum track out of sync with the rest of the kit makes for a terrible-sounding performance and potentially a lot of work to fix. Remember: Undo and Save are our friends.

Pro Tools has a Revert to Saved Session option in the event you can't undo your way back to a better sync state.

POWER TOOLS FOR PRO TOOLS 10

BASS EQ

This is dependent on the sound of the instrument and the player. Be cognizant of the similarity in fundamental frequency response between the bass and the kick drum; try to shift the emphasis on the bass EQ a little higher than the kick. For example, if you tweak the kick drum +3 dB @ 40 Hz using a peak EQ, you may want to focus on bass frequencies above 100 Hz and roll off information below 50 Hz. There is also a tendency for basses to record with a shortage of information between 1 and 3 kHz. You won't find fundamental frequencies that high, but a lot of the initial attack and clarity comes from that range in the bass. Try adding +3 dB @ 1 kHz next time you find that the bass part is not cutting through the mix.

If there are more than two electric guitar parts in your mix, you may want to consider ducking some of the bass by -3 dB @ 250 Hz just to clear out that portion of the frequency spectrum a bit. This will give the guitars a little space when their parts are played on the lower strings. It's all about separation—whether by panning or EQ, every instrument needs some space.

BASS DYNAMICS PROCESSING

Some basses just sound better in the mix with a little compression. Particularly if you're going for that '60s/'70s era Carol Kaye "Wrecking Crew" sound or the McCartney Beatle–bass vibe. Try using the BF76 compressor set on 4:1 ratio, fast attack, medium release; and adjust the input gain so that the Gain Reduction meter is riding at a pretty consistent -3 dB. The tonal coloration introduced by the compressor will even change the relationship of the bass to the other instruments from an EQ perspective, tending to emphasize the low to mid frequencies.

Fig. 9-14

A totally different approach is called for when working with jazz or R&B bass parts. Most R&B bass players I encounter would prefer to use *no* compression whatsoever on their parts. Since I usually record without compression, that's not a problem. When it comes time to mix a song with a slappin', thumbin', poppin' bass part, you will likely need to tame some of those powerful attack transients. Not like the '60s version above but rather a more surgical approach to dynamic range control that is sonically transparent. In this case, use the Dynamics 3 set on 2:1 ratio, 20 ms attack, 250 ms release, soft-knee curve, with threshold set for no more than -3 dB Gain Reduction. You will still have all the life and energy of the part as originally played, but now your outputs won't clip when things really get cooking.

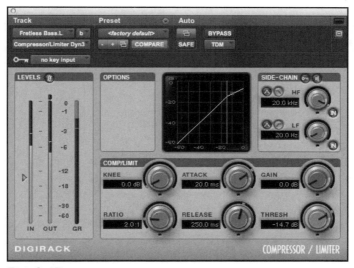

Fig. 9-15

Here's another method of locking the bass to the kick track using dynamics: insert a noise gate plug-in on the bass track, and use the Side Chain/Key function to trigger it from the kick drum.

Obviously, if the bass part is busier than the kick drum, you will be gating a lot of bass notes unnecessarily. In which case, you may find it useful to automate the noise gate bypass to turn off the effect when the bass part is more active or there are no timing issues. Next, automate the noise gate to turn on whenever there is a timing issue.

You can use this side chain/key technique with a compressor instead of a noise gate in order to duck the bass level momentarily during each kick hit. This makes the kick drum part stand out more, and may appear to clean up the low end of the frequency spectrum by removing the bass track from competition in that register.

Guitar (GTR)

Ah, guitars. My personal delight. Let's look at how to handle acoustic guitars and electric guitars.

Acoustic guitars can perform a couple of different functions in a band performance, either as a melodic or a rhythmic element (or what I like to call "tunable percussion").

ACOUSTIC GUITAR DYNAMICS PROCESSING

Acoustics love to be compressed—not too much, but just enough. Try using the Dynamics 3 compressor set on 4:1 ratio, 50 ms attack, 250 ms decay, Gain Reduction (GR) of no more than -3 dB. The slightly delayed attack time allows the picking transients to come through unaffected, while the compression tends to make single notes sustain just a bit longer at full volume. This setting should help the guitar sit well in the mix.

Fig. 9-16

ACOUSTIC GUITAR EQ

Acoustic guitars have a tendency to produce more low-end information than you need in a mix, so be prepared to insert an EQ 3 7-band plug-in on the acoustic track and reduce the amplitude of the low-shelf EQ -3 dB at around 150 Hz. This will reduce the muddiness of a dreadnaught-style guitar and help keep it out of the bass frequency range. You may find it necessary to use the High-Pass Filter (HPF) to roll off more of the low end: start at 60 Hz and sweep upward to about 100 Hz, then stop where the low end cleans up and all the other instruments are audible.

If your acoustic has old strings on it, you can make them sound a bit newer by adding +3 dB with a 10 kHz shelf EQ.

In a complex mix, it's helpful to pan an acoustic guitar track hard left or right to achieve more separation without having to make the track louder. Pan the track opposite the hi-hat or shaker to maintain separation.

Electric guitars can be rhythmic, melodic, low end, high end, clean, or distorted, sometimes changing every bar of a performance.

There is no standard formula for effects on electric guitar tracks, and many guitarists hit the studio with their signature sound dialed in and ready to roll using their own rack gear or stomp box pedals.

ELECTRIC GUITAR DYNAMICS PROCESSING

If you are mixing a guitar recorded without effects, or maybe just through an amp without processing, you might want to consider compressing that track in the mix. Using the Dynamics 3 plug-in, set the ratio at 3:1, the attack at 20 ms, and the release at 150 ms, and adjust the threshold for about -6 dB Gain Reduction. This will make the clean guitar track loud enough to be heard but not overpower other instruments or vocals. This will help you balance and will save you a lot of automation moves.

Heavily distorted electric guitars are already very compressed, so you shouldn't need to add more. If there is a lot of gain, there will likely be a lot of noise amplified along with it. A properly adjusted noise gate will eliminate the noise between notes or phrases and allow all of the fuzzy goodness to come through in the right places. Use the Dynamics 3 plug-in set for noise gate only.

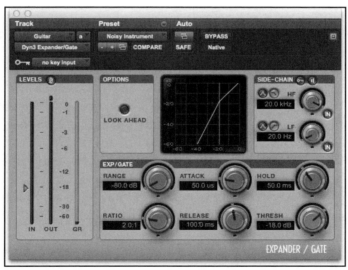

Fig. 9-17

ELECTRIC GUITAR EQ

If you succumb to the temptation to double- or triple-track all of your electric guitars, you will eventually get to the point where the layers all blend together and become a homogenous mass of guitar goo. In order to hear all the great parts on your arrangement, you may need to use an EQ to reduce some of the low- to mid-band frequencies just to make room for all of those parts. You will probably find a buildup of information around 250 to 400 Hz. Insert an EQ 3 and cut that frequency with a peak EQ set to a 1-octave bandwidth. Start out by cutting -3 dB, and sweep the spectrum to find the frequency band that cleans up the guitar sound.

Consider panning doubled tracks symmetrically in your mix (for example, at -50/+50, or -20/+20). This will separate the tracks sonically and give the impression of greater breadth across the pan spectrum.

Keyboard Tracks

SYNTHS

Modern keyboard patches come out compressed, EQed, and already hyped to the max. You may find it necessary to confine some sounds to specific frequency ranges in order to help them fit into the big picture. Compare the sound of the keys to the other chord instruments to see where some EQ cuts might help the keys fit in.

ACOUSTIC PIANO

Acoustic piano parts are a different story. While some sampled pianos are pre-processed in the box, real pianos are most definitely not. They have a broad range of frequencies and a broader range of dynamics. Each piano has its own personality as well, and a console piano records very differently from a 9-foot Steinway. A 9-foot Steinway sounds very different from a 9-foot Yamaha, and so on.

Once you decide the role of the piano in your mix, you may have to emphasize some high frequencies or add compression in order to achieve your goal. Start out conservative with your effects, and work your way up to radical. Always listen to the track with the other chord instruments and the bass to be sure all parts are easily heard.

Many of the classic Motown records were recorded using an upright piano doubled or tripled. Often, these are compressed to reduce the initial attack and increase the apparent sustain. For an old-school sound, try using a BF76 compressor set on 8:1 ratio, medium attack time, medium release time, GR of no more than -6 dB.

ORGANS

It's easy to fit a Farfisa or Vox Jaguar into your mix; they have unique sonic signatures that have a pretty narrow bandwidth. A B-3 or other Hammond-type organ with a Leslie rotating speaker is another animal entirely, particularly if the organist is kicking bass pedals.

This instrument, like piano, can occupy almost the entire frequency spectrum, so you will need to balance it in the mix primarily using level control.

You might find it interesting to use a distortion effect or guitar amp emulator plug-in on the organ. Listen to Keith Emerson of ELP or John Lord of Deep Purple—they created classic rock organ sounds that you can use as inspiration for creating your own new sounds.

Other Instruments

PERCUSSION

Tambourines: Plenty of high end on these instruments, and huge attack transients as well. If you're looking for a tambo to augment a snare part, don't do too much to the track. If it's a stand-alone eighth or 16th note part, you may want to compress the part to even out the volume levels.

Shakers provide lots of high end too. Shakers are a good complement to a hi-hat part, sound great without compression, and fit well into a mix when panned opposite the hi-hat.

Conga/bongos/djembe/other hand drums: Conga and djembe occupy low to mid frequencies, while bongos tend to fill mid- and upper-midrange frequencies. Huge dynamic swings can benefit from parallel compression. Try using a Maxim plug-in to even out the average performance level and bring up the quiet parts, then use the balance fader to let some of the transient attacks back into the performance. This will keep the part audible and natural sounding without killing your peak meters and clipping the output.

MANDOLIN/BANJO/UKULELE

These stringed instruments are similar in that they are tuned higher than acoustic guitars but tend to have less sustain when picked, strummed, or fingered. Sonically, they each have a different range of harmonics, so you will treat each one independently—particularly if they appear together in the same song.

Be cognizant of the tendency of the peak transients to really pop out of a mix. If it serves the rhythm of the song (and if the parts are played in time), this should be a great complement to the other rhythm parts. If the parts stick out too much, you can compress them lightly in order to tame the transients. We're talking maybe -3 dB of Gain Reduction.

Try panning these opposite an acoustic guitar part for more separation.

Vocals

Well-recorded vocals usually require little in the way of processing during a mix: 60 Hz high-pass filter (HPF), light compression (no more than -3 dB GR), and a tiny dusting of high-end EQ, administered in the form of +3 dB @16 kHz using the high shelf on an EQ 3.

Then again, if this is aggressive rock/punk/rap, don't be afraid to smack the compressor hard in order to get the right sound. Once again we use our tonal coloration go-to plug-in—the BF76. There is a preset called Pump that should do the trick nicely. Set the input gain control so that the GR is around -7 dB. In this instance, we are controlling the dynamics, yes, but we're mainly after the sound you get by pushing the compressor. You may hear processing artifacts in the sound (pumping), but that can be considered secondary to the urgency and power that effect brings to the vocal performance. Find the balance of power/finesse that works with your mix.

Note: Keep your overall mix level averaging -12 dB on your output meter before you add the vocals. The vocals will add another 4 to 6 dB on top of the rest of the mix.

SCULPTING A MIX

Here's how you make a real sculpture:

- **Step 1:** Get an enormous block of stone. Examine it, and develop a concept of what the end product should look like.
- **Step 2:** Chisel away large pieces of the stone to create the general shape of your sculpture.
- **Step 3:** Using smaller/finer tools to refine the shape, smooth out the rough edges and create the subtler detail.
- **Step 4:** Painstaking detail work. Sand and polish until perfect.

Note: It's important that you first develop an idea of what the final product will look/sound like. Just chipping away aimlessly will get you nowhere fast.

Here's how to apply the sculpting method to mixing:

- **Step 1:** Start with a general blend of tracks; adjust all the tracks uniformly until the peaks on your Master Fader meter average between -12 and -6. You will want to leave some headroom for any additive processing that might accumulate. Listen to the raw tracks, and get a sense of their potential and where you want to take the mix.
- **Step 2:** Make subtractive volume changes to each track as you see fit. Begin by turning down tracks that are too loud rather than turning up tracks that are too quiet. Place instruments within the stereo field based on your strategy for panning.
- **Step 3:** At this point the mix should be taking shape, albeit a bit rough. Apply EQ and compression to further refine where each instrument sits in the frequency and amplitude domains. Use subtractive EQ to create room in the frequency domain for other instruments.
- **Step 4:** Add the finishing touches to your mix. Use automation to finesse levels; choose reverb and effects to enhance the balance you've created.

Note: Track soloing is a valuable procedure at any stage in this process. Just be sure to A/B in context to keep a good perspective on how things fit together.

Thanks to James Nixon, a fine sculptor, for his help in defining this approach.

TECHNICAL ASPECTS

Dynamic Range

If you are recording in 24-bit mode in Pro Tools, your available dynamic range is 144 dB. The Pro Tools host-based mixer runs at 32-bit floating point resolution, allowing you to sum the maximum number of tracks at +12 dB without clipping the mixer. You still need to use the Master Fader to trim the final output level to avoid hardware clipping, but it's good to know you have that kind of capacity. TDM technology uses a 48-bit fixed-point mixer to yield about 288 dB of dynamic range on the mix bus. Headroom is an amazing +54 dB, yet the low-level resolution of this system is such that you can pull a fader down -90 dB and still maintain 24-bit resolution.

This means you are capable of mixing with detail and clarity at any amplitude level.

Use as much of that dynamic range as you can within the scope of the mix—don't just use the top 6 dB. Dynamic range is one of the things that made vinyl LP releases sound so good and have so much emotional impact. Loud was *loud* and soft was *soft*. Popular music in the 2000s resides almost exclusively in the top 3 decibels of the peak meter. That doesn't leave much room for subtleties. We'll discuss dynamic range in more detail in the mastering section of this book.

There is an excellent white paper on the 48-bit mix bus and mixing in the box, as well as other topics, at this site: http://archive.digidesign.com/support/docs/.

Bus Compression in Mixing

Consider using a bus compressor if you need it. How will you know if you need it? If your mix sounds right to you but the level is low on average, you may need to use a bus compressor to bring up the overall level without clipping the Master Fader. A single-band compressor deals exclusively with level and dynamic range control. The bus compressor can also tend to make your mixes "gel" better, though this is entirely subjective. By controlling the dynamic range, you are also making decisions about coloring the overall sound of your mix. Experiment with different compressors to determine which will give you the results you need to hear in your mix.

A multi-band compressor will affect frequency content as well as dynamics. This can be useful as a tool to compensate for deficiency or overabundance of frequencies in specific bands.

If your music will be mastered, either by you or someone else, be conservative in your use of multi-band compression. The goal is to make your mixes well balanced and even, and applying too much multi-band compression can make it harder to match levels and frequency response in the mastering stage.

Choose your weapons carefully.

Gain Structure

Be aware that every gain-dependent device—whether it's hardware or software, EQ or dynamics, or even reverb and delay—has a cumulative cascade effect on your overall level settings. You should be sensitive to over-modulating or -clipping any component in the signal chain. Distortion in the digital realm is not a pretty thing to behold, sonically speaking.

Gain is the term we use to describe signal amplification. There can be positive gain (e.g., +3 dB) negative gain (-3 dB), or unity gain (0 dB).

In the audio world, we use the term *unity gain* to describe the relationship between signal processing components in which gain is neither added nor subtracted in the process. If at every gain stage you calibrate settings so that there is no increase or decrease in signal volume or voltage as signal passes through, it can be said that you have achieved unity gain.

Why is this important? Because you can start with 0 dB and end with 0 dB but make one heckuva mess out of things in the middle. Here's an example: If I use a mic pre-amp that outputs 0 dB into a Pro Tools input channel, I would expect that the channel would record and output 0 dB, right? Right—so far so good. Now if I were to use a hardware insert to send a stereo mix signal from a Pro Tools Master Fader to an outboard compressor, it would arrive at 0 dB as well. But if in the process of compressing the mix I happen to adjust for -12 dB of Gain Reduction, then send it back to Pro Tools without compensation (or make-up gain), I have lost 12 dB of signal. The only way to make up that gain is to add another gain stage and boost 12 dB, thereby raising the noise floor by 12 dB; or to raise the Master Fader level +12 dB, thereby using up all of the available headroom, increasing the noise floor, and risking over-modulation from any peak transient that might make it past the outboard compressor.

In this example, we may have started with 0 dB and ended with 0 dB, but we also lost gain, added gain, and needlessly added noise and (potentially) distortion along the way. If we had observed the law of unity gain at every gain stage in the signal path, we would have avoided the problem entirely.

The bottom line is to: 1) calibrate your devices, and 2) watch your levels.

Frequency Response

You should adopt a commonsense approach to EQ, meaning that you should only use EQ if a track needs it or if you're rectifying a problem.

Try to use subtractive EQ first, then resort to additive EQ if that doesn't yield the desired result.

Use the smallest EQ plug you can to get the job done. By smallest, I mean the one using the fewest CPU cycles. For example, if you are only applying a High Pass Filter (HPF) to a vocal track, use the 1-band EQ 3 plug. It uses far fewer system resources than the 7-band EQ 3.

This practice will help manage your CPU resources and give you more processing headroom when you need it. Such as when you are mixing 60+ tracks with lots of virtual instruments.

Try to avoid using multiple EQ plug-ins on the same track, unless there is a specific effect you're going for that can't be achieved by any other means.

Hint: Insert a spectrum analyzer plug-in on your Master Fader to keep an eye on the overall frequency response of your program.

Metering

Pro Tools track meters show you the level of the signal after the final gain stage or plug-in. Here's why this is important to note:

The track meter does not show you the signal level as recorded but only the level after processing, so you will need to insert another meter as a plug-in in order to check your processing gain stages for clipping. Yes, the clip light will glow on an offending plug-in if there are more than three consecutive clipped samples, but that doesn't always tell you if there's distortion present or where that might be happening.

The meters read the output level of the track as related to the fader, even after processing. This is known as post-fader metering. Good for reference, but if your plug-ins are all clipped and the fader is down at -24 dB, your track meter will not show your signal as clipping.

When in doubt, always solo and listen to the track for distortion.

Note: I tend to insert extra meters on my Master Fader if I'm adding more than one plug-in. That way I can keep track of each gain stage before it hits the output. Usually, I'll start with an RTA in the first slot to measure the unprocessed mix bus, then a multi-band compressor, then another RTA, and finally a TL MasterMeter or vertical Dorrough meter for precision.

This allows me to meter and compare signal at three different points in the chain.

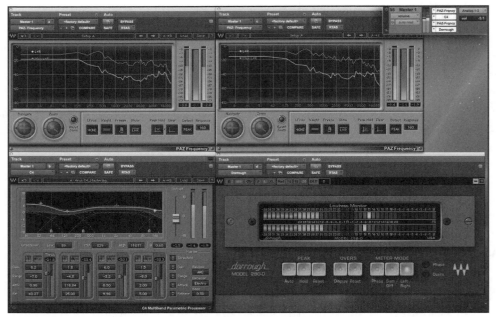

Fig. 9-18

Mixing to a Digital File

BOUNCE TO DISK

In Pro Tools you can create a mix file by using the Bounce to Disk command. This can be found in the Edit menu or initiated with a key command by pressing Option + Command + B. This will bring up a Bounce dialog that looks like this:

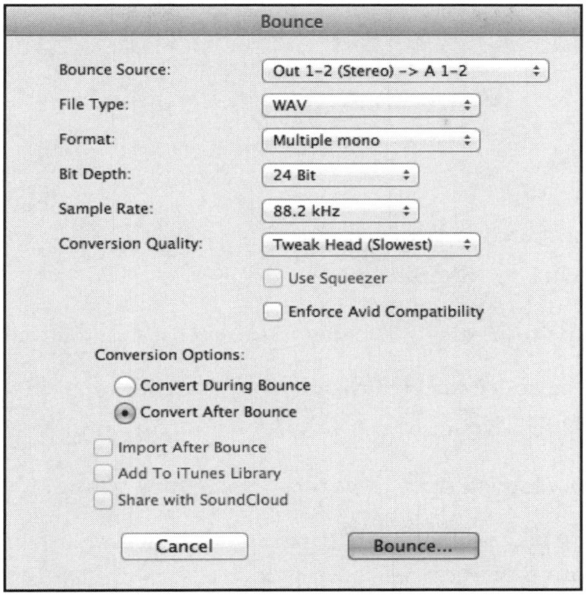

Fig. 9-19

From here you can choose the destination file format, the source outputs that will feed the mixdown, bit depth, sample rate, and stereo (or multi-track) configuration.

If you plan on mastering your mix in Pro Tools, you should use the following settings:

- WAV file format, 24-bit/88.2 or 96 kHz
- Multiple Mono files

When you enter this information and hit Enter, you will be prompted to name your file. Before you do this, you should create a new folder using the New Folder button on the bottom left of the Save dialog window. I usually place my mix folder on the top level of the session folder and name it something like "Project XYZ Final Mixes."

Having created a destination folder, be sure to save *all* of your mixed audio files there.

MIXING SUMMARY

Mixing Is Hard Work

- **Optimize:** Optimize your computer system, audio hardware, and Pro Tools software to make your mixing session go more smoothly.
- **Strategize:** Start with a strategy for mixing:

- Building the house
- Sculpting

Goals: Define your goals:

- Is this a demo?
- Is this for CD release?
- Will this be distributed electronically?
- What's the timeline for completion?

Calibration: Tune your ears by listening to mixes that sound great to you:

- Listen to these reference materials before you start your mix.
- Import full-fidelity mixes into your DAW for comparison to your own mixes.

Work it: If it sounds great right away, there's something wrong:

- In other words, it takes a lot of work to make a mix sound *right*. It will take substantially more than 15 minutes to create a great mix.
- It takes 90 percent of the time to finesse the last 10 percent of a mix.

Practice: Don't be discouraged if your mixes don't sound like Chris Lord-Alge the first time:

- Practice makes perfect.
- Repetition makes you better.

Vocals: If you have lead vocals, do your first mix with vocals balanced at just the right level.

- Then do an alternate mix with the vocals up +1.5 dB.
- Next, do an alternate mix with the vocals down -1.5 dB.
- Listen to all three; then decide which sounds best.

Quality: When you have arrived at the perfect mix, burn a CD and listen to it in your car:

- Next, listen to it on headphones.
- Then put in your earbuds, go for a walk, and listen to it.
- Next, listen on a friend's sound system.
- Finally, if it sounds good everywhere else, listen to it on headphones once again and take note of every little noise or clunk or breath that you don't want on the master. Now go back and fix those problems and repeat this entire listening sequence.

PREPARING YOUR TRACKS FOR MASTERING

If you are sending your mixes out to be mastered by a mastering engineer, you should have a conversation with him or her to cover these questions:

- How long will it take?
- How much will it cost?
- Should I attend the mastering session?
- File Resolution: Do they want 16-bit/44.1 kHz files or 24-bit/96 kHz files?
- File Format: Multiple mono files or interleaved stereo files? WAV, AIFF, or some other format?
- Delivered on hard disk, CD, DVD, or tape?
- What about adding bus compression or EQ to the mixes before I deliver them?
- What level should I aim for: peaks of -12 dB, or 100 percent modulation? Somewhere in between, perhaps?

Your mastering engineer will guide you through the answers to these questions and more, and you will learn a great deal from him or her about the mastering process.

SUMMARY OF KEY COMMANDS

OPERATION	KEY COMMAND
Select Outputs on Multiple Tracks	Shift + Option + Click on output pane
Bounce To Disk	Option + Command + B

CHAPTER 9 REVIEW

1. The two mixing methods described in this book are _____ _____ and _____.

2. When building a mix from the foundation, you can usually start from the drum tracks and work your way up through the instruments by _____ _____.

3. Instruments that are to be mixed together, such as drums, can be controlled together by assigning them to a group. The easy way to assign tracks to a group is by highlighting the names of the tracks and pressing _____ + ___.

4. You can use Track _____ to apply software plug-in processing to _____ tracks, ____ inputs, _____ tracks, and _____ faders.

5. Applying EQ to drum tracks should be done on the individual track _____ rather than on a sub-mix.

6. Kick drums and bass guitars often share the same frequency range, usually between ___ and ____ Hz. You can use the _____ plug-in to shape the sound of each instrument to make room in the spectrum for both, thereby clearing up the low end.

7. Operating Pro Tools in 24-bit mode gives you a theoretical dynamic range of _____ dB.

8. Observing the law of _____ means making sure that your audio I/O is calibrated, and that at each gain stage, no gain is added or taken away.

9. You should use the most CPU-economical plug-in to do the job. When inserting a high-pass filter on an audio track, use a ____-band EQ 3 plug-in to conserve system _____.

10. Pro Tools track meters display the _____ gain stage before output. In order to accurately measure the difference between amplitude as recorded and amplitude as processed, put a meter in the _____ position.

11. The command for Bounce to Disk is _____ + _____ + ___.

12. From the Bounce to Disk menu, you can choose audio file format, _____ _____, _____, and mono or stereo file format, as well as _____ source and conversion options.

Mastering Overview

Also referred to as a type of audio post-production, mastering is the final step in the production process when preparing your mixes for distribution or duplication. The main idea is to optimize the sound of music mixes for playback on a wide array of sound systems, and in a variety of media ranging from vinyl LP to CD to compressed data file formats.

I describe it to my mastering engineers like this: I give you a bunch of good mixes, you give me back a cohesive *album.*

Whether you are mastering for yourself or a client, you should go into a session with fresh ears and an objective view toward achieving the best possible sound quality.

WHAT DOES A MASTERING ENGINEER DO?

- **Quality Control:** The main task of a mastering engineer is to ensure that a song (or collection of songs) has sonic integrity and adheres to generally accepted professional standards.
- **Critical listening:** A mastering engineer needs to be able to listen clearly, make objective evaluations, and determine what process or processes to employ in order to adjust the audio for best sound translation. The mastering engineer will use software and hardware tools to manipulate dynamics, and apply corrective EQ to the mixes in order to achieve this goal. In the case of a CD or vinyl release, the mastering engineer will also establish an appropriate amount of time between songs and ensure that there are proper fade-ins and fade-outs on each song, with no unwanted count-offs or end-of-take chatter to mar the listening experience. In general, an experienced mastering engineer will apply as little processing as possible in order to achieve the desired outcome.

When Do You Need Mastering?

Almost always, if the goal is to have your music played on a wide array of playback devices and sound systems.

You Should Have Your Music Mastered If ...

- Your mixes were done by different engineers.
- Your mixes were done in different studios.
- Your mixes were done at different times.
- Your tracks were recorded in different sessions at different times or feature different players.
- Your mixes come from a variety of media or file formats.

In the case of a compilation, you should have your completed project mastered if the songs came from different albums or artists.

Should You Master Your Own Mixes?

It depends on the circumstances. In practice, by the time you're done mixing, you are often too close to the project to make truly *objective* qualitative decisions about the EQ or dynamics, especially after days, weeks, or months of making highly *subjective* qualitative decisions. Besides, if you mix a song to the best of your abilities, there should be no room for you to improve upon it, right?

An exception would be in the case of extreme budget limitation. If you own your own Pro Tools rig, it can definitely be more cost effective to take on the mastering step yourself. Though it's often worth the added expense to get a pair of educated and objective ears on your mixes.

Bob Ludwig, one the top mastering engineers in the world, has an important view of this aspect of the process:

With the record industry in a state of entropy and with similarly declining budgets, many producers and artists are forced to attempt to master their own music. It is said that it takes ten thousand hours of learning to master one's craft, which is why most of the world's greatest mixers (who spent their ten thousand hours learning how to mix) do not master their own work.

Note: I would encourage engineers to try their hand at mastering; it's a valuable experience. It's an informative process and will facilitate understanding the full scope of completing a recording. You never know—you may be good at mastering and really enjoy doing it.

Thinking Like a Mastering Engineer Versus a Mixing Engineer

It's hard to separate yourself from the recording and mixing process, but a mastering engineer has to listen more objectively and in relative terms. It means finally letting go of the snare drum sound or the vocal reverb sound, or even the balance between the background singers. It means listening for surpluses or deficiencies in the frequency spectrum of the mix (too much of this, too little of that), then finding the proper EQ and/or compression settings to compensate. To that end, conduct the mastering session separately from the mixing process. Make sure that you are objective enough to make judgment calls on EQ or compression or overall level. A mastering engineer should be concerned with making all of the songs in a collection sound like they belong on the same album, or at least were recorded by the same artist. Grammy®-nominated engineer David Miles Huber masters his own mixes in 5.1 surround, but he does it as a separate session after the mixes are completed. David imports his mixes into a new session and applies processing as necessary to maximize the sonic quality of his work. We will build on this approach as we create our mastering session.

BASIC MASTERING TOOLS

The tools available to you in the mastering process are similar to the tools used in mixing, but they are used somewhat differently. They are:

- Volume-based effects
- Time-based effects
- Reconstructive tools

Volume-Based Effects

While you can't change the volume of each individual instrument in a song that's already been mixed, in the mastering process, you can adjust the overall volume of a song, a portion of a song, or a group of songs. You can also fade in or out as a transition into or out of a song. You can also adjust the EQ characteristics of a song or a portion of a song, depending on the desired effect. Again, the idea of mastering is to make the songs sound similar in relative level and overall EQ.

Time-Based Effects

These would include phase modification tools, stereo enhancement, delay, and reverb. On rare occasions it may be necessary to add reverb in the mastering session, but if the mastering engineer noticed a problem in the mix (e.g., reverb on only one side of the stereo field or a phase problem with reverb return), he or she would probably refer the mix back to the mixing engineer to be remixed.

It would be rare to add delay in the mastering stage, but more unusual things have happened.

Reconstructive Tools

These include noise reduction, hum removal, hiss removal, and pop/click removal software. These are typically available as DAW plug-ins but often act as stand-alone software applications as well.

MASTERING IN PRO TOOLS
What You Can Do In Pro Tools

- Sequencing.
- Adjust levels, fades.
- Fine-tune EQ and compression.
- Edit top and tail, edit length.
- Determine overall and relative levels.
- Remove noise.
- Bounce each song as a master file.

What You Can't Do in Pro Tools

- Burn to CD or DVD.
- Create or edit PQ sub-codes.
- Check a CD master for errors.

PRO TOOLS IN THE MASTERING SUITE

Gateway Mastering in Portland, ME, uses four Pro Tools systems. This from owner Bob Ludwig:

We often use a hybrid of analog and digital processing in our mastering, as we still receive many analog tapes, and we also will go from the digital domain to analog and back in order to use unique pieces of analog gear and to get some sound colors that are only available in the analog world.

It used to be that we rarely used any plug-ins on Pro Tools, because the sound quality did not measure up to stand-alone digital hardware, but this situation has been rapidly changing. With the advent of powerful processing cards and boxes offered by Waves APA, Universal Audio's UAD-2 Quad DSP board, TC Electronics' PowerCore Firewire, and other accelerators, the DSP power of most outboard digital gear can now be had within the Digital Workstation and all the good things that it implies (automation, AudioSuite, etc.). Some of the new digital modeling of classic analog gear sounds very close and often offers more flexibility than the original units.

We aren't entirely there yet; some stand-alone digital hardware, like the Weiss DS-1 de-esser or the Weiss EQ1-LP linear phase IIR equalizer, have massive latency in order to do the amazing things they do. Their native latency is far beyond the longest delay times Pro Tools can compensate for. Still, there is no reason not to believe that sooner rather than later, most massively DSP-intensive devices will be made available for Digital Audio Workstations, so the future is obviously heading toward all DAW processing.

DIY MASTERING IN PRO TOOLS

- **Start with the Final Mixes:** If you are mastering your own mixes, be sure that you are using the latest and best-sounding mixes for your project. If you have followed the file-naming conventions as discussed earlier in this book, you should be able to easily locate and identify the latest versions of each mix.
- Import audio at a high resolution.
- Depending on the final destination, Pro Tools mastering sessions should be created according to the following specifications:
- **CD Mastering—24-bit/88.2 kHz:** Use this setting for making a Red Book (audio disk) CD master, as well as for making audio files for web distribution.
- **Mastering for Visual Content—24-bit/96 kHz:** If you are mastering audio for video, whether DVD or a video for social media distribution, use the 96 kHz sample rate.
- **Sample Rate Conversion:** Even if your final destination is 44.1 kHz or 48 kHz, your mastering session sample rate should use the higher multiple of the destination sample rate to make the best use of the higher-resolution signal processing afforded the higher sample rates.
- The common thinking here is that the conversion from 88.2 to 44.1 kHz—or from 96 to 48 kHz—is a simple mathematical division by 2, not some odd rate conversion from 96 kHz to 44.1 kHz, or 44.1 to 48 kHz, or some other number. While there is some debate about whether or not modern computers can handle that odd-rate math conversion without sonic artifacts, it makes sense to err on the side of being conservative with regard to the quality of your final audio.
- Why not use 192 kHz sample rate? Mainly because audio convertors are not as accurate at that high rate of processing and may actually introduce distortion. This may not be as relevant in mastering as in recording, but if you are planning to use hardware inserts to perform external processing with analog gear, you will definitely be passing through several AD/DA conversion stages.

- Also, audio files at 24-bit/192 kHz take up a lot of disk space, data bus throughput, and CPU processing horsepower, and don't necessarily yield additional *usable* frequency response (remember, we can only hear up to 20 kHz, approximately).

BUILDING A MASTERING SESSION

Build a session with a new track for each song. You will be able to customize plug-ins and signal path for each song, depending on what you think it needs. This gives you the opportunity to experiment with different sequencing options, cross-fades, and more—without disrupting settings on other songs or modifying edits or fades.

Assembling Tracks

Determine the running order, and assemble songs/tracks in that order from top to bottom. If you are mastering more than one song, this makes for a good visual representation of your running order and how songs flow together. If you decide to change the running order, you can easily drag tracks around to rearrange the sequence.

Monitoring

Compare your mixes, your mastered mixes, and your reference material often. Use the solos to hear each track. On processed tracks, you will need to bypass plug-ins in order to hear the original mix without processing. Compare to your selected reference music to keep a good perspective on the sound of your mastered audio. Calibrate your playback system for 85 dB, C weighted. Use this as your average listening level, but vary the level from time to time in order to avoid listening fatigue. Be sure that you are using well-balanced speakers that allow you hear the low frequencies down to at least 30 Hz, or you may be missing a large portion of the information in that octave.

Signal Chain

Assign metering *first* in the insert chain on each track, including the Master Fader.

Any plug-ins you add should appear after the meter, giving you an opportunity to keep an eye on levels pre- and post-processing.

Add another meter at the end of the signal chain to observe your final levels.

Experiment with EQ and dynamics plug-ins and the order in which they appear. There may be subtle differences in the outcome of each process, and you should be aware of what each option does to your audio.

Construct your Window Layout scheme so that you can see all processing and metering at the same time on the desktop.

The mastering signal chain may include processing components linked in this order:

- High-pass Filter below 10 Hz
- Meter/RTA
- Compressor
- Multi-band Compressor
- Equalizer
- Limiter
- Meter/RTA

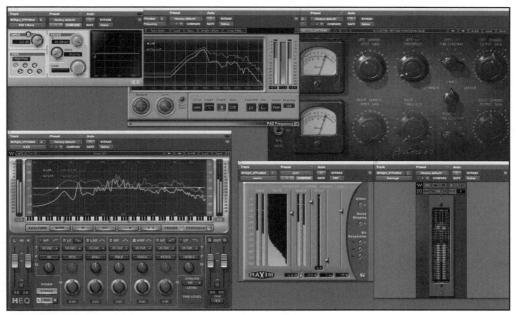

Fig. 10-1

Using Level Automation

Once you have arrived at a good dynamic and EQ balance, you may find it necessary to balance overall level from cut to cut. You can use the Level Fader to accomplish this, but if the level needs to change within a song, you can use the level automation to draw in the appropriate levels. These levels can be easily adjusted or modified and stored with the session for immediate recall.

Dynamic Range Control

In the mastering stage, compression is used to fine-tune dynamic range and is generally most effective when added in small increments.

Parallel Compression

Sometimes called "New York" compression, this refers to adding compression in such a way that allows you to hear both the compressed and uncompressed signals at the same time.

This can be useful when you want to compress a mix heavily to bring up the energy and volume level but still want to hear some of the dynamics and peak transients.

Some plug-ins, such as Maxim, utilize a mix control allowing you to determine the balance between compressed and uncompressed signal directly from the plug-in window. If you are using a dynamics plug-in without this feature, or wish to use an external compressor to accomplish this, use these steps to set up parallel audio processing:

- **Step 1:** Click the Send button of the audio track to which you wish to add parallel compression. Select "new track…," create a stereo aux input named "SongNameComp," and click Create.
- **Step 2:** Set the Send level to 0 dB by Option-clicking the fader.
- **Step 3:** Assign a compressor plug-in to the new aux input, and adjust to taste. Add other processing on the aux input as necessary or desired.
- **Step 4:** Adjust levels on the "SongName" and "SongNameComp" track level faders to achieve the right balance between uncompressed and compressed audio.

Serial Compression

Since inserts cascade in a series, adding a compressor as a plug-in on the audio track will compress the source audio as well as any processing that comes before the compressor plug-in.

USING MORE THAN ONE COMPRESSOR ON A TRACK

It may be necessary to use more than one compressor when you need to control particular transients independent of the overall compression effect.

If some instruments in the mix are particularly peaky (high-attack transients), set the first compressor in the chain to process with a fast attack, fast release, then set GR to taste.

- Insert a second compressor to bring up overall level and smooth out dynamics.
- Use a longer attack time (> 500 ms).
- Use a longer release time (< 1 second).
- Reduce gain by no more than 2 or 3 dB.

Multi-Band Compression

The Swiss army knife of the mastering realm. We have discussed multi-band compression in at least two other places in this book. In the context of mastering, we need to look at multi-band compression as a powerful tool to accomplish sonic restoration as well as sonic enhancement.

It is important to consider how to set the variable crossover points to be used in dividing frequencies for independent processing:

- **Low to Middle Bands:** Crossover between the low-band and mid-band should be somewhere below the range of your lead instrument or vocal. Try crossing over at 200 Hz or below; otherwise, your processing may interfere with mix balances. For example, imagine if the crossover point were 500 Hz—smack in the middle of the vocal range; the singer's lower notes might be boosted along with the kick drum, while the middle and higher notes might be attenuated with the rest of the mid-range. Not a very realistic way to treat a mix.
- **Middle to High Bands:** Again, setting this crossover relative to but *above* the range of the vocal or lead instrument will preserve the balance as intended in the original mix. A crossover setting of 3 to 4 kHz would put you out of the vocal range but still enable you to control the upper mid-range tendency to be strident.

REPAIRING A TRACK USING MULTI-BAND COMPRESSION

I had a client bring in a mix that sounded like the drummer paid for the session—the snare was easily 6 dB louder than anything else in the mix. As it turns out, the drummer *was* sitting next to the mix engineer, coaching him through his first mix in his new basement studio.

By using a multi-band compressor with one band tuned specifically to respond to the narrow-band center frequency of the snare drum sound, we were able to reduce the gain of that band by -6 dB for just the few-hundred-millisecond duration of the snare hits. This reduced the volume of the snare enough to make the mix usable.

EQ

Application of EQ will be to taste, but you should listen to your reference recordings again to hear the optimal balance between low, middle, and high frequencies. Then try to match the approximate balance between frequencies using your EQ.

Note: In raising particular high-frequency bands, be careful not to turn the recording into a hi-hat song. By changing the EQ balance to bring out vocal breathiness, for example, you might alter the delicate balance achieved in mixing the rest of the instruments.

Create a Master Fader

This gives you an opportunity to add an overall compressor, EQ, or other processing to the cumulative output of your session.

Using it sparingly and using a very high-quality limiter can really make the sound of your tracks more cohesive at this stage.

The Master Fader also gives you a method for trimming final volume up or down and for metering your final output.

Create a Pre- and Post-Processing Monitor Bus

If your audio interface has at least four outputs and you have a mixer or the ability to switch monitor sources, you should create a separate monitoring path for A/B comparison of pre- and post-processing of your audio.

The setup is a bit more complex but definitely more flexible in the long run.

- **Step 1:** In your I/O page (Setup > I/O), create a new output path called "Solo Bus," and assign it to outputs A 3–4.
- **Step 2:** Go to the AFL/PFL Path drop-down menu, and select Stereo A 3–4 as the solo bus. This assigns the output of the solo bus to physical outputs 3–4 of your audio interface.
- **Step 3:** In the AFL/PFL Mutes drop-down menu, select A 1–2. This mutes the main stereo output 1–2 whenever you hit a solo button. (Note: Remember this later; you'll need to set it to "none" when mixing.)
- **Step 4:** For each audio track, click the Send button and create a new aux input named "SongName AUX." Set the send level to 0 dB (Option-click on the Send fader). Set the output of each audio track to "no output."
- **Step 5:** All of your processing and plug-ins will need to be inserted on the aux input that corresponds to each audio track. You can color code the track pairs (e.g., "SongName" and "SongName AUX") to make them easier to identify.
- **Step 6:** Now, soloing the "SongName" track will output the unprocessed signal to your I/O 3–4 outputs for instant A/B comparison listening without having to turn off each plug-in individually. Just be sure to calibrate the 1–2 and 3–4 outputs to the same volume level.

Note: Be sure to bounce your files to disk using the A 1–2 outputs in order to hear and print the files with signal processing.

OVERALL LEVEL OPTIMIZATION

Listen to the transitions repeatedly, and listen to the entire collection of songs from beginning to end to be sure that the levels from song to song, and the overall level of the project, are well balanced and appropriate for the style of music you are mastering.

Even though a ballad may have been mixed with peaks of -1 dB, that doesn't mean the track should be presented at that level in context with other songs.

Likewise, though a pounding rock song may have been mixed with peaks of -12 dB, that does not mean it should appear that way in context.

The only way to determine the appropriate relative level from track to track is by listening carefully from beginning to end, comparing all tracks.

The Level Wars

Much carnage has been wrought in the name of loudness, beginning notably with the Metallica *Black* album. If you can, avoid the temptation to subscribe to the theory that louder is better when it comes to mastering. Again, Bob Ludwig:

There are times an uneducated A&R person may reject a mix because they refuse to change their playback level, and mixes that are done with dynamic range and lower average levels are rejected out of hand. This unfortunate casualty of the Level Wars causes people to try to master their own work. Of course, Pro Tools offers many tools that a professional mastering engineer now uses, so some people think because they own a DAW they are now a mastering engineer. People need to do what they need to do, but often the result is that otherwise good engineers actually damage the musicality of their own work. Instead of making it more musical, they merely make it louder. This is a crime against art.

If someone decides to "pre-master" their mixes before giving them to the artist to listen to, we prefer to be supplied both the "listening" mix and the original pre-squashed mix so we have something we can work with. It is a sad fact that once someone puts a very loud, squashed reference out in the world, many people's knee-jerk reaction is to prefer this louder version without evaluating what damage is being done to the musicality. They don't stop to consider the human body's proven hearing physics that are trained to "tune out" stimuli (music) that is static and without dynamics.

FINAL STEPS

When all of the creative work is done, there still remains the technical work of bouncing the mastered files and prepping them for final delivery.

Checklist for Bouncing Final Mastered Files

- Establish final running order.
- Fine-tune all timings and transitions between songs or tracks.
- Create fades as necessary.
- Set beginning and end points for each song file to be bounced.
- Check all levels to be sure there are no digital clips or "overs."

- Check level song by song and in context overall.
- Double-check to be sure that all your plug-ins are active and all external processing devices are powered up and connected.
- Document all external processor settings to keep track of revisions.
- Make sure that your track output routing is set to your main stereo outputs.
- Check your hard drive to be sure you have enough space for the bounced files.

Bouncing Your Mastered Files

Triple-check to make sure all appropriate tracks are un-muted and un-soloed, and that all your plug-ins are active.

In the Edit window, select the Start marker of your first song, then Shift-click on the End marker, creating a region selection within the timeline.

Choose the Bounce menu (Option + Command + B), and create a new folder on the same disk as your sequences. Name the folder "MyProject Mastered Mixes."

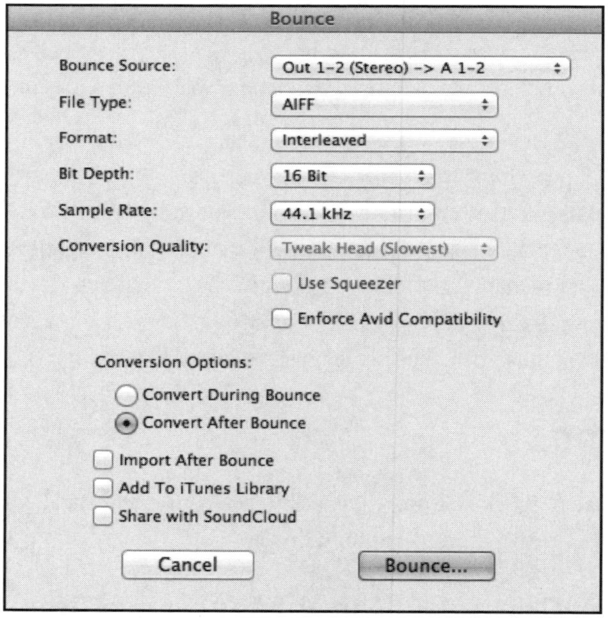

Fig. 10-2

For CD masters, create 16-bit/44.1 kHz AIFF files, using the highest conversion settings available.

For DVD- or video-bound content, create 16-bit/48 kHz AIFF or WAV master files. Check with the author or editor of the project for any additional specs. Some video projects have very specific audio level requirements, particularly if they are destined for television broadcast.

Film projects may require delivery of stems, or stereo sub-mixes of your tracks. Be sure to ask for these specs before completing your mastering.

Name the bounce "SongNameMaster_01," and click OK.

Monitor the bounce carefully to be certain everything sounds right, detect errors, and be sure the bounce content and length is correct.

Repeat this sequence for each song or track. When you have completed this process, you should have all of your final mastered and bounced files located in one folder, properly named and easily identifiable.

Creating the Final Master CD

You can use any third-party program to burn a master CD. Follow these steps:

- **Step 1:** Open a new session in your CD authoring software, name it "MyProject CD Master01," and save it to the same disk directory as your mastered mix files.

- **Step 2:** Drag all your mastered mix files into the session, and put them in the proper running order.

- **Step 3:** Remove any default timing gaps between tracks. Because you established the precise running times of each track on your Pro Tools mastering session, you will not need any gaps between tracks.

- **Step 4:** If there is an option for entering metadata into the CD authoring directory, now is the time to populate those fields. Include disk name; ISRC codes; artist, publishing, and copyright information; and any other information pertinent to project identification.

- **Step 5:** Burn two master disks. If you have a client, burn three disks.

- **Step 6:** Listen to each, checking for errors. In particular, check for phase coherence in mono.

- **Step 7:** Seal one copy and set it aside for duplication. Set another aside as the client reference copy, if applicable.

- **Step 8:** Use the remaining copy to check *very carefully,* listening end to end using headphones. Check for quality on a variety of systems before sending any copies to the duplicator or the client.

- **Step 9:** Once this CD passes all of your listening tests, you can mark or label each of the disks as masters and feel relatively confident in sending the remaining copies to their respective destinations. Any CD listening or reference copies can be made directly from one of the CD masters.

Delivering a Master for Duplication

If your CD authoring program is capable of exporting an edit list with P and Q sub- codes, save that as a text file with your mastered files as well. The duplication plant may request a copy of this document along with the master disk.

Send the clearly labeled, unopened master CD to the duplication plant, along with the PQ subcode text file. Include all information about the project that you can supply. Most manufacturers have a stringent submission process that identifies the information needed before they accept projects.

In some cases a duplicator may accept hard drives, DVDs, or specialized DDP files. Check with your duplicator of choice for their delivery specifications.

Delivering a Master for Online Distribution

Q: Do I need to master my music for MP3 distribution?

A: For file format, yes; sound quality, no. Some distributors require a specific format, but they will usually tell you what they need or can convert the files themselves. There is no obvious reason to master specifically for MP3 files, as they can just as easily be ripped from the master CD at any data rate required. Just be sure you have preserved some dynamic range in your mastered tracks.

Aggregators usually ask for both uploaded files and market-ready CDs for physical distribution. Again, check with your distributor of choice to determine the deliverables.

Documentation: Keep meticulous notes on all of your processes and filenames; create a text document and include it with your mastered files for future reference or from which to prepare revisions.

Backup Versus Long-Term Archival of Your Data

When everything has been mixed, mastered, and delivered, it's time to think about storing your data.

BACKUP

Data backup is considered a short- to medium-term solution for storing data, and usually involves transfer to hard drive, CD-R, DVD-R, BluRay, or other optical media. These formats are not designed for long-term storage but will suffice for three to five years.

Hard drives are designed to last up to three years, per manufacturer standards, and then only if exercised (mounted) every three months or so.

Optical media is not designed for long-term storage, regardless of manufacturer claims. Be prepared to migrate your data to newer formats about every three to five years. Refer to the "Backup" section earlier in this book for references to P&E Wing Backup guidelines.

ARCHIVAL

Data isn't data unless it lives in three places. That means three different physical formats in three different physical locations.

Professional data tape storage is considered to be the standard of choice for enterprise-level IT departments.

Exabyte tape is the standard of choice for the Library of Congress, in addition to immediate online access via enormous RAID servers.

Some institutions still rely on analog tape for reliable long-term storage. When you consider that tapes from the 1950s still exist—and are playable—it speaks highly of the longevity of the technology.

Again, you should refer to the P&E Wing document relating to Archival and Delivery Standards for professional audio projects.

MASTERING SUMMARY

- Treat mastering as a separate process once mixing is completed.
- Often we are too close to our own work to be objective about the sound. Take some time off between mixing and mastering, and listen to your other reference material to gain perspective on your ideal frequency response target.
- Determine how loud your songs need to be compared to others in the market. Compare your reference music to your levels.
- Use other mastered projects as aural reference. Pick several examples in a similar genre that sound right to you.
- Run through the pre-bounce checklist before you bounce final files.
- What's the final destination format? If this project is destined for CD, you'll need 16-bit/44.1 kHz AIFF files. If it is destined for DVD or video, you'll need 16-bit/48 kHz AIFF or WAV files. If it is for online distribution, your distributor will tell you what it needs.
- Bounce all your files to the same folder, named appropriately.
- Create more than one CD master; don't send the duplicators the one with fingerprints all over it!
- Make sure you back up your files.

SUMMARY OF KEY COMMANDS

OPERATION	KEY COMMAND
Set Fader Level to 0dB	Option + Clicking a fader

CHAPTER 10 REVIEW

1. The _____ session should be created as a separate session for mixing, as you will be using different processing and signal _____.

2. The three basic tools used in mastering are _____-based, _____-based, and _____ tools.

3. Pro Tools as a mastering platform allows you to sequence tracks, adjust _____ and _____, and apply processing, but does not allow you to burn a _____ or _____ directly from the program.

4. Create a new Pro Tools session for mastering using the data rate of ___-bit/_____ kHz for mastering a CD, and ___-bit/___ kHz when mastering for video.

5. _____ should be the first plug-in on audio tracks, including on the Master Fader.

6. The two ways to use compression in mastering are _____ connection of compressors, and _____ compression, a.k.a. "New York" compression.

7. When bouncing mastered songs, the file format should be ___-bit/_____ kHz AIFF for CD and MP3-bound projects, and ___-bit/_____ kHz AIFF for video projects.

In Closing

I hope this book helps you make better music. At the very least, I hope that you are inspired to practice your craft and keep your learning curve vertical. Keep studying, read up on new technologies and old processes. Until next time—work hard, play hard, and keep getting better!

Frequency Chart

Here is a graphic that will help illustrate the spectrum of human hearing as it relates to both frequency in Hertz and the range of various instruments in relation to the piano keyboard. Use this as a guide to identifying frequencies contained in musical performances.

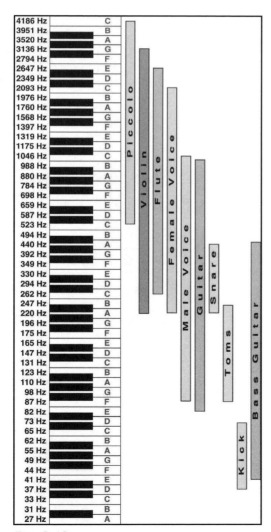

Fig. 9-16

Glossary

Here are some commonly used audio terms or abbreviations that will clarify portions of this book:

Auth. An abbreviation for *authorization*.

bad. A negative subjective opinion held by this author. Synonyms include *inconsistent, less-than-stellar,* and *poor.* There is no consistently measurable threshold beneath which something is bad. Use your best judgment.

channel. An audio path; may be mono or multiple channels. Customarily associated with recording consoles and tape recorders, channel can also be used to describe the audio signal path into and out of a DAW. MIDI channels are independent data streams that can be routed to specific input and output devices, both internal and external to the DAW.

comp. An abbreviation for *composite.* To combine/compile the best parts of multiple takes into a single master take, as in to comp a vocal track.

DAW. An abbreviation for *Digital Audio Workstation.*

dB (FS). An abbreviation for d*ecibels full scale.* 0 dB(FS) is equivalent to maximum amplitude at the threshold of clipping, 100 percent modulation of digital signal, or no more headroom.

dB. An abbreviation for *decibel.* One-tenth of a bel (the bel is seldom used in measurement). Though dB can reference a number of measurements, we will be primarily be using **dB (SPL)** to measure loudness in the studio and **dB (FS)** to reference headroom and maximum signal level.

dBVU. An abbreviation for *decibel volume units.* Used for measuring average audio signal amplitude. 0 dBVU is equivalent to about -14 dB(FS). 0 dBVU is standard reference for +4dB balanced audio systems, and equates to AC current of 1.23 volts (for the tech geeks out there).

DI. An abbreviation for *Direct Injection, Direct Input,* or *Direct Interface.* An electronic audio device used to match impedance and level, usually between musical instruments and recording devices or PA systems. Can be active or passive. Also called *DI Box.*

good. A positive subjective opinion often promoted by this author. Equivalent terms include *great, brilliant, killer,* and *awesome.* There is no known scientific method for measuring good; use your own criteria.

GTR. An abbreviation for *guitar.*

menu. A Pro Tools menu is a list of functional options that can be accessed from the top of the Main Edit window or within other pop-up windows.

pane. A smaller component within a window, typically providing access to a specific set of parameters or options. This book refers to Insert panes, Send panes, Track panes, and other such "sub-windows."

pass. Common usage: "Give me another *pass* at that guitar solo." Same as **take.**

peak meter. Designed to respond accurately to very fast audio transients, such as drum hits. This is the type of meter emulated in Pro Tools displays.

PNO. An abbreviation for *piano.*

PPM. An abbreviation for *Peak Program Meter.* See also **peak meter.**

SPL. An abbreviation for *sound pressure level,* as measured in **dB (SPL).**

take. Refers to a recorded performance, as in a vocal *take.* Same as **pass.**

TCE. An abbreviation for *time compression, compression,* and/or *expansion.*

track. (noun) Depending on the context, this can refer to a recorded song or a recorded performance, and in Pro Tools, refers to a session playlist created to record or play back audio, video, or MIDI information.

track. (verb) The act of performing or recording a song or parts of a song—e.g., when recording a jazz piece, one usually tracks all of the musicians at once.

VU meter. Typical use of an analog VU meter is to measure the average amplitude of an audio signal over time. Hence, the rise time and fall time of a VU meter are each about 300 ms. Not good for reading peak program amplitude.

window. A portion of the onscreen display, which provides visual display and access to a set of Pro Tools functions. Examples are the Edit window, the Mix window, and the Transport *window.*

Appendix: DVD-ROM Video Tutorials and Pro Tools Sessions

VIDEO CONTENT

The DVD-ROM included with this book contains a number of video tutorials designed to help you thoroughly understand the features and techniques explained in *Power Tools for Pro Tools 10*. Use these videos to learn more about the Pro Tools environment and to gain greater understanding of the processes described in the text.

Videos 1–4 introduce you to the world of Pro Tools.

Videos 5–7 discuss screen layout, basic operation, and editing functions.

Videos 8–18 show how to effectively configure your virtual studio in order to record basic tracks, record overdubs, mix with automation, and master a final product.

Video 19 summarizes the process of working in Pro Tools 10.

1. Introduction

   Welcome to the world of Pro Tools 10, one of the most powerful DAWs in the world.

2. What's New in Pro Tools 10

   Whether you're new to Pro Tools or a veteran user, this video will quickly introduce the newest features and functions in this latest version of Pro Tools.

3. Launching Pro Tools

   Understanding how to open existing sessions or create new ones is the first step in Pro Tools proficiency. This segment shows:
   - The proper order for powering up a system
   - Where to store audio and session files
   - How to efficiently manage the DAW from the first mouse click.

4. How to Use the Session Files

   Copying tutorial material from the DVD-ROM to your hard drive, opening sessions, and keeping track of data is important to your learning experience and to your workflow. This tutorial helps ensure that you don't lose your assets!

5. Edit/Mix Window Layout

   Getting around in Pro Tools is easier when you understand the window layout. This tutorial will guide you through the:
   - Edit window
   - Mix window
   - Top menu bar
   - Edit modes

6. Transport Functions

   Pro Tools navigation is simple and elegant, yet has many configuration options for customizing the creative work environment. This segment focuses on:
   - Counters and status displays
   - Record options
   - Playback options
   - Creating and managing markers
   - Creating custom Window Configurations

7. Data Management

   This tutorial digs deep into the best ways to get data in and out of Pro Tools. It demonstrates methods to easily create and locate templates, session file versions, and more. Overviews of these important functions are included:
   - Import audio
   - Import session data
   - Export as AAF/OMF
   - Bounce to disk

8. Building a Virtual Studio

   Pro Tools lets the user configure a mixer so that it provides exactly what's needed to record each song. Explore the various tools available to design the ideal virtual console and see how to use that design as a starting place for future sessions.

9. Using Direct Plug-ins

   Plug-ins are fundamental creative building blocks in the development of virtually every mix. This video demonstrates the use of plug-ins, inserted directly on a recorded track, to control dynamics, adjust EQ, and control pitch.

   It also shows the differences between—and recommends some uses for—serial and parallel processing. This segment helps you avoid some of the biggest (and most common) processing mistakes made by beginning DAW users.

10. Using Auxiliary Inputs

    Whether adding reverb to tracks or creating a headphone mix, the auxiliary input is a very powerful weapon in the recording arsenal. Learn to maximize flexibility and minimize system resources using aux buses.

11. Recording and Playback

    Pro Tools can be operated as a simple recording device, or a nimble and highly configurable DAW. Learning the array of recording and playback commands will let you configure transport capabilities to match your workflow. In this video, we will cover use of the following:
    • Transport Window Options
    • Record Options
    • Playback Options
    • Loop Recording with Playlists

12. Pro Tools Playlists

    Tracking with playlists can make it easy to work with scratch tracks, click tracks, or alternate versions. In this segment, we will examine how to use playlists when editing basic tracks, overdubbing instruments, and comping vocal takes.

13. Setting up a Rough Mix

    At some point in the recording process you will need to create a reference mix, or rough mix, for yourself or others to evaluate. This segment will show you how to quickly set up a basic rough mix, add effects, and bounce the mix to disk.

14. Automation

    Pro Tools offers an automation system that is easy to use, yet very powerful. This tutorial gets you started using automation quickly and effectively.

15. Bus Processing

    Turn a good mix into a great mix just by inserting some simple processing tools at the end of the mix chain. See how bus processing with dynamics or EQ adds a bit of polish to the overall sound of your mix.

16. Creating the Final Mix File

    Take a step-by-step look at the process of bouncing your final mix to disk. This video demonstrates output options for Pro Tools and provides important considerations regarding the creation of files that are suitable for the mastering process.

17. Setting up the Mastering Session

    Mastering is the final step in the recording process. Once you're proficient at building a virtual mixer and using plug-in processing, you can use those concepts in a slightly different way to create a mastering session.

18. Creating Mastered Song Files

    Now that you've made it through the mixing and mastering process, it's time to bounce your final mastered song files. This tutorial walks through options for the creation of files that will be uploaded to a digital distribution service or burned to a CD for duplication.

19. In Conclusion

    This video segment contains final comments from the author.

AUDIO CONTENT

The Pro Tools 10 sessions used in these video exercises are included on this DVD-ROM. They provide an opportunity to get some hands-on experience using professionally recorded multitrack masters! Use them to explore the vast array of tools and techniques available to Pro Tools power users.

Chapter Review Answer Key

CHAPTER 2 REVIEW

1. Pro Tools 10
2. delay, I/O
3. iLok
4. 10
5. Complete Production Toolkit
6. delay, TDM
7. HD TDM or HDX, PCI-e, HD TDM or HDX
8. HD Core, HD Accel
9. usage, processing
10. DAE or system
11. Higher, RTAS
12. high, CPU
13. short, long, maximum
14. buffer
15. N, I/O
16. internal, external
17. ADAT, S/PDIF
18. I/O settings
19. Shuffle, Slip, Spot, Grid
20. Zoomer, Trim, Selector, Grabber, Scrubber, Pencil
21. Smart
22. mouse click, keyboard

CHAPTER 3 REVIEW

1. All of the above
2. True
3. AIFF, WAV
4. Spacebar, 0
5. 5
6. Wait for Note, Metronome, Conductor
7. Time Code
8. False
9. Shift + Spacebar
10. Control + click
11. a) Normal
    b) Record
    c) Loop Record
    d) Destructive Record
    e) QuickPunch
12. playlist
13. QuickPunch

CHAPTER 4 REVIEW

1. -2.5dB, -3dB, -4.5dB, and -6dB
2. output, routing
3. pre, post-fader
4. plug-ins, interface, external
5. voice, latency or delay
6. direct, sends
7. Command + Drag
8. delay or latency, hardware
9. 10, 10
10. Master fader
11. Option + C
12. group, command
13. tempo
14. transport

15. edit, mix
16. m , . /
17. enter, 999
18. Command + S
19. Strip Silence
20. Consolidate

CHAPTER 5 REVIEW

1. half speed
2. Track
3. peak level
4. dynamic
5. An I/O device with at least 2 outputs
6. follow main pan
7. Omni
8. Save As…
9. selection, placement
10. True
11. the instrument sounds in the room
12. re-amping
13. True
14. Command, spacebar, F12, 3
15. pitch
16. reverb
17. double tracking or doubling
18. stacking, doubling
19. Tuning
20. comping
21. Grid, Groups
22. playlist
23. QuickPunch
24. False

CHAPTER 6 REVIEW

1. Strip Silence
2. consolidate
3. timing
4. quantizing
5. Clip Conform
6. Time Compression, Expansion
7. False
8. Polyphonic, Rhythmic, Monophonic, Varispeed
9. pitch
10. MIDI Editor, Score Editor, MIDI Event List
11. MIDI Track Offset, MIDI Track Offset

CHAPTER 7 REVIEW

1. audio clip, processing
2. Real-Time Audio Suite
3. Time Division Multiplexing
4. ten
5. Control, Command, Click
6. Option + Click
7. Audio Suite, Auxiliary
8. RTAS, AAX, HD TDM
9. equalizer
10. 1, 5, 7
11. subtractive, additive
12. frequency bands
13. 10:1
14. sibilance
15. pitch change, auto pitch correction
16. Phase-reverse
17. delays
18. slap delay, short delay, medium delay, long delay
19. distortion
20. stereo

CHAPTER 8 REVIEW

1. Volume, Pan, Mute, Send level, Send pan, Send mute, Plug-in parameters
2. Off, Read, Write, Touch, Latch, Trim
3. Command + 4
4. automation enable
5. overwrite
6. thin
7. auto, automation lanes
8. Trim

CHAPTER 9 REVIEW

1. Building a House, Sculpting
2. frequency spectrum
3. Command + G
4. Inserts, audio tracks, aux inputs, instrument tracks, master faders
5. insert
6. 50 and 100Hz, EQ3
7. 144dB
8. Unity Gain
9. one-band, resources
10. final, first insert
11. Option + Command + B
12. bit depth, sample rate, output source

CHAPTER 10 REVIEW

1. mastering, flow
2. volume-based, time-based, reconstructive tools
3. levels, fades, CD or DVD
4. 24-bit/88.2 kHz, 24-bit/96 kHz
5. Metering
6. serial, parallel
7. 16-bit/44.1 kHz AIFF, 16-bit/48 kHz AIFF

Index

POWER TOOLS SERIES

HAL•LEONARD®
www.halleonardbooks.com

0512